KT-394-007

Acknowledgements

Very many veterans of 1st Royal Tank Regiment and 2nd Royal Tank Regiment have contributed to the making of this book. Alas, many of them have reached the 'green fields beyond' so *Battles with Panzers* is dedicated to the memory of the several thousand tank warriors who fought in the two terrible world wars, fell and are buried in France, the Western Desert, Burma, Italy, North West Europe (and possibly in Germany). A special thank you is due to the family of the late Kenneth Chadwick, author of *Seconds Out*, and also to Lieutenant-Colonel James Bouverie-Brine, Field Marshal Lord Michael Carver, Richard Clifton, Colonel Tom Craig (text and photographs), Lieutenant-Colonel Peter Dey (text and photographs), Lieutenant-Colonel J. Dingwall, L.J. Dinning, Sergeant Doyle, Major S.R.F. Elmslie, Lieutenant-Colonel George Forty, A.W. Green (citations, photographs), Tom Harland, Jeffrey Hill-Tout (text and photographs), R.G. Knight, Geoff Knights, Major-General A.R. Leakey and Lieutenant-Colonel George Forty for permission to quote from *Leakey's Luck*, A.E. Lee, Colonel John Longman, W.G. McGinley, Jack Moat, Colonel Sir Frederick Pile, Major Norman Plough (text, photographs and maps), Bert Rendell, Peter Roach (permission from publishers), Major-General G.P.B. Roberts, Major Mark Rudkin, Bryan Watkins, Peter Watson, Kenneth Ward, Major John Wollaston and David Fletcher, Nancy Langmaid and the staff of the Tank Museum.

Finally, grateful thanks to the Colonel Commandant Royal Tank Regiment for permission to include photographs of Mitchell's Tank *v.* Tank battle; Captain C. Robertson VC and Captain R.W.L. Wain VC.

Preface

In the last three years of the First World War, as Field Marshal Sir Douglas Haig confirmed in his final despatch of the war, the tank battalions played a vital role in victory. Some twenty-seven years later, at the end of the Second World War, Field Marshal Bernard Montgomery echoed the same sentiment.

Shortly after General Montgomery arrived in the North African desert, destined to transform Britain's Eighth Army and march from victory to victory, he caused a sensation among his men. A dedicated professional infantryman (of the Royal Warwickshire Regiment), he chose to put the cap badge of the Royal Tank Regiment – a gleaming silver First World War tank – on his beret and wore it with pride throughout the rest of the war. Shortly after the end of hostilities in 1945 he wrote:

We learnt our lesson the hard way – as is so often the case in the history of British arms. It took the early successes of the German panzer divisions in 1940 to convince us that the tank, if used properly, was a decisive weapon in modern land warfare. By then it might have been too late. But we were saved from disaster because of the efficient tank schools which the Regiment had established in peacetime and by the splendid body of reservists which they had trained. These made it possible to effect a rapid expansion of our tank forces, Regular and Territorial, and eventually to put into the field a hard core of highly efficient armoured units – which bore the brunt of the fight for two long weary years. Finally at Alamein in October 1942, we gained the advantage over the enemy, utilising our superior numbers and equipment – after which we never looked back. And it was the same in other theatres of war. The Regiment won praise wherever it fought.

I know this better than most. It was my great honour and privilege to have had under my command at varying times during the late war most of the units of the Royal Armoured Corps – Regular, Territorial and units specially for the war. Among all these, I can speak with authority of the technical efficiency, and tenacity and skill in battle of the units of the Royal Tank Regiment.

When the Second World War was over, the Regiment asked me, an infantry soldier, to become one of its colonels commandant and it was a notable moment for me when my appointment as such was approved by the Sovereign – Colonel-in-Chief of the Regiment. Let us never forget the immense debt which the whole nation owes to the officers and men of the Royal Tank Regiment. I have always considered the Royal Tank Regiment to be outstanding in the Royal Armoured Corps – second to none when it comes to efficiency in battle. By determination in peace and valour in war, the Regiment worthily established, and has unflinchingly maintained, the right to its inspiring motto – 'Fear Naught'.

Field Marshal Viscount Montgomery of Alamein KG, GCB, DSO

BATTLES WITH
PANZERS

MONTY'S TANK BATTALIONS
1 RTR & 2 RTR AT WAR

PATRICK DELAFORCE

SUTTON PUBLISHING

First published in 2003 by
Sutton Publishing Limited · Phoenix Mill
Thrupp · Stroud · Gloucestershire · GL5 2BU

Copyright © Patrick Delaforce, 2003

All rights reserved. No part of this publication may be reproduced, stored in
a retrieval system, or transmitted, in any form or by any means, electronic,
mechanical, photocopying, recording or otherwise, without the prior
permission of the publisher and copyright holder.

Patrick Delaforce has asserted the moral right to be identified as the author
of this work.

British Library Cataloguing in Publication Data
A catalogue record for this book is available from the British Library.

ISBN 0-7509-3244-9

SANDWELL LIBRARY & INFORMATION SERVICE	
I1794901	
Cypher	30.07.03
940.41241	£17.99

Typeset in 10/12pt Plantin Light.
Typesetting and origination by
Sutton Publishing Limited.
Printed and bound in England by
J.H. Haynes & Co. Ltd, Sparkford.

Contents

Introduction

This book is the sequel to *Taming the Panzers*, the history of the 3rd Battalion Royal Tank Regiment (3 RTR) in the two world wars, and is the history of the two senior battalions, 1 RTR (First of Track) and 2 RTR (Second to None).

1 RTR (originally 'A' Company, 'A' Battalion, 1st Battalion RTC, then 1 RTR) had an outstanding role in the First World War. Of the four Victoria Crosses awarded to the whole Royal Tank Corps, 1 RTR won two of them. Involved in the first ever tank *v.* tank engagement – the first 'Battle with Panzers' – they won the day. They fought almost non-stop throughout the Second World War from the early days in the North African desert, through El Alamein and the hot pursuit to Tripoli and Tunis, to the invasion of southern Italy, until Montgomery summoned his desert legions for the invasion of north-west Europe. As the spearhead of 7th Armoured Division they fought their way through Normandy, northern France, Belgium and Holland towards Berlin.

2 RTR (originally 'B' Company, 'B' Battalion, 2nd Battalion RTC, then 2 RTR) fought in all the major battles on the Western Front from 1917 to the end of the war, including Messines, Ypres, Cambrai, the German offensive of 1918 and the great Allied push in the summer of 1918. Altogether eleven large-scale battles were fought and 116 awards gained. In the Second World War 2 RTR fought in France in 1940, in Cyrenaica at the astonishing victory of Beda Fomm and in Operations Battleaxe and Crusader, before being sent to Burma where they fought a heroic rearguard action (partly supporting the Chinese Army). Finally they were brought back to Europe via Iraq to fight the length of Italy up to the Austrian frontier.

No wonder Field Marshal Bernard Montgomery was so proud of 'his' tank battalions.

Part One

FIRST OF TRACK
(1 RTC/RTR)

1 RTC/RTR in the First World War

The gestation and birth of the first 'land machine' capable of breaking the lethal deadlock of the Western Front was long and complicated. The original advocates very early in the First World War were Colonel E.D. Swinton and Lieutenant-Colonel Albert Stern. A memorandum entitled 'Attack by Armour' and written by Winston Churchill helped create great interest in a 'tank' type of machine, and enthusiasm for such a weapon was shared by Lloyd George and, to a lesser extent, Sir Douglas Haig. The design team of Fosters of Lincoln (W. Tritton and Lieutenant W.G. Wilson RNAS) produced a machine known variously as 'Centipede', 'Mother' or 'Big Willie', which was made to specific dimensions (length 31ft 3in, width with gun sponson 13ft 8in and height 8ft). Trials of the Mark I tank took place at Hatfield Park on 2 February 1916 and were successful – which meant that the Armoured Car Section of the Machine-Gun Corps, later known as the Heavy Section Machine-Gun Corps (HSMGC), was in business! Six companies lettered A to F were formed, each comprising 25 tanks. Half of the first batch of 150 tanks would be 'male' tanks armed with two 6-pdr guns firing cannon shell plus three automatic Hotchkiss or Madsen rifles. The other half would be 'female' tanks armed with Vickers machine-guns. Their role was to destroy enemy posts and defend 'male' tanks from infantry attacks. The crew of eight would have a young officer in command, a driver, two gearsmen, two gunners and two loaders. In the 'female' tank four machine-gunners replaced the two gunners and two loaders.

Each company consisted of four sections, each with six tanks, plus one spare tank. Each section had three 'male' and three 'female' tanks, and was divided into three sub-sections. Each company establishment was 28 officers and 255 other ranks. (In addition, there was an administration branch consisting of one officer and four other ranks and a workshop branch consisting of three officers and fifty ORs.)

Major C.M. Tippetts from the South Wales Borderers commanded 'A' Company and their recruitment area was Merseyside, Blackburn, Burnham, Oldham, Leeds, Halifax and Wakefield. Training with the new intake, initially with only a few tanks, took place at Bull House camp at Bisley and later at Lord Iveagh's Elvedon estate near Thetford. Lance-Corporal (unpaid) A.E. Lee recalled:

> We were moved from the huts of Bisley camp to tents at Siberia Farm about a mile away. Our training was extended to include the .303 Hotchkiss Light Automatic Rifle and the 6-pdr Hotchkiss Naval Quick Firing Gun. Gunnery training was difficult. Practical training with live ammunition was easy as far as the .303 Vickers and Hotchkiss were concerned as we had the use of the Bisley ranges [but] the 6-pdr gun could not be used there. We were taken to Larkhill on Salisbury Plain for firing practice.

Winston Churchill, formerly First Lord of the Admiralty, suggested that the crews of the 'landships' should be trained in gunnery by the Navy. Lee again: 'Large numbers of us were sent to Whale Island (HMS *Excellent*) for training. The old Petty Officer Instructors went to great lengths to ensure we became efficient gunners.' Classification tests were fired from Monitors in the English Channel. 'We learnt by a system of trial and error and somehow by sharing our knowledge we got results,' noted Lance-Corporal Lee. 'Soon every man in the crew became a competent driver working on the principle that every man must be able to do the job of everyone else in an emergency. We worked hard at training for 6½ days every week.'

The wireless transmitters had a limited range of 3 miles but could not be used in action because of engine noise and vibration. Semaphore and morse code were used ineffectively and carrier pigeons were 'deployed' with varying success. Young officer tank commanders would often walk ahead of their tanks checking that the going was hard enough with an ashplant stick. With its 105hp Daimler engine, each tank, loaded with crew, 300 rounds for the guns and 20,000 rifle rounds, weighed 28 tons, 8 cwt.

Lee recalled some of the names of 'A' Company's tanks. They included 'Autogophaster' and 'Otasel', while one male/female sub-section was christened 'The One-eyed Riley' and 'Riley's Daughter'. Others included 'Active', 'Adder', 'Alert', 'Ardent', 'Arrogant', 'Arrow' and 'Arethusa'. The tanks in Lee's own section were named after popular London verses, such as 'Oh, I Say'; 'Look Who's Here'; 'Watch Your Step'; 'We're All In It' and 'So Search Me'. His own tank was 'Keep Smiling'. Lieutenant C.E. Palmer-Bott commanded and the other crew members were F.H. Banner, O. Boulton, E. Fillingham, F.T. Preece, J. Duncan and L.C. Chapman.

Visitors to see the new weapons of destruction and the training programme included King George V, Lloyd George, the Prime Minster, Winston Churchill and Earl Haig. The latter was so impressed that he altered his plans to break the stalemate on the Somme front. Besides Swinton, another key visitor was a Major Hugh Elles RE from GHQ France who came to check on the new 'Caterpillar' project. Word got out to the public about these activities, and various unofficial nicknames were created, such as 'The rag-time ASC' and 'Fred Karno's army'.

In August 1916 'A' Company was given ten days' 'overseas' leave and on their return to camp packed up their equipment and kit. They entrained for

Southampton and thence travelled by ship to Le Havre. The cranes at Southampton could not lift the heavy tanks, which had to be loaded at Avonmouth. Men and machines were reunited at Yvrench, a small village near Abbeville, where the 3-ton sponsons were bolted on to each side of the tanks. 'C' and 'D' Companies had landed in France ahead of 'A' and 'B', and were first into action. The battle of the Somme had started on 1 July 1916 and during the course of that day the British Army suffered some 60,000 casualties. 'C' and 'D' Companies went into action on 15 September with 60 tanks in 'penny-packets' supporting XIV, XV and III Corps of the Fourth Army. Of these, 36 tanks reached the front line around Flers and Guedecourt and fought with some success.

Winston Churchill wrote in his memoirs:

The ruthless desire for a decision at all costs led in September to a most improvident disclosure of the caterpillar vehicles. . . . Fifty of these engines, developed with great secrecy under the purposely misleading name of 'tanks', had been completed. They arrived in France during the early stages of the Battle of the Somme for experimental purposes and the training of their crews. When it was seen how easily they crossed trenches and flattened out entanglements made for their trial behind the British lines, the force of the conception appealed to the directing minds of the Army. The Headquarters staff, hitherto lukewarm, now wished to use them at once in the battle. Mr Lloyd George thought this employment of the new weapon in such small numbers premature. He informed me of the discussion which was proceeding. I was so shocked at the proposal to expose this tremendous secret to the enemy upon such a petty scale and as a mere make-weight to what I was sure could only be an indecisive operation, that I sought an interview with Mr Asquith, of whom I was then a very definite opponent. The Prime Minster received me in the most friendly manner, and listened so patiently to my appeal that I thought I had succeeded in convincing him. But if this were so, he did not make his will effective, and on September 15, the first tanks, or 'large armoured cars' as they were called in the Communiqué, went into action on the front of the Fourth Army attacking between the Combles ravine and Martinpuich.

It rained through October and much of November. Lance-Corporal Lee's section was based in Thiepval village and his 'Keep Smiling' tank was on its way to the front line when the attack was postponed. The battleground of the Somme became a quagmire, so the tanks were abandoned well forward under skeleton crews and 'A' Company returned to camp at Aveluy Wood.

Towards the end of the Battle of the Somme 'A' Company was involved in several supporting actions. At St Pierre Divion 'female' tank 544, commanded by Lieutenant H.W. Hitchcock, reached the start line to support the Black Watch. What follows is the official report of the action near the River Ancre on 13 November, written by Corporal A. Taffs:

At five minutes before Zero hour the engine was started and at Zero hour car No. 544 advanced and was directed by Lieutenant Hitchcock on its course till about 7am when it reached the German front line and was temporarily unable to proceed as tracks would not grip owing to the condition of the ground. This had already occurred in No Man's Land. Up till now none of our troops had been seen and the car was surrounded by the enemy. About this time Lieutenant Hitchcock was wounded in the head and gave orders to abandon the car, and then handed the command over to Corporal Taffs. Three men and Lieutenant Hitchcock got out of the car; he was seen to fall at once, but no more was seen of two of the three men who had evacuated the tank. The third man was pulled back into the tank after he

'A' Company A13 tank 'We're All In It' abandoned sideslipped into a trench. (*Tank Museum 410/A5*)

had been wounded in the forearm, and as the enemy were shooting through the open door, it was immediately closed. Fire was at once opened upon the enemy who retired to cover and opened on the tank with machine-guns and rifles. Corporal Taffs decided not to abandon the tank but decided with the help of the driver Lance-Corporal Bevan, who had been previously wounded about the face by splinters of his prism, to carry on and try to get the tank forward to its objective. They managed to extricate the tank by using the reverse and then drove forward as far as the German second line where the tank crashed into a dugout and was hopelessly engulfed and lying at an angle of about 45 degrees thereby causing the two guns on the lower side to be useless and the two guns on the upper side only capable of firing at a high angle. The tank was now attacked by the Germans with machine-guns and also bombed from the sides, front and underneath. At about 8am as none of our troops had yet been seen, probably owing to the thick mist which prevailed during the whole action, Corporal Taffs sent a message by Carrier Pigeon asking for help. This message was received by 2nd Corps who passed it on to the 118th Infantry Brigade who gave orders to the Black Watch to render all assistance possible. About 9am the tank was relieved by a party of the Notts and Derby Regt who were soon followed by the Black Watch. Corporal Taffs and the remainder of the crew left the tank when our line was established well in front of it and was safe from capture by the enemy.

The crew of the tank were Lieutenant H.W. Hitchcock (killed); Corporal A. Taffs; Lance-Corporal R. Bevan (ASC Driver) (wounded); Lance-Corporal S.A. Moss; Gunner W.A. Stanley (wounded); Gunner W. Miles (killed); Gunner F. Ainley (wounded) and Gunner A.W. Tolley.

The bodies of Lieutenant H.W. Hitchcock and Gunner W.J. Miles were found and identified today. Gunner W. Stanley was seen being conveyed to hospital after the action. The guns have been removed from the tank by a salvage party today, and brought back to camp.

Corporal Taffs and the men who remained in the Tank with him, undoubtedly did splendid work by remaining at their posts. I would specially bring to notice the names of 40429 Corporal Taffs A. and M2/106388 Lance-Corporal Bevan R.

14/11/16   Signed C.M. Tippetts, Major, Commanding 'A' Company, Heavy Section, MGC

Five of the crew were awarded Military Medals. At Beaucourt Sergeant D. Davies and Gunner H. Thomas were awarded Italian bronze medals, Sergeant W. Gibson the MSM and Lance-Corporal W. Fenton the Military Medal for repairing tanks under fire in a workshop 'party' near the River Ancre.

Lance-Corporal Lee wrote of the tankless company at the end of 1916, based at Fleury:

We had no sergeants left [and] I was the senior corporal. Practically everything we had possessed had been lost with our tanks and nothing had been replaced. We hadn't seen a canteen or shop since September. There wasn't a buttonstick or brush between us. We had come to France with only one suit. Uniforms were in rags. We must have looked a motley crowd as we shuffled on to parade after a three-day train journey, a six-hour night march and two hours sleep.

As part of the expansion from company to battalion, they were joined by a large batch of reinforcements from England. Their senior officer (a troop lieutenant) put *all* the veteran 'remnants' in their rags on a charge. Fortunately Corporal Lee woke up 'A' Company's senior surviving officer who restored the 'status quo'. The company spent Christmas 1916 in Eclimaux and stayed there until the spring of 1917 when they were reunited with their Mk IV tanks at Wavrans railway station.

Hugh Elles was promoted to operational command of the four 'rather forlorn little companies, living from hand to mouth'. A large area of some 24 acres between the River Ternoise and the main Hesdin–St Paul road was taken over for use as central workshops and stores. Colonel Elles made his headquarters at Beauquesne and his total staff expanded to 1,200 (plus 500 Chinese labourers).

A driving and mechanical school was needed as there were always two or three hundred tanks being repaired. In all about 3,000 tanks arrived from England; they were transported from Le Havre to Erin station where eleven rail lines led into the 'Tankodrome' main enclosure. Each new tank had to be tested and equipped before it could be issued to an active unit, and nearly every battlefield tank 'casualty' was returned by train to Erin.

By the end of 1916 the four companies had expanded to battalion size and were formed into two brigades. 'C' and 'D' formed 1st Brigade, and Lieutenant-Colonel A. Courage commanded 2nd Brigade with 'A' and 'B' Battalions. 1st Brigade (now known as Heavy Branch, Machine-Gun Corps) took part in the Battle of Arras which started on 9 April – Easter Monday. The Mk IV tank also saw action in the summer of 1917 when Earl Haig mounted a major offensive in Flanders. It had the same engine as the Mk I, but performance, reliability and safety were all improved. Two of the modifications were the provision of thicker armour and an external fuel tank. In all, 1,200 Mk IV tanks were eventually built. In June the title 'Tank Corps' was adopted and two months later there were nine tank battalions in France. Major J.F.C. Fuller arrived as Chief General Staff Officer and under Brigadier-General Hugh Elles the new Royal Tank Corps (from 28 July) became a genuine fighting force.

'A' Battalion fought in the Battle of Messines in June 1917 equipped with 38 new Mk IV tanks (plus six Mk Is converted into supply tanks). Courage's 2nd Brigade supported the Second Army in their attempt to capture the enemy's salient on the Messines ridge, overlooking the Ypres sector. On 7 June British infantry were supported in their attacks on Wytschaete village and Joye Farm. For this action Second Lieutenants C.W. Duncan, F.B. Keogh and J.M. Bailey were each awarded the Military Cross. Another six men were awarded the Military Medal: Sergeant F. Brash carried a wounded man to safety in the Oosttaverne line; Corporal C.H. Clements rescued Private Bryant from No-Man's-Land and carried him to Joye Farm; Private J.H. Robson, although wounded in the knee, kept on firing and disabled twenty enemy soldiers; Private L.H. Brokenshaw drove his tank for thirteen hours and Private R.F. Francombe for seven hours until disabled by gunfire; Private T.G. Housley steered his tank across the Damm Strasse.

Lance-Corporal Lee described the Battle of Messines: 'The two-day battle starting on 7 June had as objectives (1) to drive the enemy off the high ground at Wyschate [*sic*] Ridge and straighten our front line, (2) deny the enemy use of the high ground for observation purposes and (3) guard our right flank during the coming attack on Paschendale [*sic*].' Nineteen great mines laid by the tunnelling companies – totalling a million pounds of ammonal explosive – were exploded under the enemy's front line. Lee again: 'Zero hour was 03.10. Our part of the attack included a section of Wyschate Ridge. Along the top ran a sunken road called the "Damm Strasse". This was fortified and used as the enemy front line. We were to operate in pairs, therefore my tank "Revenge" and sister tank "Iron Ration" worked together.' Lee noted that all the tank names had been changed to start with the letter 'a'. He preferred 'Avenger', but 'Apple' and 'Apricot' were allocated to his pair. These were deemed 'most unsuitable for fighting tanks', so the crafty crews painted out the original names with a mixture of water and lime, which the rain soon washed off!

At 03.05 hours the order came 'Everyone into the tanks and start up'. The hands of our watches seemed hardly to move. . . . The last minute seemed like an hour. Then suddenly the earth seemed to split open as the guns started to fire. The noise was stupendous. We heard afterwards that the sound had been heard in England. There was very little enemy fire and we met no opposition in the enemy front line – everything must literally have been blown to pieces. . . . The ground was perfect and visibility fine. We had no difficulty in putting the [enemy] guns out of action and letting the infantry move forward. Five times during that morning we were called aside to help the infantry deal with machine-guns.

The afternoon was a repeat of the morning. There were no trenches to attack; the defence consisted principally of groups of machine-gunners. Most of them were strongly positioned . . .

with firm ground. We had no trouble dealing with them. If they were dug in, we were able to drive through them and if they were in pill-boxes we simply drove round the back of them and a few 6-pdr shells into the doors quickly dealt with them.

Twice 'Revenge' and 'Iron Ration' were ditched in marshy ground – but fortuitously not at the same time! Lee again: 'We had practised the towing-out of ditched tanks. Every tank carried a heavy steel cable for towing, shackled to eyebolts front and rear and carried over the top of the tank between the tracks.' 'Revenge' and 'Iron Ration' reached the final objective – the 'green' line – by about 04.00 hours slightly in advance of the infantry, and simply kept on going! 'Shooting at everything that moved and looked a worthwhile target, we moved into enemy territory. Suddenly we came under very heavy machine-gun fire and rifle fire from a large farmhouse in the middle of a field.' 'Revenge' went left and 'Iron Ration' right, firing as they went. Soon the 6-pdr shells set the farmhouses on fire and about 300 Germans broke out and ran for a belt of trees 100 yards away. 'Between us we had them caught in a crossfire. Very few reached the trees.'

Colonel Swinton had by now become one of the leading tank tactic experts and his rules for tank warfare were promulgated as 'Tank Tips' although they were largely ignored by GHQ! Major (later Major-General) J.F.C. 'Boney' Fuller was the first GSO2 of the new Tank Corps appointed to Elles's staff in December 1916. He organised the 'Instructions on Training' and became the leading tank tactician in the First World War.

TANK TIPS

- Remember your orders
- Shoot quick
- Shoot low. A miss which throws dust in the enemy's eyes is better than one which whistles in his ear
- Shoot cunning
- Shoot the enemy while they are rubbing their eyes
- Economise ammunition and don't kill a man three times
- Remember that trenches are curly and dugouts deep – look round the corners
- Watch the progress of the fight and your neighbouring tanks
- Watch your infantry whom you are helping
- Remember the position of your own line
- Shell out the enemy's machine-guns and other small guns and kill them first with your 6-pdrs
- You will not see them for they will be cunningly hidden. You must ferret out where they are, judging by the following signs: Sound, Dust, Smoke
- A shadow in a parapet; a hole in a wall, haystack, rubbish heap, wood-stack, pile of bricks. They will be usually placed to fire slantways across the front and to shoot along the wire

- One 6-pdr shell that hits the loophole of a MG emplacement will do it in
- Use the 6-pdr with care; shoot to hit and not to make a noise
- Never have any gun, even when unloaded, pointing at your own infantry, or a 6-pdr gun pointed at another tank
- It is the unloaded gun that kills the fool's friends
- Never mind the heat
- Never mind the noise
- Never mind the dust
- Think of your pals in the infantry
- Thank God you are bullet-proof and can help the infantry, who are not
- Have your mask always handy

On 31 July the 2nd Tank Brigade supported General Jacob's II Corps advancing on the Gheluvelt plateau in the Hooge sector. Enemy artillery fire from a strong-point nicknamed 'Clapham Junction' knocked out all but one of the 19 tanks that managed to get into the action. More than 20 others were delayed, got ditched or broke down. 'A' Battalion was engaged on the Westhoek Ridge where Captains H. Carew and E.D. Blackburn were awarded Military Crosses. Lance-Corporal T. Murdoch and Private H. Utting gained Distinguished Conduct Medals when their respective tank commanders were put out of action and they managed to bring their tanks and survivors back to safety. Murdoch then returned to retrieve the carrier pigeons used to convey messages to supporting infantry. 'Surbiton Villa' was another enemy strong-point which gave 'A' Battalion trouble. Corporals A. Dean, A. Lee, A.M. Murch and Privates E. Birnie, E.W. Wilkinson and J. Duncan all received Military Medals for the outstanding feats in this action. Duncan drove his tank under fire for 10 hours. Corporal Lee described his role in the Third Battle of Ypres:

> We reached our day's objective at Surbiton Villa about 200 yards in front of our advanced infantry. At the bottom of a valley one of our tank tracks broke through the soft surface and we slid sideways into a deep hole. With one gun pointing earthwards and the other to the sky we were helpless, our unditching beam being shot away an hour before. We could see the enemy about 100 yards in front massing for a counter-attack.

Fortified by a noggin of rum the resourceful Lee, assisted by Pat Brady, a former infantry machine-gunner, got out of the tank unseen by the enemy. Each had a machine-gun and a box of ammunition. They crawled to shell-holes in front of the ditched tank, where they 'waited until the enemy reached point-blank range, then we let them have it! The surprise was complete. The attack was broken up and the few demoralised survivors taken prisoner by the arriving infantry.' In the subsequent counter-attack 'Iron Ration' arrived amidst the heavy shelling and was struck by a direct hit that 'completely wrecked her. The ground was a shambles. Everyone was either dead or badly wounded. The sponson and guns had taken most of the impact. The blast had driven forward into the tank killing everyone inside in

Captain Clement Robertson VC.
(*By kind permission of the Colonel Commandant of the Royal Tank Regiment/Tank Museum 1399/A6*)

the enclosed space but it had blown me clear before the splinters started to spread.' 'Iron Ration's undicthing beam was used to haul 'Revenge' out of her hole to fight again. In September Corporal Lee, now sporting a new haircut and a clean uniform, received the Military Medal from General Elles at Tank HQ.

Early in October, towards the end of the Third Battle of Ypres, 'A' Battalion supported the 21st Division in several actions near Polygon Wood, north of Gheluvelt and Poelcappelle. For three days and nights Captain Clement Robertson and his batman Private C.S. Allen surveyed and taped the ground ahead towards a bridge over the Reutelbeek and the enemy strong-points on the far side. For his extraordinary courage Robertson was awarded the Victoria Cross – the first for the Tank Corps. Private Allen and Sergeant D. Davies were awarded the Distinguished Conduct Medal and Corporal F. Jarvis the Military Medal. Robertson's citation reads:

From 30 September to 4 October this officer worked without a break under heavy fire preparing a route for his tanks to go into action against Reutel. He finished late on the night of 3 October, and at once led his tanks up to the point for the attack. He brought them safely up by 3am on 4 October and at 6am led them into action. The ground was very bad and heavily broken up by shell fire and the road demolished for about 500 yards. Capt Robertson, knowing the risk of the tanks missing their way, continued to lead them on foot. In addition to the heavy shell fire, intense machine-gun and rifle fire was directed at the tanks. Although knowing that his action would inevitably cost his life, Capt Robertson

'A' Battalion Mk IV female tank with fascine boarding train at plateau railhead on the eve of the Battle of Cambrai. (*Tank Museum 867/E4*)

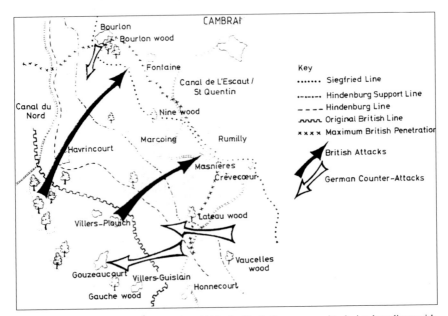

At the Battle of Cambrai, 20 November 1917, the Tank Corps committed nine battalions with 378 Mk IV tanks with 54 more held in reserve.

deliberately continued to lead his tanks when well ahead of our own infantry, guiding them carefully and patiently towards their objective. Just as they reached the road he was killed by a bullet through the head, but his objective had been reached and the tanks in consequence were enabled to fight a very successful action.

By his very gallant devotion, Capt Robertson deliberately sacrificed his life to make certain the success of his tanks.

★ ★ ★

The greatest tank battle of the war took place in November 1917. It was the intention of the British Third Army to smash through the various defences of the Hindenburg Line north-eastwards towards Cambrai. A grand total of 476 tanks were deployed, 36 to 'A' Battalion plus six in reserve. All three tank brigades took part, with 'A' Battalion allotted to the 20th and 29th Divisions of III Corps. Each brigade had 18 supply tanks and 3 signal tanks with wireless. Some 32 tanks were fitted with grapnels designed to pull away wire not destroyed by artillery fire, while two were loaded with bridging material and fascines. The final tank carried telephone cable linking the forward troops to Army HQ. From Bray-sur-Somme the nine tank battalions entrained for the front line, along a start line some 13,000 yards

Captain R.W.L. Wain VC.
(*By kind permission of the Colonel Commandant of the Royal Tank Regiment/Tank Museum 1399/A4*)

long. 'A' Battalion started near Havrincourt Wood, commanded by Lieutenant-Colonel Lyon. The company commanders were Major J.C. Tilly and Majors Lakin and Thorpe.

Captain Richard Wain, a section commander, had fought at the Somme in January; he was wounded in July and again on 22 September. He was killed in action at Marcoing, near Cambrai, on 20 November and was awarded the Victoria Cross – the second for 'A' Battalion. As his section crossed the first Hindenburg Line and approached the enemy support line his tank 'Abu-Ben-Adam II' received a direct hit from a mortar shell at short range while attacking Good Old Man Farm. When the smoke and fumes of the explosion had died away he found that he and one badly wounded private were the sole survivors. Staggering out of the tank, they salvaged a Lewis gun from the wreckage and rushed straight at the enemy strong-point, Wain firing as he went. They succeeded in taking half the garrison prisoner. Already seriously wounded, Wain picked up a rifle and continued firing at the retreating enemy until he was fatally wounded in the head. Bleeding profusely, he carried on clearing the enemy out of the strong-point but shortly afterwards died of wounds. His VC citation reads:

> During the attack the tank in which he was became disabled by a direct hit near a German strong-point in the Hindenburg Support Line, at L24a 3.6 which was holding up the attack. Capt Wain and one man were the only survivors, and they were both seriously wounded. While the infantry were held up there, this officer, in spite of his wounds, rushed from behind the tank in front of the enemy strong-point with a Lewis gun and captured the strong-point, taking half the garrison prisoners. Although his wounds were very serious, Capt Wain picked up a rifle and continued to fire at the retiring enemy until he received a fatal wound in the head. Although bleeding profusely from wounds, this gallant officer refused attention of stretcher-bearers in order to carry on clearing the enemy out of the strong-point.
>
> It was due to this gallant act by this officer that the infantry were able to advance.

King George V presented the Victoria Cross to Wain's proud parents at Buckingham Palace on 20 April 1918. By 0800 hours the first objectives were secured, but Ribecourt held out until 0920 hours and the enemy resisted 'A' Battalion around Havrincourt in cellars and dug-outs. Flesquieres held out but 'A' and 'I' Battalions swept forward in the right centre of the advance. But at Grand Ravine sixteen tanks were knocked out. By 1600 hours the main tank battle was over.

Captain W. Bayley, the battalion reconnaissance officer, and Major J.C. Tilly had an unofficial race on the 20th Division front. The battalion had captured the bridges at the canal bend near Marcoing on the way towards the Hindenburg support line. Now Tilly, riding on a mule, and Bayley, running briskly, set off under the muzzles of several German batteries to gain the battalion's second objective: the railway bridge at Marcoing and the canal locks between Marcoing and Masnières. With revolver shots they put to flight a German demolition party and then cut the electric leads of the mine under the bridge. Soon eight 'A' Battalion tanks arrived and three others secured the lock east of Marcoing. The indomitable Major Tilly, still on his mule, set off again on a recce mission towards Cambrai, together with Major Lakin on a horse. Reaching the outskirts of Cambrai the pair were politely saluted by German medical orderlies, and returned unscathed to their own lines by 1500 hours. Unfortunately the following British cavalry and infantry of 29th Division showed little sense of urgency and the opportunity to exploit into Cambrai was lost.

Eight 'A' Battalion tanks supported 20th Division on the right flank in the bend of the Marcoing canal. For two hours they drove to and fro along the German front line under heavy fire from field guns and machine-guns pinning down the British infantry.

Lance-Corporal Lee was in Captain Raikes's section, helping the Notts and Derby infantry clear Marcoing. Crossing the canal bridge, they patrolled in front of it. During the counter-attack on the 21st Lee was wounded in the face, arm and leg, but considered his wounds not too serious. Later he reported to the nearest dressing station and the MO asked him how long it was since he had been wounded. When he answered 'Four or five hours', the MO was furious. 'You fellows in the tanks never come down straight away after being wounded.' He gave Lee the maximum anti-tetanus injection over the heart instead of in the arm! Via No. 6 General Hospital at Rouen, the Tank Depot at Le Treport and Le Havre, Lee travelled back to Blighty.

Seven 'A' Battalion officers won decorations. At Noyelles Captain D.T. Raikes MC gained the coveted Distinguished Service Order and Captain C.O. Rich a bar to his Military Cross; Military Crosses also went to Captain George Ingham, who led an attack on Nine Wood, and Second Lieutenant T.J. Shaw for actions at Gauche Wood and Villers Guislan; Captain M.J. Miskin supported the Border Regiment around Marcoing and won the Military Cross; Second Lieutenant J.M. Bailey gained both the Military Cross and the Croix de Guerre after the battles of Messines, Ypres and now Cambrai; finally Second Lieutenant G. Matthews was awarded the Military Cross for an action at Noyelles. In addition, Corporal A. Mayglothling won the Distinguished Conduct Medal at Noyelles after all his crew were wounded and four Lewis guns hit. Fire broke out four times but he still managed to rescue his crew. Corporal W.H. Stickler won the Distinguished Conduct Medal at Marcoing. Military Medals were won by Sergeants L.C. Lose, C.G. Sayers and J.E. Gardner, Corporal H.J. Edwards, Lance-Corporals L. Chandler and T. Murdock and Privates A.D. Summers, P.D. Springham, W. Smith and R.J. Murray. On 30 November a strong German counter-attack overran British troops in the villages of Gonnelieq and Villers-Guislain and surged forwards towards Gouzeaucourt. The 2nd Tank Brigade with 36 tanks of 'A' and 'B' Battalions supported the 1st Guards Brigade in the fierce fighting around Bourlon Wood which eventually halted the German advance.

During the Battle of Cambrai the Royal Tank Corps had forced a 6-mile salient into and through the Hindenburg Line at a cost of some 600 casualties. 'A' Battalion received awards for seven officers and twelve other ranks. Major J.C. Tilly, the acting battalion CO, received a belated Military Cross.

★ ★ ★

During the winter of 1917/18 two new tank developments occurred. The new Mk V that replaced the Mk IV tank had Hotchkiss guns instead of Lewis guns and was powered by a Ricardo 150hp engine that produced greater power (although the maximum speed was still only 4.6mph!). Thicker frontal armour of 12–14mm-thick steel gave greater protection. New epicycle gears designed by Major W.G. Wilson enabled drive *and* steering to be performed by one man. The Mk V had a crew of eight (but with 6ft extensions – three extra panels on each side – could carry 20 to 25 infantry) and could cross 13ft-wide trenches. The new fast pursuit tank called the Whippet was not allocated to 'A' Battalion. The second development was the German A7V 'fortress' tank of which a batch of 20 were produced. It weighed in at 30 tons, was 24ft long and was armed with a 57mm gun plus six Maxim machine-guns. It carried a crew of 18 and was powered by twin Daimler engines driven by a sophisticated gearbox.

The great German offensive started on 21 March 1918. Some 63 divisions advanced on a 43-mile frontage and within three days had made huge gains. The 4th Tank Brigade with the newly numbered battalions included the 1st, 4th and 5th under command of the British Fifth Army in the Peronne area. In their withdrawal to Haricourt, Moislains and Mauripas a considerable number of 1st Battalion tanks were unable mechanically to complete the journey and were consequently destroyed. For some time the main role in this defensive battle was that of manning Lewis gun posts in the trenches. The River Ancre was crossed and at 0440 hours on the 21st a huge bombardment fell on the British Army. On the 22nd all tanks were ordered from the Tankodrome to Buire Wood and on to Three Tubs Wood and thence to Moislains. Tank no. 2048 under Second Lieutenant Dudley had to be destroyed. On the 23rd the battalion took up position on the high ground north-west of Moislains, with 'A' and 'B' Companies lining the ridge at 50 pace intervals, with 'C' in reserve. A petrol dump and two more tanks had to be blown up. Second Lieutenant MacFayden had to destroy his tank but stayed with the wreck and used salvaged Lewis guns to inflict huge losses on the advancing enemy at Bouchhavesnes. Further withdrawal then took place north of Clery-sur-Somme and on the 24th they fell back to a line east of Haricourt. A considerable number of tanks failed mechanically and had to be destroyed, but Captain Dorman and his section fought back bravely near Hem, as did Captain Fraser near Mauripas before returning to Mericourt at midnight. Lieutenant Oldham had a notable action at Curlu. Major Thorpe established a line of Lewis gun posts in trenches 700yd east of Mericourt. The rest of the battalion withdrew to the north-east of Bray and on the 25th fell back to the Bois de Tailles. Captain Keogh with nine tanks engaged the enemy at Méaulté.

On the 26th a gun team consisting of Captain Sunnikin, Lieutenant Ehrhardt and Sergeant Scott, despite being hemmed in on three sides by the enemy, inflicted heavy casualties on the Germans. All the supply tanks withdrew to Heilly, where a bridge over the River Ancre remained intact. The battalion finally rallied on the 27th at Franvillers and together with Australian infantry the Lewis gun teams held a ridge south of Brizieux, while surviving tanks supported the Australians at Mericourt and Bonnay. The enemy was halted for the time being on the Morlancourt to Villers-Bretonneux line. A church service was held on Easter Sunday.

It was a desperate, nightmarish time and the British Army was almost 'in extremis'. Many brave individual actions brought deserved awards, notably to Lieutenant E.A. Oldham at Curlu and Hem. Captain F.B. Keogh, Lieutenant D. Mann, Second Lieutenant MacFayden with eight tanks covered the withdrawal of 105 Infantry Brigade on the Bray–Albert road near Méaulté; Captain F.S. Sunnikin at Bois de Tailles excelled in a rearguard action covering the infantry withdrawal from Bray; Major M.L. Dakin DSO won a Military Cross for actions at Maricourt and Bray. Distinguished Conduct Medals went to the Lewis gun teams – Corporal W.G. Hurby, Sergeant R. Scott and Private W.J. Ford. The recce officer Captain H.L. Elton won the Military Cross, and Captain R.C. Young and Major J.C. Tilly each won a bar to his Military Cross, the former at Maricourt and the latter as second-in-command of the defences of the Bray–Corbie road.

★   ★   ★

On 1 April 'C' Company took over all the surviving fighting tanks, and 'A' and 'B' Companies were formed into Lewis gun teams. Fortunately on the 5th 'B' Company collected ten Mk IV tanks from Beauval, and 'A' picked up twelve Mk IVs the next day from Vignacourt. The battalion moved to Behencourt and on the 9th went to Frechencourt. At this time 4th Battalion RTC took over the reserve Lewis gun responsibility. While attached to the 3rd Tank Brigade the laager in the Bois d'Aquenne was heavily shelled on the 17th with mustard gas, used here for the first time, and 6 officers and 32 ORs of 'A' Company were evacuated to hospital. The battalion then concentrated in the Bois d'Abbé. When Lieutenant-Colonel Broome fell sick on the 18th, Major J.C. Tilly again resumed command. To prevent attacks by the Royal Flying Corps three stripes (in white, red and blue) were painted on the roof of every tank.

In the previous month fourteen of the new German A7V tanks spearheaded four 'storm' divisions on a 4-mile frontage around Villers-Bretonneux. On 24 April some of these monsters appeared in support of the German 77th Division aiming at Cachy, then held by the British 8th Division.

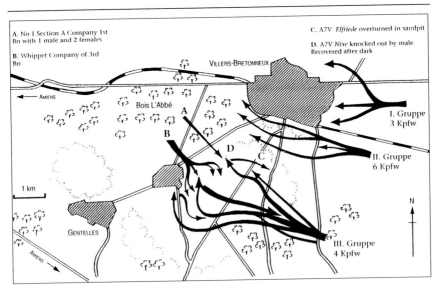

A. No 1 Section A Company 1st Bn with 1 male and 2 females

B. Whippet Company of 3rd Bn

C. A7V *Elfriede* overturned in sandpit

D. A7V *Nixe* knocked out by male. Recovered after dark

VILLERS-BRETONNEUX

AMIENS

Bois L'Abbé

I. Gruppe 3 Kpfw

II. Gruppe 6 Kpfw

1 km

GENTELLES

AMIENS

N

III. Gruppe 4 Kpfw

Villers-Bretonneux, scene of the first tank *v.* tank battle, April 1918.

Captain J.C. Brown's 1 Section of 'A' Company was still recovering from the mustard gas attack. The section consisted of a rather battered male Mk IV tank under Second Lieutenant Frank Mitchell plus two 'female' tanks, also Mk IVs. Captain Brown went forward on foot towards the Cachy switch line and at 0945 hours the three Mk IVs moved off close to the Bois d'Aquenne. Three German A7Vs of Group III had become lost in the fog (No. 504 'Schnuck', No. 525 'Siegfried' and No. 561 'Nixe'). At about 1020 hours 'Nixe' had opened fire; shells hit the two female Mk IVs and forced them to retire from the battlefield. Second Lieutenant Mitchell closed towards 'Nixe' and his left-hand gunner scored three hits on the A7V, causing six casualties. The remainder of the crew evacuated their tank. This is Mitchell's account of the action:

I informed the crew and a great thrill ran through us all. Opening a loophole, I looked out. There, some 300 yards away, a round, squat-looking monster was advancing; behind it came waves of infantry, and further away to the left and right crawled two more of these armoured tortoises. So we had met our rivals at last! For the first time in history tank was encountering tank!

The 6-pdr gunners crouched on the floor, their backs against the engine cover, and loaded their guns expectantly. We still kept on a zigzag course, threading gaps between the lines of hastily dug trenches, and coming near the small protecting belt of wire we turned left. The right gunner, peering through his narrow slit, made a sighting shot and the shell burst some distance beyond the enemy tank. No reply came. A second shot boomed out, landing just to the right, but again there was no reply. More shots followed. Suddenly a hurricane of hail pattered against our steel wall, filling the interior with myriads of sparks and flying splinters. Something rattled against the steel helmet of the driver sitting next to me and my face was stung with minute fragments of steel. The crew flung themselves flat on the floor. The driver ducked his head and drove straight on. Above the roar of our engine sounded the staccato rat-tat-tat-tat of machine-guns and other furious jets of bullets sprayed our steel side, the splinters clanging against the engine cover. The Jerry tank had treated us to a broadside of armour-piercing bullets.

Taking advantage of a dip in the ground . . . we manoeuvred to get the left gunner on to the moving target. Owing to our gas casualties the gunner was working single-handed, and his right eye being swollen with gas, he aimed with the left. Moreover, as the ground was heavily scarred with shell-holes, we kept going up and down like a ship in a heavy sea, which made accurate shooting difficult. His first shot fell some fifteen yards in front, the next went beyond, and then I saw the shells bursting all round the tank. He fired shot after shot in rapid succession every time it came into view.

Nearing the village of Cachy, I noticed to my astonishment that the two females were slowly limping away to the rear. Almost immediately on their arrival they had both been hit by shells which tore great holes in their sides, leaving them defenceless against machine-gun bullets, and as their Lewis guns were useless against the heavy armour plate of the enemy they could do nothing but withdraw.

Now the battle was left to us, with our infantry in their trenches tensely watching the duel like spectators in the pit of a theatre. As we turned and twisted to dodge the enemy's shells I looked down to find that we were going straight into a trench full of British soldiers, who were huddled together and yelling at the tops of their voices to attract our attention. A quick signal to the gearsman seated at the rear of the tank and we turned swiftly, avoiding catastrophe by a second.

Then came our first casualty. Another raking broadside from the German tank and the rear Lewis gunner was wounded in both legs by an armour-piercing bullet which tore through our steel plate. We had no time to put on more than a temporary dressing and he lay on the floor, bleeding and groaning, while the 6-pdr boomed over his head and the empty shell cases clattered all round him. . . . We turned again and proceeded at a slower pace. The left gunner, registering carefully, began to hit the ground right in front of the Jerry tank. I took a risk and stopped the tank for a moment. The pause was justified; a well-aimed shot hit the enemy's conning tower, bringing him to a standstill. Another roar and yet another white puff at the front of the tank denoted a second hit! Peering with swollen eyes through his narrow slit, the gunner shouted words of triumph that were drowned by the roar of the engine. Then once more he aimed with great deliberation and hit for the third time. Through a loophole I saw the tank heel over to one side; then a door opened and out ran the crew. We

First battle with panzers. 1 Battalion RTC Lieutenant Mitchell's male Mk IV *v.* German ATV tank, 24 April 1918. (*By kind permission of the Colonel Commandant of the Royal Tank Regiment/Tank Museum 1305/B4*)

had knocked the monster out! Quickly I signalled to the machine-gunner and he poured volley after volley into the retreating figures.

My nearest enemy being now out of action, I turned to look at the other two, who were coming forward very slowly, while our 6-pdr gunners spread havoc in the ranks of the advancing German infantry with round after round of case shot. [This consisted of iron balls strung at intervals on steel wire; the effect can be imagined.] Now, I thought, we shan't last very long. The two great tanks were creeping relentlessly forward; if they both concentrated their fire on us we would be finished. We fired rapidly at the nearest tank, and to my intense joy and amazement I saw it slowly back away. Its companion also did not appear to relish a fight, for it turned and followed its mate and in a few minutes they had both disappeared, leaving our tank the sole possessor of the battlefield.

The remaining A7V tanks withdrew. Later that day Captain Groves's and Lieutenant Holton's sections threw back enemy infantry attacks around the Bois d'Aquenne. Two days later 'A' and 'C' Companies supported the French Foreign Legion and the Moroccan Division, in which action Captain Groves and Second Lieutenant Wilson particularly distinguished themselves. Wilson broke through the enemy line, drove through the ruined village of Villers-Bretonneux and attacked some German heavy guns with case-shot and machine-gun fire. He then patrolled some enemy trenches and caused enormous losses by enfilade fire. After these actions 'A' Company handed over its remaining tanks to 'C' Company, south of the Somme, before returning to Franvillers Wood. On the 28th Second Lieutenant J.E. Jones helped the French infantry in an attack on Mangard Wood. In the course of clearing numerous enemy machine-gun nests he and all his crew were wounded; on their return Jones insisted that his crew should be evacuated in the ration cart before he allowed himself to be treated. He received the immediate award of the Military Cross. Other awards for the April actions went to Captains C.F.S. Groves and J.L. Loveridge for supporting the Moroccans and also to CSM D. Robertson DCM and Corporal W.G. Mursley DCM who both received French decorations. For the tank battle Captain F.C. Brown gained a bar to his Military Cross, and Second Lieutenant F. Mitchell received the Military Cross. In the Bois l'Abbé and Mangard Wood actions Privates Boyson, Gardner, Baird, Vallance, Dinwoodie and Spencer received Military Medals and Wallace the Distinguished Conduct Medal.

★ ★ ★

The great Battle of Amiens started on 8 August 1918 with a series of objectives east of the town on the Bapaume–Peronne line. Three Army corps were involved, III to the north of the River Somme, with the Australians to the south and the Canadians on their right flank. Lieutenant-Colonel M. Hankey commanded IV Tank Brigade, with four battalions including the 1st allocated to the Canadian Corps. The 1st was one of only two units issued with the new Mk V Star tanks, and their role was to support 4th Canadian Division. The plan was simple. Thirty Mk V tanks each carrying two infantry machine-gun sections would drive straight through to the third objective, deposit the machine-gunners and then send back fifteen tanks to help the Canadian infantry in their advance. However, a German battery knocked out nine of the ten 'A' Company tanks and eventually only eleven out of the original thirty rallied. Strongpoints in Fresnoy and Le Quesnel held up the advance. At the cost of 3,500 casualties the Canadians captured over 5,000 prisoners plus 161 guns. The overall attack was suspended on 11 August, by which time only 67 of the 415 tanks that started the action remained battle-worthy. But the Battle of Amiens shattered the confidence of the German Supreme Command. General Ludendorff wrote: 'August 8 was the black day of the German Army in the history of the war.'

The men of the 1st Battalion earned 12 Military Crosses and a Distinguished Conduct Medal for this battle and 11 Military Medals for actions around Beaucourt-en-Santerre. Major G. Hampson won the Distinguished Service Order near Cayeux Wood and Major Henry Beauchamp, the battalion chaplain, received the Military Cross. He was always in the firing line assisting the wounded.

Most tank battalions went into reserve until 18 September to retrain and reform as part of the preparations for the grand assault on the famous Hindenburg Line. This ran from just east of Arras south-eastwards for 40 miles to St Quentin. The First American Army and the Fourth French Army with 515 French Renault light tanks attacked in the southern sector between Reims and Verdun. The British First and Third Armies attacked on the line of the Canal du Nord. The action started on 27 September. IV Tank Brigade, which included the 1st Battalion, led the Australian Corps' attack on a 3-mile sector between Bellicourt and Vendhuille where the canal ran underground. From the Tankodrome at Mannacourt the battalion moved up to their start line, as this account relates.

The battalion operated with the 30th American Division and by means of taped routes approached to just behind the front line. At 5.30am on the 28th all the tanks went over to the attack, the object of which was to breach the Hindenburg Line and secure the tunnel entrance to the Canal de Torrens. 'A' Company, consisting of twelve tanks, moved forward to the north of Bellicourt, while 'B' Company worked south through Nauroy. The extremely heavy mist, combined with the dense smoke barrage, made the maintenance of direction a very difficult matter and the compasses in the tanks proved of immense value. Eight tanks of 'A' Company were able to reach the Hindenburg Line, where they crushed a thick belt of wire and succeeded in silencing a large number of machine-guns. They then went on to their final objective, but two received direct hits and two were ditched, only four arriving at the further end of the tunnel. Of 'B' Company seven cars made good progress and cleared much ground east of Bellicourt and north of Nauroy. During this operation two of their cars received direct hits and two had to stop owing to mechanical trouble and were burnt. Great success attended this operation against the enemy's strongest line of defence, though, had observation been better, much better results would have been achieved.

A very good action was fought by Second Lieutenant Hapgood's tank, which was ditched in the Hindenburg Line within 20 yards of the enemy. The enemy was strongly established at this point and directed very heavy fire on to the tank, with trench mortars, machine-guns and even hand grenades. Notwithstanding this, Lieutenant Hapgood held out for two days until the arrival of some Australian troops, who succeeded in dislodging the enemy. This officer and his crew then unditched the tank and proceeded to the rallying point.

The battalion rallied in the valley behind Haricourt on the evening of the 29th and the next day salvage work and repairs to damaged tanks were put in hand.

The American 30th Division had penetrated the Hindenburg Line's main and support lines and had reached Nauroy – a 2-mile advance aided by 33 British tanks of 1st (and 4th) Battalions.

Major M.J. Miskin won a bar to his Military Cross for actions at Bellicourt and Beaurevoir, and Private R.L. Hutchinson the Military Medal for taking a tunnel crossing near Bellicourt.

On 8 October the Third and Fourth British Armies launched a combined attack on their 17-mile front southwards from Cambrai. The tanks of 1st Battalion supported the Fourth Army. Second Lieutenant A. Wilson dealt with enemy posts at Les Folies and helped the South Africans at Hamage and Petite Folie farms in front of Beaurevoir. His courage was rewarded with the award of the Military Cross. Private B. Hamilton gained the Military Medal by knocking out a field gun north of Sonia Wood. Most of the German defenders had retreated to the River Selle line near Le Cateau after being forced out of the Hindenburg Reserve line at Beaurevoir. This is the account of 1st Battalion's actions during October:

On 1 October 'C' Company rejoined the remainder of the battalion and on the 3rd 'A' Company was merged into 'B' and 'C' Companies for further operations. These two composite companies moved forward to a valley on the 5th, continuing their journey the following day to the final starting point. Until the evening of the 7th all available time was spent in final adjustments and reconnaissance, and at 5.30am both companies went into that action which followed on the continued pressure of the previous week and which completely broke down the enemy's resistance on this front. The success of the operations was complete. The infantry drove the enemy before them and, whenever necessary, tanks moved up to deal with difficult situations. Both at Hamage Farm and Les Folies Wood sections of 'B' Company distinguished themselves, a battery of six guns being engaged and captured by Lieutenants Watson and Wilson at the former place. One car only was hit, the remainder rallying without casualties.

On that and the succeeding evenings a wonderful spectacle was seen in the burning of the enemy dumps and supply centres. The glow from these conflagrations lighted the sky and the surrounding country for many miles and bore witness to the precipitate retreat into which the enemy had been forced by the day's action. Destroyed bridges and crossroads marked the trail of the beaten and demoralised enemy, and the ensuing days found the battalion following in his wake at top speed. Perhaps the most gratifying part of this advance was the deliverance of villages and inhabitants which had been under the unenviable rule of the Germans since the autumn of 1914. In many cases excess of joy resulted in tears and every imaginable kind of gift was showered by the grateful villagers upon their rescuers.

The battalion finally halted in a small clearing north of Maretz and from 11 to 16 October the time was fully occupied in preparing for the next battle and reconnoitring the forward area. Much attention was paid to the River Selle which was reported by civilians to be an impassable obstacle. In spite of this information two visits were made by the battalion reconnaissance officer, Captain Bradbeer and the 'B' Company RO, Lieutenant Thornbank, to the banks of the river which were in no-man's-land, and eventually suitable crossings were found. The enemy's position was very strong here owing to the natural obstacle of the river and the huge railway embankment on the Le Cateau line. On the 15th all tanks in the battalion, consisting of one composite section of four tanks belonging to 'B' Company and two composite sections, also of four tanks, belonging to 'C' Company, moved up to their lying-up points in a small orchard north of Escaufourt, where they were camouflaged and the crews returned to rest in preparation for the action.

A start was made from here at 1am on the morning of the 17th, a previously taped route being followed. During the night gas shelling by the enemy was intense in all the valleys, and the difficulty of passing through these poisonous clouds was increased by the presence of a dense mist and the smoke from our own barrage which came down at 5.30am. While this barrage was going on observation was impossible but it just lifted as 'B' Company, which was leading, arrived at the banks of the river. Just prior to this the battalion sustained a great loss by the death of Major Miskin, who was killed by a shell while leading his company. All tanks succeeded in crossing the river and from there proceeded to engage the enemy who were resisting strongly along the embankment. The resistance was eventually overcome, numerous machine-guns being silenced, and the infantry in the course of a strong attack dislodged the enemy from his positions. All tanks, with the exception of one which received a direct hit, returned to the rallying point and from there proceeded to the old camp at Maretz as GHQ Reserve.

Lieutenant C.R. Thornback and Second Lieutenant T.A. Heywood won their Military Crosses in the River Selle attack south of Le Cateau, and the latter drove his tank across the river! Corporals Body and Collins and Privates Brown and Duncan all won Military Medals in the same battle.

Further attacks were made by the Third and Fourth Armies but resistance was still strong – on 17 October some 3 miles of ground were gained in the centre and on 4 November progress was made on a 30-mile front towards Mons and Malberge. The last tank engagement of the war took place the next day when eight Whippet light tanks advanced beyond the Forest of Mormal.

★   ★   ★

On 4 November a revolution broke out in Germany. The fleet mutinied but Ludendorff was confident that his armies could keep on fighting on the new Antwerp–Meuse line of defences. Nevertheless the Armistice was signed at 11am on 11 November. The war was over. During 1919 further decorations arrived for the men of the 1st Battalion, including five Distinguished Conduct Medals and three Military Crosses, one to Captain J. Macmillan RAMC. Since their arrival in France in 1916 the battalion had won 2 Victoria Crosses, 1 Distinguished Service Order, 3 bars to Military Crosses, 39 Military Crosses, 21 Distinguished Conduct Medals, 1 bar to a Military Medal, 60 Military Medals and 5 Military Service Medals.

The German frontier was crossed on 1 December and Cologne was occupied on the 6th, with the colours of the Tank Corps carried on the armoured cars of 17th Battalion. Field Marshal Sir Douglas Haig in his final despatch paid tribute to the Tank Corps:

Since the opening of our offensive on 8 August tanks have been employed on every battlefield. The importance of the part played by them in breaking up the resistance of the German infantry can scarcely be exaggerated. The whole scheme of the attack on 8 August was dependent upon tanks and ever since that date on numberless occasions the success of our infantry has been powerfully assisted or confirmed by their timely arrival; so great has been the effect produced upon the German infantry by the appearance of British tanks, valuable results were achieved by the use of dummy tanks painted on frames of wood and canvas.

CHAPTER TWO

Between the Wars

Most of the twenty-five tank battalions were disbanded in 1919/20 but a few, including the 1st Battalion (which became the Tank Depot battalion) remained on permanent establishment. They did not serve in Russia nor in Ireland. Lieutenant-Colonel G.B. Matthew-Lannowe commanded the battalion at Bovington. Demobilisation was the main concern of the RTR veterans.

Peacetime soldiering after years of bloody fighting is of course an anti-climax. Back came the parades and drill, PT, endless tank maintenance, the courses, guard duty and, above all, sport, with army boxing, rugger, soccer, cricket, hockey, PT, cross-country running and athletics. The RSMs and the squad sergeants (the backbone of the British Army) were in their element. Bull was paramount. Distinctive coloured patches were worn on both shoulder straps of jacket and greatcoat (red for 1 RTR, saffron for 2 RTR), and the lanyard or whistle cord round the left shoulder of the service dress jacket was of the same colour. The RAC gunnery school was at Lulworth camp, a few miles from Bovington near Wareham in Dorset. All recruits received their basic training on courses lasting about thirty-six weeks. In the tankmen's honour the square in Bovington was renamed Amiens Square, while the street names were changed to commemorate famous people or places – such as Robertson Avenue, Elles Road, Swinton Avenue and many others.

Very little of consequence occurred for some considerable time. Training was simple. The squadrons trained in the summer and at the end of September the tanks were put away into heavy preservation in the hangar or Tankodrome. The light tanks would make occasional circuits of the training area at a modest speed in case of breakdown. Guns or machine-guns were fired only rarely, although there was a Command Machine-Gun Cup competition. The real 'work' began in the afternoon. The boxing team would train. The cross-country team would train. The athletic team would train. Fierce inter-company/squadron and inter-hut games took place. In the summer cricket, swimming and water polo competitions were organised.

In 1921 the 1st (Depot) Battalion moved a short distance down the road from Worgret camp at Wareham back to Bovington (which became known as the RTC Depot on 16 June 1925). The 'Geddes Axe' fell on the Tank Corps and investment in tank design almost ceased. The huge Machine-Gun Corps was disbanded and the few survivors joined the 3rd Tank

1st (Depot) Battalion on parade with the Tank Corps Band marching along King George V Road, Bovington. (*Tank Museum 10/C4*)

Battalion. The regimental band was formed in February 1922 and the famous black beret introduced uniquely to the Royal Tank Regiment on 5 May 1924.

F.J.C. Wollaston (subsequently a major) was a tank commander in the late 1920s. He wrote about the Carden-Loyd carriers and light tanks deployed by 1 RTC. Initially he was a hull gunner and second driver on the T74 Mk II Vickers tank.

The original MG carrier, designed by Carden and made in Loyd's garage, used the engine and transmission of the 'T' Model Ford. The controls were clutch pedal half down, disengaged – full down, low gear – right back, high gear. Middle pedal reverse (with clutch in neutral) right pedal – brake. A hand brake, which also held the clutch pedal half down. Tiller bar steering (the first I think). The drive was two sprockets at the front through a differential – so that whatever slowing was applied to one side when steering added to the speed of the opposite track. A little tricky when learning to drive, and resulted in a lot of starting handle twisting. The hand throttle slid on a serrated quadrant to the right front of the driver. The engine was between the crew, and the driver rested his elbow on the cover when working the controls. The ignition lever was on a quadrant – to the right of the throttle (the two controls forming a half circle).

The Vickers machine-gun was fitted on the right side on a frame. This was pushed by the gunner's right foot to elevate the gun, and had a few degrees' traverse. It could be locked in position and the foot removed from the pedal.

The programme for new recruits consisted of five weeks of drill and more drill, and a great deal of PT, followed by thirteen weeks of tank driving and maintenance. The adjutant would take drill parades twice a week. At the end of the eighteen-week period the squad marched to Wool railway station in their smart new blue 'patrols' carrying black swagger canes with silver crested knobs. After leaving for the battalions with 'real' tanks (Mk IVB light tanks with machine-guns only or medium tanks with 3-pdr guns and Vickers machine-guns), there followed a six-week gunnery training course at Lulworth. (The Army food there was considered superior to that produced at Bovington or Tilshead, so this was a popular stint.) Finally the training programme ended at the RTC Depot with pistol drill and firing, 24-hour guards, PT tests, ceremonial drill and passing out parades. Typical Army 'bull' in fact!

King George V visited Bovington in June 1922 and witnessed a variety of demonstrations. A searchlight tattoo was held at Cove Common and many schemes, 'raids' and 'attacks' were carried out. An American military mission toured the Aldershot command and a tank demonstration was laid on for them.

When Brigadier C.F.N. Broad DSO formed the 1st Tank Brigade at Tilshead on 1 April 1931 the 1st (Depot) Battalion, which had rather stagnated since the end of the First World War, took on a new role. The new 1st Light Battalion was equipped with armoured car companies, and a third with eight Morris Martels and eight Carden-Loyd machine-gun carriers. These 'tankettes' soon became known as 'light tanks', as John Wollaston relates:

> Mr Carden went on to design the light tanks. The Mk III light tank with a Rolls-Royce engine had a Wilson self-changing gearbox. This was controlled by a pre-selector unit on the driver's right side. The gear lever was a few inches long and would select any gear to which it was moved. To change gear the clutch pedal was depressed. It follows that having changed gear, the lever was moved to the next one required, e.g. when reversing one immediately selected first gear; in first – two and so on.
>
> The engine was shining black and silver, with an enamelled rocker cover and staybright aluminium sump. It was a straight six, with twin carbs – fitted with starter carbs instead of chokes. Armament was a Vickers MG mounted in a turret.
>
> There was a distinct snag with the steering. The system used was clutch and brake. In this the two operations are perforce separate. If the clutch to one track was disengaged when decelerating, the braking effect of the engine made the tank dive in the opposite direction. It was referred to as 'reverse steering'. I used to teach my section drivers to keep pulling and beat the reverse effect. I did hear of drivers being taught to use the reverse steering. The result of going out of control was a spate of tanks turning over. This led to commanders discussing the number of accidents their drivers had had; and a discovery that every road we used was banked, which caused them.
>
> Actually, running smoothly at over 20mph, steering along a winding road was a dream. Like steering a modern heavy car fitted with power steering. There was no intercom. I used to signal movements with my feet. A double tap on the back of the driver's seat was 'advance'. On the move it was 'speed up'. A slight press in the middle of the back, just above the seat, was 'slow down' and a hard pressure 'stop'. Turning was by pressure on the arms. It was so effective I was fully in control of speed and direction.

Exercises were carried out each year but from 1927 onwards such training was taken more seriously. Lieutenant-Colonel F. Pile ensured that the Light Battalion could move at speed over long distances and was even able to move at night. An Experimental Mechanised Force was formed in the same

Tank Corps Review, 1935. Medium Mk III, Light Mk II A and B. (*Patrick Delaforce*)

year, consisting of armour, infantry, artillery and support services. In the next year, 1928, two 'War Office Exercises' with the Light Tank Battalion as part of an infantry brigade were successful. Salisbury Plain was the usual exercise 'territory', and the Light Battalion was then billeted in Kandahar Barracks, Tidworth. Their forty-eight Carden-Loyd machine-gun carriers acted as light tanks. That year the conversion of horsed cavalry to armoured fighting vehicles started amid much controversy. Winston Churchill, then the Chancellor of the Exchequer, demanded that the cavalry units be abolished or mechanised!

In 1934 the Light Battalion distinguished itself on one such exercise, as Lieutenant (later Brigadier) John Sleeman recounted:

I was commanding No. 1 Troop, 'A' Company, 1st Light Battalion, and we were about to start on a raid (of approximately 150 miles) skirting Andover, Salisbury and Amesbury, to come in on the enemy's rear.

Just as we were starting to break out northwards the new orders arrived. The infantry were allowed by the umpires to surround the area and lie on the road like the members of Gandhi's 'disobedience campaign' in India. They were guided by officers' wives who had arrived by car earlier. As we closed in on them they would not move, and others attempted to climb on to the tanks, while the artillery were allowed to bring up their field guns and block the roads at point-blank range, in full view. In spite of these difficulties we succeeded in breaking out northwards and rallied at first light as 'A' Company, near Swindon as planned.

When Lieutenant-Colonel J.A.L. Caunter MC took over command from Lieutenant-Colonel G.A. Rosser in 1935 the 1st Light Battalion had 'spotlights' or searchlights fitted to their light Mk II tanks with most encouraging results for more efficient night firing. The battalion carried out a brilliant night attack in mid-September during the Southern Command exercise. The 'enemy' was a complete infantry division which emerged from its position after dark and moved forward in several columns to reinforce the front. Under Caunter's command the 1st Light Battalion had previously passed round the enemy's flank and gone into harbour early in the evening. Informed of the enemy's move Caunter sent his battalion out to intercept and harry the infantry columns. After a 24-mile dash in rain and darkness his column of Mk V tanks caught the enemy infantry on the road and threw them into confusion. The fitted searchlights were invaluable and paralysed the defenders. It was the biggest and most successful armoured night attack that had ever taken place. Caunter (nicknamed 'Blood' because his favourite oath was 'Buckets of Blood') introduced the tank cooker so that crews could feed themselves. It was nothing elaborate – just a perforated tin filled with sand and an enamel pot.

The battalion was based at Cambrai Barracks. Sergeant John Wollaston noted:

We were now fitted out with Mk III light 2-man tanks, originally with Meadows 6-cylinder engines but later replaced by Rolls-Royce engines (said to be £10 cheaper). The tanks cost £1,700 each. Manoeuvres at Tilshead were for three weeks starting on 12 August. In late December orders came for the immediate move to Egypt on temporary duty. The battalion sailed from Southampton on 31 December 1935 on an Anchor line ship TSS *California*, 16,791 tons, requisitioned from the North Atlantic run with the full crew. The sergeants travelled 'tourist' class, waited on hand and foot. All the ORs were in cabins. The Marconi telegram service ceased at Gibraltar. We sailed through the Med in wireless silence. From Abbassia Barracks, Cairo, we moved to Mersa Matruh with 63 tanks, 'A' Company of Vickers Medium ('D' Company 6 RTR) and the rest light tanks. In October we moved back to a tented camp near Abbassia and sailed back to the UK on the TSS *Laurentic*, diverted to Port Said after disembarking at Haifa. Back to Cambrai Barracks, Perham Down near Tidworth. Two years later – back to Egypt on HMTS *Nevasa*, 9,000 tons. All below warrant rank sleeping in hammocks. We took 58 Mk VIB tanks near the end of their track mileage (2,000). My tank arrived at Beda Fomm with 5,000 tracked miles – a record! Families started to join us in September.

Bert Rendell joined 1 RTC in 1934 and wrote after the first Egyptian tour:

From Alexandria to Mersa Matruh, due to the volcanic areas we passed over and to the speed we were asked to maintain, plus the deep sand, even worse with the sandstorms raging, track plates and track pins began to break: for 'rookies' to encounter all this, we simply arrived in bits and pieces. Heaven help us if there had been an enemy awaiting us at Mersa Matruh. This was a bad time for us all: water was short, food was poor and the sandstorms seemed to go on for ever. Having brought our battalion of tanks up to a war standard, we moved up to the [frontier] wire and the Italians on the other side watched us appear. We both watched each other.

Young Second Lieutenant Rea Leakey arrived by troop ship at Alexandria in March 1938. He was one of a group of RTR officers that included Peter

Page, Captain Teddy Mitford and Derek Thom. They moved into tented accommodation adjoining Helmieh Barracks, 10 miles outside Cairo. The pay was good and the sports facilities excellent, especially at the Gezira club in the heart of Cairo. Leakey was a brilliant all-round sportsman, excelling at athletics, rugger, cross-country (desert) running, cricket and boxing. In the Army of Egypt boxing competition he fought against his batman Private Tyler and lost, suffering two black eyes and a broken nose. His CO 'Blood' Caunter discouraged tennis although Leakey was due to play the famous German player, Baron von Cramm.

1 RTR moved from Cairo by train to Mersa Matruh, a small harbour town about 100 miles west of Alexandria. A move was then made westwards to await the possible attack by Mussolini's vast army based in Libya. Leakey wrote:

> Our time at Matruh was not wasted. Almost every day parties used to go out on reconnaissance, finding out where the going was good, plotting in each fold in the ground and, above all, learning to navigate. Once away from the sea, there are very few landmarks, no roads or railways which can be used to plot one's position. Each unit had its expert navigator whose task it was to ensure that he could give a map reference of his position whenever asked. He plotted a course as would a mariner and steered his vehicle on that bearing with the aid of a sun compass and noting the distance measured by his speedometer. On his wireless aerial he flew a large black flag. At the end of a 50-mile trip across the desert it was not considered bad if he finished up 2 miles from his destination, but more often than not his destination would be a mere map reference and nobody could dispute his accuracy. There was no quick method of fixing an exact point on a featureless desert.

Bert Rendell, by now a lance-corporal at Perham Down, described his first experience of Egypt: 'The regiment were given 56 new Mk VI tanks with Meadows engine in 1936/7. A three-man tank with driver, gunner, radio/operator and commander. The gunner could not fire and operate the No. 9 radio at the same time. In practice the commander takes the 0.5 gun and the operator the .303 gun.' Rendell was a good football player and a better boxer who won the welterweight title in the boxing competition. He passed the Mechanic I test with a star on his arm. 'We had become a wonderful bunch of lads and our "esprit de corps" was high. Those were happy days. Pay was 32 shillings and threepence a week.'

On 27 October 1938 Caunter wrote a report on searchlights mounted on tanks: 'Best shooting is done by tanks from where no searchlights are shining. If left on for more than 15 seconds hostile gunners on a flank may be able to lay [guns] on the light. Batteries will not stand up to a long continuous use. The entirely new operation of what may give us a decisive and cheap victory should we ever have to use them in real fighting.' These 1 RTR tank-mounted searchlights were christened Canal Defence Lights (CDLs) for security purposes. Their potential remained a secret. A brigade of CDL tanks was eventually formed in the UK and moved into France for the 1944 invasion but for various reasons it was never used in action.

The 1st Battalion adjutant from 1935 to 1938 was Captain R.L. Scoones, the quartermaster was J. Noel DCM and the RSM R. de Vere (J. Taylor from 1937 to 1940). The chief instructor at the RTC School, Bovington, was Lieutenant-Colonel J.C. Tilly, who noted in July 1936: 'I saw Major R.M.W. Gross the other day home from Egypt. The Light Battalion had 9 tanks running out of 63 and no spares. He says things are chaotic there.' The Italian invasion of Abyssinia had caused a crisis that meant a mobile armoured division with a 'cavalry' brigade and a 'pivot' group needed to be reinforced (in September 1938) by 1st Light RTR and 6 RTR with medium tanks. The formidable and efficient General Percy Hobart arrived on 27 September. The battalion now had a mixture of 2-man Mk III tanks, some faster 2-man Mk IVs and some new 3-man Mk Vs. The latter had Christie-suspension and were powered by a 600hp Napier aero-engine fitted transversely between the rear sprockets. They were fast and lively. When young Second Lieutenant Michael Carver arrived he found that the average transport officer on his monthly vehicle check would simply run down a list asking the driver 'Lights OK?', 'Horn all right?' 'Propshaft bolts OK?' – and take the driver's word for the condition of the tank. Carver had a different approach. He appeared in overalls with all the necessary tools and checked each item himself individually. Carver noted:

> Tony Lascelles came from 2 RTC and was made adjutant. The commanding officer was a fiery, hot-tempered, energetic and enthusiastic man, known as 'Blood' Caunter. He could get very excited and was said to have been seen on an exercise in Egypt shouting into his binoculars and beating the side of his tank with his microphone. He certainly kept everyone on their toes. . . . He was an unimaginative man and I did not like him much. I suspect that he did not much approve of me.

Caunter was promoted in July 1939 to command the new Army Tank Brigade in the UK.

Sergeant Doyle of 'C' Squadron recalled training in the desert in the summer of 1939: 'Reveille was at 5.15, PT from 5.30 to 6.30 with every officer and man: breakfast for the 59 tank crews (in battle training) the rations per man were one packet of biscuits, one tin of bully beef, one calico bag with dried prunes, dried figs plus two pints of water per day.' They travelled from Tilbury Docks on the SS *Orama*, sailing via Port Said, and the band had played 'Auld Lang Syne'. Doyle's friend 'Ginger' Stratford had visited Naples en route and noted Mussolini's troops in shabby uniforms, their boots tied up with string, and baggy pants. They had unshaven faces.

Doyle, who later drove Captain Rea Leakey's A-9 tank (No. T7201) noted:

> We had no problems with the new A-9 tanks, 22mph maximum as the 1st (Light) Battalion had been equipped with Mk IVa, IVb 3-man light tanks capable of 40mph. With these slow cruisers we had lost a little of our sting but compensated for it in the heavier firepower, three Vickers machine-guns, one in each of the sub-turrets either side of the driver, third one co-

1 RTR King's Birthday Parade, June 1938. (*A.R. Leakey*)

axially mounted with the 2-pdr anti-tank gun in the main turret. The six-man crew [consisted of] OC, gunlayer, driver/operator (man the radio, load main turret gun) and two sub-turret gunners and the driver.

Doyle noted that the lack of green vegetables, fruit and bread caused severe desert sores, the scratching of which led to severe festering. One trooper had a hole in his arm the size of an egg. The figs and prunes had the opposite effect on that intended! The uninspiring diet was bully beef and biscuits, soused herrings in tomato sauce and MacConochies tinned stew.

Michael Carver again:

On arrival in Egypt we moved into a tented camp in the garrison of Helmieh, near Heliopolis on the eastern outskirts of Cairo, where we shared a permanent officers' mess with the 31st Field Regiment, Royal Artillery. A few offices were in huts, but everything else was in tents. This became unpleasant in April, when the *khamsin*, the hot wind from the south, blew, covering everything with sand and dust and making life utterly miserable. It would start in the east and work round through the south to the west, usually taking about 48 hours to blow itself out. Apart from this and the muggy heat of July and August, it was a pleasant life.

After Caunter's promotion 'Booming Bill' Watkins, a humourless but efficient and kindly man according to Carver 'after six months was promoted to command the Heavy Armoured Group [1 Royal Tank Regiment and 6 Royal Tank Regiment – renamed in April 1939] and was replaced by 'Moley' Molesworth, a dead-beat major who had been passed over for promotion for years. Charles Ward acted as brigade-major to Watkins . . . Mr Cook was the highly efficient regimental quartermaster sergeant of 1st Royal Tanks.' Carver was, however, very proud of his regiment. 'The soldier of the Royal Tank Corps of those days was the cream of the army. My soldiers were of a high standard in every respect, in intelligence, in behaviour and in their willingness to tackle anything.'

So 1st Battalion Royal Tank Regiment with their beat-up little tanks prepared for war in the western African desert.

CHAPTER THREE

The Western Desert, 1939–40

The 'First of Track' at Mersa Matruh received a telegram from HQ Heavy Armoured Group: 'Mobilise, All Troops are now on active service from 4 September.' They had moved from their 'peace station' at Helmieh, Cairo, on 25 August 1939 and their strength was as follows. 'A' Echelon had 56 tanks, 17 officers and 151 ORs (including 10 Royal Corps of Signals). 'B' Echelon had 14 3-tonners, 6 30-cwt and 4 15-cwt (water) trucks, plus 4 Rolls-Royce armoured cars (with a total staff of 46), and its personnel totalled 6 officers and 310 ORs. At HQ Heavy Armoured Group detached were 5 officers and 29 ORs, and at HQ Armoured Division there were 3 officers and 36 ORs.

Lieutenant-Colonel H.R.B. Watkins was Battalion CO until 28 September, when he was replaced by Major W.E. Molesworth MC. The majors were L.S. Harland MC, H.B.M. Groves MC, F. Brown, C.E. Ward and briefly Reggie Keller (who was destined to command 3 RTR in the heroic battle at Calais and the disastrous Greek campaign in 1940). The captains were E.A. Fulcher, L.G. Hynes, C.H.W. Rice, J.G.S. Compton, E.C. Mitford (destined later to command RTR battalions and a brilliant desert navigator), R.G.M. Stevenson and A.C.T. Sassoon. The lieutenants were R.M.P. Carver (destined to command 1 RTR on his way to becoming a Field Marshal), E.A. Lascelles (adjutant), Cruikshank, Dennis Coulson, Simonds, Peter Page and Rea Leakey (two well-trained desert navigators), Stapleton, Bouverie-Brine, Sir F.G.L. Coates Bt, Forster, Hotham, Williamson, Noel DCM (quartermaster), Yeo, Derek Thom, Holliman (another RTR CO in the making) and Captain R.P. Hendry RAMC. Second lieutenants were Richards, Manby, Franklin, Ball, Hadfield, Jones and Poston (future ADC to General Montgomery). The RSM was J. Taylor.

During September the battalion was on 6 hours' notice to move. This did not deter HM King Farouk of Egypt from inspecting 'his' defenders on the 13th. Training for war was stepped up – TEWTS (Tactical Exercises Without Troops); exercises in attacking an enemy convoy; battle drill; navigation exercises; aircraft recognition by the RAF (during which a Gloster Gladiator crashed, killing its pilot). Training exercises included (a)

1 RTR officers, Egypt, 1939. (*A.R. Leakey*)

advance to contact, (b) unit change of direction and (c) W/T control, including jamming enemy frequencies and changing from W/T to R/T. A night training exercise took place on the 26th, which included forming a brigade leaguer at night, changing leaguer at night, the use of searchlights (canal defence lights mounted on tanks) and action on 'alarm' signals. The War Diary states that on the 28th a *khamsin* stopped training, but the last week in October saw full-scale manoeuvres around 'Charing Cross' and Mersa Matruh, then on 3 December the battalion returned to Cairo. At the end of November the unfortunate and unlucky 'Hobo', Major-General Percy Hobart, was sacked by General 'Jumbo' Maitland Wilson (the cavalry generals were still in the ascendancy!) and Major-General O'Moore Creagh MC, another cavalry officer, became the new divisional commander. General Hobart's legacy – indeed his philosophy – was this. He wrote:

I decided to concentrate on dispersion, flexibility and mobility this season; to try to get the division and formations well extended, really handy and under quick control. To units unused to the speed and wide frontages made possible by mechanisation these matters presented considerable difficulties. There is the isolation due to the wide intervals necessary in the desert, involving the necessity of being able to keep direction, to navigate a unit, to keep a dead reckoning, to learn to watch for small indications and to use one's eyes in spite of mirage . . . it has not yet become instinctive for crews and commanders to get down at *every* halt and look round their vehicles *at once*. Many oil leaks, loose bolts etc. would be seen and remedied and subsequent demands on fitters avoided. Crews should make it a point of honour to keep their vehicles running without outside assistance.

Hobart devised numerous exercises, such as his 'Mosquito' tactics using small, highly mobile, harassing movements, and 'Leaguering' in triangular or square defensive positions at night with armoured vehicles on the perimeter and 'soft' vehicles in the centre. In addition there were divisional 'recovery' exercises, others for 'B' Echelon evacuation and for both 'A' and 'B' Echelons in refilling and replenishing.

Officers and men learnt to navigate by reference to the sun, a compass and the stars at night, plus keen observation of minor landmarks – scrub, a ruined stone hut, a wrecked car. Soon they learned to live in the desert. Each formation, however, had a navigation officer leading the way. They learned how to take up 'hull down' positions for tanks behind sand dunes, from which only their turrets would be visible to the enemy. Desert driving needed new skills; sudden hollows, sharp rocks, occasional boulders and deep or very soft sands were all potential hazards. The tank squadron learned to conserve petrol, food and especially water, which was usually rationed.

On 16 February 1940 the Mobile Division officially became the 7th Armoured Division and soon acquired the famous Jerboa as its divisional sign. Initially the tough little desert rodent appeared somewhat ill-nourished (his first cousins – coloured black for the 4th Armoured Brigade and green for the 7th Armoured Brigade – looked healthier) but the final version when the division invaded Normandy appeared prosperous, well-fed and very confident!

1 RTR arrive in Egypt. (*James Bouverie-Brine*)

1 RTR. From the back row, the group includes Kendall, Graham, Stuart, Lobb-Stuart, Gill Smith, Hoare, Hearst, Paton, Banks, O'Lawl, Humphries (Revell?), Roberts, Kilbain and Streather. (*James Bouverie-Brine*)

Exercises continued throughout early 1940 with demonstrations for the Press and newsreels, and another showing the Egyptian Army how to use tanks in the desert. In April 1 RTR with the 8th Kings Royal Irish Hussars formed part of the 4th Light Armoured Brigade. Firing exercises took place on the AFV Ranges on 27 May.

All tanks now carried the divisional formation sign and their serial number in white on red on right and left front dustguards. Squadron tactical markings were of solid colours specified for tank battalions – red for A, yellow for B and blue for C. Tanks of 1 RTR were named with the initial letter 'A' following First World War tradition, in white on the battalion's red. Names included 'Arnold', 'Ada', 'Aberdeen', 'Alsace', 'Anglesey', 'Achilles', 'Andromeda' and 'Agrippa'. Various experiments in tank camouflage were tried. Plain sand colour was used until mid-1940, then Colonel Caunter's disruptive scheme of radiating light and dark wedges was adopted. The triangles radiating from the rear were designed to draw the eye and the enemy aim astern of the tank's movement.

Mussolini declared war on Great Britain on 10 June and immediately 7th Armoured Division began harassing operations against Marshal Graziani's Italian Army. He had fifteen divisions in all, totalling 215,000

troops, with eight of the divisions based in Tripolitania and seven in Cyrenaica. The 50,000 Allied troops consisted of the Desert Rats, two-thirds of the 4th Indian Division, one-third of the New Zealand Division and the 16th British Infantry Brigade. Little Bertie Rendell, now a full corporal, was sent to the Sidibish area on a boxing/PT course. On his return to the frontier he 'saw Italians on the other side of the line handsomely dressed with wonderful feathers stuck in their hats'. Major Groves MC, OC 'B' Company, captained the 1 RTR cricket side when the opening batsmen Trooper Albert Cole and Corporal Appleby made 127 runs and 133 runs respectively against the Royal Signals at the Gezira sportsground. Sir Freddie Coates, troop leader in 'A' Squadron, made W.G. McGinly a sergeant. After suffering four bouts of malaria, and having a 'dicky heart', McGinly was downgraded medically to B2; he became a gunnery instructor and quietly returned himself to his squadron commander Major 'Fay' Compton!

Lieutenant Rea Leakey described how the recently promoted Brigadier 'Blood' Caunter led an immediate raid:

Starting 14 June, Caunter's protection troop, two cruisers and three light tanks of 1 RTR plus 'A' Company of 1 KRRC set off on a two-day march 150 miles to take Fort Capuzzo. 'Blood' led the way in a cruiser tank, round the rear of the fort, belted 2-pdr AP shells through the fort's metal doors, out came 16 officers, 200 men. The Italian captives were taken to the frontier town of Sollum. But six casualties occurred when two tanks were blown up on mines. We blew up the fort and retired west behind the frontier wire. Five days later the Italians sent 50 tanks, 30 guns and a Battalion of lorried infantry from Sidi Azeiz, 20 miles across the frontier to three miles short of the frontier wire. Fifteen cruisers of 1 RTR with 2-pdr guns massacred the Italian tanks with their thin armour plating. In an hour all over – the majority of Italians surrendered.

Leakey's driver Trooper Doyle noted:

First attack was on Fort Capuzzo with troop, guns and Rifle Brigade infantry. The enemy had mobile A/tank guns, screened by motorcycle and sidecar-mounted MGs. In the engagement T7201 [his tank] fired 21 rounds, but Sergeant-Major Rabson's tank fired 101 shells. The gun barrel was red hot; limited vision through 3-inch glass block, with visor down produces very narrow slits, about 1/8th-inch in diameter in the visor itself. Driver often blinded by dust and smoke of enemy shells, blocking out what is happening outside. Radio operator/gun loader totally blind, buried in the bowels of the tank, handling the ammo, reloading after the gun is fired and recoiled. The OC tank directs driver on course and speed, indicates target and range to gunner, which guns to be used, also controls two sub-turret gunners with their MGs. At the same time transmitting and receiving on radio to conform to battle routine.

Opposite, top: Helmeih, August 1939. 1 RTR's Mk VIB light tanks just off to the desert. (*James Bouverie-Brine*)

Opposite, centre: Mk VIB light tanks en route to the desert, August 1939. (*James Bouverie-Brine*)

Opposite, bottom: Desert manoeuvres, February 1939. Leo Sassoon, Gus Holliman, Ferdy Hutchison and Tick Tock, at Athill. (*James Bouverie-Brine*)

1 RTR A-9 cruiser 'Arnold' in desert, 1940. (*Tank Museum 83/B3*)

1 RTR cruiser tanks, Abbasia, May 1940. (*Imperial War Museum E-95*)

Sergeant F.J.C. Wollaston wrote:

> In June 1940 we were at our peace station near Cairo on internal security duties. We were equipped with 2- and 3-man Light tanks – ideal for the job. Apparently there were 18,000 Italians in Egypt and GHQ was worried.
>
> A pre-arranged plan to evacuate families was implemented. All with children were sent to Palestine. The whole train-load, plus husbands where available, were given lunch at the Slade Club, Abbassia Barracks – strangely it was quite a jolly occasion. We then walked across to the station inside the Cantonment. Most of the families went on to South Africa. The remaining wives were drafted into suitable jobs to relieve servicemen. In July we were re-equipped with cruiser tanks A-9 and A-10 (crews 6 and 5) retaining a few light tanks Mk VIB (crew 3). We then rejoined 7th Armoured Division and were immediately sent up to the Libyan Frontier and relieved 6 RTR south of Fort Capuzzo – the only tank regiment on the frontier. [The 11th Hussars, nicknamed the Cherry Pickers, were running their own war against the Italian frontier forces]. Dummy tanks were used to replace the other units and all retired south of Mersa Matruh for rest and refit.

In July the battalion took part in an exercise with 4th Indian Division to Mena having moved the tanks by train to 'Charing Cross'. The tank strength was 23 cruisers and 26 light. Major-General O'Connor, commander of the desert forces, visited the battalion on 30 August.

September was the month when 1 RTR really went to war. The CO, Lieutenant-Colonel Molesworth, went sick on the 16th and Major F. Brown took command. Major L.G. Hynes of 'B' Squadron had a successful shoot at an enemy concentration of vehicles around Nagfet El Nas and Dar El Brug. Trooper Doyle of 'C' Squadron wrote:

> Our first advance into action, the A-9 battle strength dwindled. Bogie wheels on suspension were twin rimmed retaining a solid tyre to assist in absorbing shock between track and hull of tank. Tyres would develop a failure when they expanded and became loose. Smell of burning rubber meant a replacement would be needed. Also chain link pins wore out, the chain stretches, then snaps. T7201 was so bad that Captain Leakey, squadron leader, gave up, moved to another tank. [Other problems were] worn out steering clutches and brake bands seized up; engine power traverse failures; main gearbox failure; leaking radiators; disintegrated fans. Basic radio procedure taught to all tank crews to enable them to take their fair share of night watches in laager. The navigator's tank travelled in straight 'legs' determined by sun compass, bino compass or prismatic compass, thus enabling remainder of regiment to zig-zag to find the best terrain to traverse.

The Italians had made a determined advance on the 13th with eight battalions of tanks and six infantry divisions. Leakey again:

> The orders were 'to make a fighting withdrawal, but under no circumstances were tanks to be lost in battle'. The Italian artillery bombardment mostly hit empty desert and their bombers gave us a larger dose than usual. When the dust and smoke cleared we saw the most fantastic spectacle. The Italian Army was advancing towards us led by more cyclists – then came the tanks, again in parade order and followed by row after row of large black lorries.

This was the start of a week-long battle during which 1 RTR and its supporting arms slowly withdrew from the frontier on 13 September and headed back towards Mersa Matruh. The Italian Army reached Sidi Barrani, a small town some 60 miles across the border, and continued into Egypt.

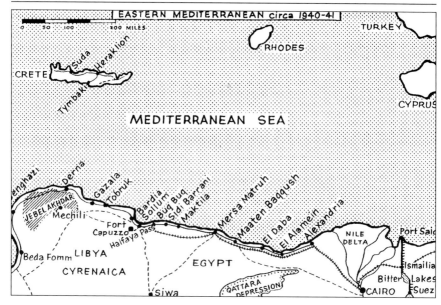

Battleground in the Eastern Mediterranean, *c.* 1940–1.

1 RTR Cruiser tanks on the way 'up to the Blue'. (*Imperial War Museum E-104*)

They built and fortified a line of camps stretching 30 miles inland from the sea. Leakey commented: 'the older officers just could not "take it". Thus I got command of a squadron and went from lieutenant to major overnight.'

During the week 11–18 September Captain Cruikshank's 'B' Squadron was part of 'Campbell Force', with Second Lieutenants Richards and Bockinsale and Sergeants Horry, Burgess and Hall. Using their artillery box barrage ('hell on earth', it was reported) around Sidi Oman they knocked out two enemy tanks, many lorries and destroyed many infantry.

At twenty-four, Lieutenant Leakey was the oldest member of T7201's crew. He regarded his driver Trooper Doyle as a good mechanic who took great pride in his vehicle. The wireless operator and turret gun loader was a regular soldier, a Welshman named Adams. Trooper Milligan, the main turret gunner, came from Dublin and the two sub-turret gunners were 'very young'. Leakey noted that 'living in the desert was tough, we had no beds, no caravans and water was very scarce: shaving was forbidden, no mobile laundries, never changed clothes ('did we stink'), bully beef and biscuits our fare; no alcohol, desert is a clean place, we were healthy.'

Several attacks were made by 1 RTR on Fort Capuzzo. The second time the enemy was well dug in and in a 20-minute hard battle 1 RTR withdrew. Leakey noted it as the 'only defeat at hands of Italians'. He then led three tanks with the powerful CDL searchlights west of Fort Capuzzo in a night attack, destroying enemy vehicles moving up from Bardia.

Actions took place near Abu Nuh with 'A' Squadron led by Captain Peter Page in his tank; Squadron HQ was Captain J.G.S. Compton in a cruiser A-9 tank; Second Lieutenant Sassoon led 1 Troop with three light Mk VI tanks, with Sergeant Atkin and Sergeant Parsons. Captain Page and Sergeant Shields led 2 Troop with two light Mark Vs; Second Lieutenant Read, Sergeant Alexander and Corporal Craik with three A-9 cruisers formed No. 3 Troop; Sergeant Pugh and Sergeant McGinley with A-9 cruisers formed No. 4 Troop.

Sergeant Pugh's tank was hit by 20 shells from an enemy field gun but the crew were rescued. The squadron fired 1,250 rounds of .303 and 0.5 ammunition at 300 enemy soldiers clustered around a disabled cruiser tank, and about 50 of them were killed or wounded. Four enemy lorries carrying anti-tank guns were knocked out, a petrol lorry was set on fire and 18 smaller lorries were engaged at 600 yards.

In October training out of the line continued at Bir Shanen and Matruh. General Wavell, Commander-in-Chief Middle East Forces, visited 1 RTR on 19 November. Lieutenant Yeo became adjutant and Captain H.A. Lascelles became OC 'C' Squadron. The tank state was reduced to 20 A-9 and A-10 cruisers and 22 light tanks. The Cherry Pickers and other sources reported enemy activities (in terms of military enemy transport or MET) around the Italian fortified camps. Captain A.R. Leakey with 3 light tanks counted the Italian traffic going down Halfaya Pass: Sidi Barrani 150; Sofafi East 35; Maktila 150; Sofafi North-west 28; Tumarr West 200; Sofafi South-west 48; Tumarr East 60; Rabia 30; Maesrd 150 and Niheiwa 300.

1 RTR A-9 at speed – good going! (*James Bouverie-Brine*)

1 RTR A-9s at speed – not such good going! (*James Bouverie-Brine*)

1 RTR tanks on desert road. (*James Bouverie-Brine*)

Sergeant F.J.C. Wollaston wrote a report on the local topography:

It may be appropriate at this stage to explain the topography of the area. The sea cliffs running south from Bardia swing inland at Sollum and become an escarpment to the south-east. Sollum is on the first sandy beach below the cliff escarpment. The local water is discoloured and brackish. As a result Sollum had a distillation plant years before the war. It was a small village. A track along the coast eastward ended at Sidi Barrani (40 miles). A tarmac road zig-zags up the 700-foot escarpment, passes Fort Capuzzo just over the frontier, and so on west across Libya. At the top of the escarpment the Egyptian Army has 'A' Company-size barracks. A few miles inland along the escarpment is Halfaya Pass. A track leading south from the coastal track (Sollum–Sidi Barrani) zig-zags up this pass. Then swings west and south out into the desert and back to the coast at Tobruk – 65 miles due west. This is the Trigh El Abd. Further south the escarpment ceases to be an obstacle to vehicles. The vast majority of our troops moved between Alexandria and Libya in this area.

We cooked by crews except for the evening stew which came in with the replenishment lorries. We washed and shaved every day. My crew had a sponge bath and washed (KD) clothing every three days. We took turns using the two extra gallons of water issued daily to all tanks: it came from Birs, old rain cisterns. The water truck went out most days and filled up.

In December Lieutenant-Colonel Jerram DSO, MC and four officers of 7 RTR visited for three days to see life up at the front. Brigadier 'Strafer' Gott, soon to be a famous desert hero, visited on the 3rd and the next week the CO, Lieutenant-Colonel Culverwell, returned from sick leave.

Operation Mars, the codeword for 1 RTR's role in the next attack on the Italian Army, was received early in December.

CHAPTER FOUR

Operation Compass and the Beda Fomm Battle

The Western Desert Force was commanded by Lieutenant-General Richard O'Connor, a much-decorated hero of the First World War. He and Generals Wavell and Wilson planned in great secrecy the 'Five-Day Raid', later named Operation Compass. It was a daring, well-planned and well-coordinated attack intended to isolate, surround and subdue all of Marshal Graziani's fortified camps. The 7th Armoured Division would lead the 4th Indian Division and the 16th British Infantry Brigade through the 20-mile gap between Nibeiwa and Sofafi camps on the southern flank. O'Connor now had the newly arrived, powerful infantry tanks, Matilda Mk IIs, with thick armour that was to prove almost impregnable to Italian guns. The Royal Navy would bombard the Italian defences between Maktila and Sidi Barrani.

Captain Leakey attended a briefing in Cairo on 26 November known as 'Training Exercise No. 1'. On 9 December 1 RTR moved to Bir el Illiqiya in reserve and three days later took up observation of Sofafi camp and then went on to Qaret el Reiweibet. The Italian Air Force bombed the column on the 14th, killing Troopers Dobbon and Clarke. By the 16th 1 RTR were north-west of Capuzzo aerodrome, where they destroyed four Breda 65s, two CR32s and a Savoia. Captain Leakey was awarded the Military Cross for this attack. They then headed for Buq Buq on the coast via Bir Bzen, cutting the Bardia–Tobruk road.

On the first day of the Five-Day Raid it was evident that the Italians had been taken completely by surprise. They were woken up in their camps by tanks shooting at them from the centre of their 'fortress'. Their shells bouncing off the 7 RTR Matildas was another horrible shock. 1 RTR had advanced some 12 miles through the gap in the wire. 'As we came over a small ridge we saw about twenty Italian tanks cutting across our front to the north', wrote Leakey.

They were M-13 tanks about the same size as our cruisers and mounted similar guns. Over the air I gave out orders to my C Squadron: 'Enemy tanks ahead, form battle line on me and standby to engage.' My eight cruiser tanks raced forward to their battle positions, while the light tanks who were in the lead moved across to either flank of the cruisers. They could do no good in this battle. The squadron on my right performed a similar manoeuvre. The stage was set rather like a battle at sea. The Italians spotted us and turned to engage us. In no time the air was alive with the scream of velocity shells.

Operation
Compass,
December
1940.

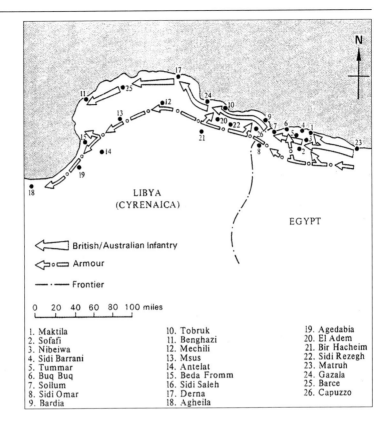

LIBYA
(CYRENAICA)

EGYPT

1. Maktila
2. Sofafi
3. Nibeiwa
4. Sidi Barrani
5. Tummar
6. Buq Buq
7. Sollum
8. Sidi Omar
9. Bardia

10. Tobruk
11. Benghazi
12. Mechili
13. Msus
14. Antelat
15. Beda Fromm
16. Sidi Saleh
17. Derna
18. Agheila

19. Agedabia
20. El Adem
21. Bir Hacheim
22. Sidi Rezegh
23. Matruh
24. Gazala
25. Barce
26. Capuzzo

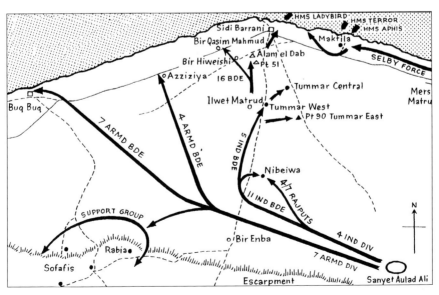

Operation Compass. The Battle of Sidi Barrani, 8–10 December 1940.

Two RTR tanks were hit but eventually eight M-13s were left behind!

Sidi Barrani was isolated and captured on the 10th, after the 4th Indian Division with the Matilda tanks of 7 RTR had surrounded and captured most of the key Italian fortified camps. 1 RTR tank state was 16 A-9 and A-10 cruisers, plus 16 light and two scout-cars. The squadron commanders were 'A', Major Compton; 'B', Major Hynes; and 'C', Major Lascelles. In mid-January all the vehicles of 6 RTR and the 3rd Hussars were transferred to 1 RTR. Eight light tanks from 6 RTR were formed into a sub-unit under Captain Rea Leakey, as part of 'C' Squadron.

General O'Connor now had the bit between his teeth and slowly, inevitably, his forces advanced. First the Indians plus 7 RTR, then the 6th Australian Division plus 7 RTR, stormed and captured all the towns and ports along the way – Sollum, Bardia, Tobruk and Derna. The 7th Armoured Division acted as sheepdogs, cutting off each town and corralling in their thousands Graziani's wretched army. 1 RTR 'celebrated' Christmas Day by containing Bardia. Each trooper received a tin of bully beef to himself and a double rum ration, but there were no turkeys and no Christmas puddings.

During January 1941 the battalion saw desultory actions outside Derna. 7th Armoured Division's orders for 1 RTR were to head for Mechili to cut off the Italian garrison's escape. Some 70 miles of the march was across unmapped country – the going was bad, with deep wadis, and it rained

Italian artillery fire on the horizon. (*James Bouverie-Brine*)

constantly. At Mechili orders came to move with all speed to cut the coast road at Beda Fomm, 70 miles west of Benghazi. Leakey again: 'This march of 150 miles was a complete nightmare, most of the time I was too tired and bruised by my bucking tank. It was bitterly cold, either raining or blowing a sandstorm. We ['C' Squadron] were leading the most southerly column. It took us 36 hours to reach the coast road. No more than forty-five British tanks survived this terrible journey.'

However, 1 RTR took a relatively minor role in the great battle of Beda Fomm on 5/6 February which effectively destroyed the Italian Army escaping from the coastal ports. What follows is the commanding officer's report.

Account by Lieutenant-Colonel G.J.N. Culverwell of action taken by 1 RTR on 5/6 February 1941

2030   Regiment less light squadron (6 Mk VI AB under Major Lascelles) left Msus for Antelat. Strength 10 cruisers (A9 and A10), 8 light tanks (Mk VIB), 1 Troop RHA under command.

0230   Arrived 4000 yds north-east of Antelat. In touch with 7 AD but only intermittently with 7 AB. In the morning, maintenance carried out. One A9 recovered after an accident. A Patrol (two, each of two light tanks) sent on tracks north and north-west of Antelat.

1200   'B' Echelon arrived, all vehicles filled up and the regiment moved to Beda Fomm arriving at about 1400 hours.

1405   2 i/c 7 AD met commander 1 RTR and gave him the situation report. Commander 1 RTR decided to get in touch with commander 2 RTR and reconnoitre the area. Just as I was leaving, the sole remaining light tank, to the north-west of unit, reported medium tanks to the north. I gathered the 3 Hussars were in this area as they had been reporting vehicles throughout the march from Antelat. I therefore formed the opinion that these vehicles were friendly. I instructed the squadron reporting the tanks to identify the vehicles and if they were the enemy to destroy them. I then handed over command of the battalion to Major Brown. On arrival at HQ 2 RTR heavy firing was heard and a number of M13s were seen moving south. These were obviously being engaged by 1 RTR. I immediately returned to the area in which I had left RHQ. I found troop RHA coming out of action and 1 RTR rallying, having engaged one squadron of 14 M13s and another of 16 A13s and one A9. Major Cruickshank being hit on the track. Orders were then received to attack the enemy column on the road. Visibility was poor and it was raining heavily. The regiment moved on a bearing of 295°, two up, A Squadron (Major Fellows) right, B Squadron (Major Hynes) left, one light tank to the north. Course was accordingly altered to 2700. Left Squadron (Major Hynes) reported enemy halted on road in sight at about 1000 yds. Shortly afterwards right squadron (Major Fellows) reported a column consisting of transport only at the same range. Fire was opened by both squadrons. I ordered them to close to machine-gun range after a few minutes. Position of RHQ was approx. 400 yds from the road. B Squadron moved up to the hull-down position about 500 yds from the road, and engaged the enemy column with mg and 2-pdr fire. A Squadron then moved up, crossed the road, and proceeded south engaging guns to the west and firing on transport to the east. About this time B Squadron were fired on from north-east by a 2-pdr with a white trace. Visibility was now such that it was impossible for troop RHA to come into action as it was impossible to distinguish our own troops from the enemy.

1730   I informed the 7 AB that I promised to withdraw squadrons to rally in daylight. I then ordered squadrons to withdraw and to rally on me. Desultory artillery fire was still continuing on RHQ at the rate of about 2 per minute. In view of this I moved RHQ 100 yds east, fire was accordingly lifted and moved in our direction. This manoeuvre was twice repeated, indicating direct observation. In view of this and also because the 3 Hussars and 2 RTR appeared to be on the move, and as no squadron had yet rejoined and it was now dark, I ordered squadrons to rally at Beda Fomm. RHQ moved to this area at about 1800 hours. The regiment finally rallied at about 2100 hours. One A9 was left in this area with a track off. The crew repaired this at about 2030 hours and reported they were on the move to rejoin the unit.

2100   The regiment moved to area x0767 as ordered. Actual position not stated owing to faulty navigation due to poor weather conditions. Prior to this A Squadron (Major Fellows) had been sent to form a road block as ordered by 4 AB.

Over 20,000 well-equipped Italian soldiers with 120 new M-13 tanks were determined to fight their way through to Tripoli. The battle raged all along the 10-mile column until the white flags went up.

At 1430 hours Major N.C.B. Fellows spotted sixteen M-13s to his front on a ridge about 2,000 yards away. On being engaged by 'A' Squadron the enemy turned north. A few minutes later Major L.G. Hynes of 'B' Squadron reported fourteen M-13s and a large lorry moving east, and ordered his four cruisers and one light tank into battle line; halted in hull-down position, they engaged the enemy heavily. Major Loder-Symonds, the RHA FOO, drove beside 'B' Squadron in a Morris truck and brought his 25-pdrs into action, soon damaging four of the enemy AFVs. Hynes surveyed the road ahead:

> It was the most wonderful sight it has ever been my lot to see; for miles in each direction the road was packed tight with lorries and guns and cars and buses and tanks – everything you can think of. We fired everything we had at them and the whole road began to seethe like an ants nest, with Italians running in all directions. They fought back at us with their guns and we got several hits but no harm was done.

After the battle Hynes, with four tanks and two lorries at his disposal, was given a batch of 6,000 prisoners to take back to Benghazi. Placing two of his tanks at the head of the column and the other two at the rear he marched his prisoners over the desert and supplied them with food and water for three days. On the way he secured food from the smashed-up Italian supply lorries. He solved the water problem by sending a big tanker and a water cart to and fro all day long to the nearest well (or bir). Hynes was puzzled because many of the Italian tanks were manned by men wearing naval uniforms. None of the Italians showed the least inclination to escape, and even seemed happy that the fighting was over. The 7th Armoured Division captured 20,000 prisoners along with 1,500 lorries, 112 tanks (some of which were later used by the British) and 216 guns. It was a great victory. Among the decorations awarded were Military Medals to Trooper W.F. Walpole and Corporal Harry Bennett.

On 17 February all tanks over haulage-mileage and requiring extensive repair were handed in to the Advanced Divisional Workshops and the light tank 'runners' to the 3rd Kings Own Hussars. The surviving cruisers were left with ADW. Meanwhile 1 RTR, tankless but victorious, set off for Mena camp by the pyramids in Cairo, via Bir Habbas, Michili, Tmini, Tobruk (where canteen stores including beer were obtained), Bardia, Sollum, Capuzzo, Buq Buq, Mersa Matruh, Fuka and El Baba. By the 28th most of them were enjoying the fleshpots of Cairo.

CHAPTER FIVE

1 RTR in the Siege of Tobruk

Victory turned to humiliating defeat within two months of Beda Fomm. Churchill and General Wavell deployed British and Commonwealth formations to help the gallant Greek Army defend itself from Mussolini's unwarranted attack. Hitler was furious and for a variety of reasons sent his Panzers and Stukas into Greece. And a certain General Erwin Rommel – a brilliant panzer commander – landed in Tripoli on 12 February. On 31 March Rommel's mainly Italian forces, spearheaded by 120 formidable Mark IV and Mark III tanks and supported by Luftwaffe attacks, burst through the inexperienced 2nd Armoured Brigade to reach Antelat. Arriving at Msus, he feinted an attack on Mechili and then moved on to Derna and Gazala, and finally surrounded Tobruk. On 6 April his forces captured Generals O'Connor and Neame, who were travelling without any escort.

The inexperienced 9th Australian Division withdrew eastwards along the coastal road, commanded by the tough Major-General L.J. Morshead. General Wavell flew into Tobruk and gave orders for its defence. The Royal Navy escorted a convoy into Tobruk harbour carrying a brigade group of 7th Australian Division from Egypt. In a large, old freighter – rather to their surprise – came 'B' and 'C' Squadrons of 1 RTR (with RHQ) in SS *Thurland Castle*, together with 16 A-9 and A-10 cruisers and 20 Mk VIB light tanks (plus 4 Matildas of 4 RTR).

For a month lorry-loads of 1 RTR men with plenty of money saved up had entered Cairo where they met Egyptians only too anxious to help them spend it. Their fun was short-lived, however. On 6 April 1 RTR received urgent orders to call in every available man and draw tanks from the workshops. That evening officers visited all the hotels, cafés, bars and cinemas in Cairo, rounding up as many men as they could find. The tanks were put on flats which took them to Alexandria, where they were laboriously hoisted on board ship. On disembarkation at Tobruk the tank crews worked feverishly. No wireless sets had been fitted, while the guns were still in crates and covered in grease. The main AFV workshops in Tobruk were very efficient and quickly produced 'renovated' tanks to help the defenders. There were about 15,000 Australian troops in the garrison, plus British tanks and some 8,000 British troops, comprising the 51st Heavy

Captain A.R. Leakey, Egypt, 1941. (*George Forty*)

1 RTR Matilda tanks in Tobruk. (*Imperial War Museum E-5541*)

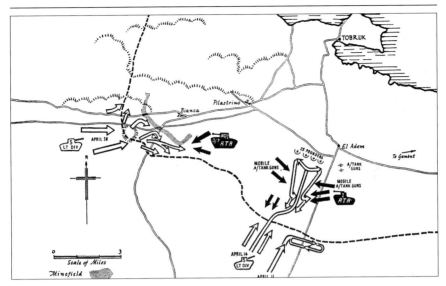

Rommel's attacks on Tobruk, 11, 14 and 30 April 1941.

AA Regiment, the Northumberland Fusiliers machine-gunners, the 51st Field Regiment RA and two troops of 1 RHA with 25-pdrs, and a few 'refugees' from 2nd Armoured Brigade.

Lieutenant-Colonel Culverwell was 1 RTR's CO, Major George Hynes was OC 'B' Squadron (his second-in-command was Lieutenant James Bouverie-Brine, who kept an excellent daily diary of the siege), Major Rea Leakey was OC 'C' Squadron and Lieutenant John Wollaston was the Intelligence Officer. The resourceful George Hynes managed to locate and occupy a cave directly his squadron landed. Over the next few weeks they turned this into living and sleeping quarters with a honeycomb of galleries and dug-outs. It boasted a canteen and a mess kitchen, and even had electric light (using old Italian batteries recharged by a motorcycle dynamo).

The Tobruk perimeter was 30 miles in length and the anti-tank ditch was shallow and provided little obstacle. However, the Italian pill-boxes and dug-outs were in good shape and the Australians quickly enhanced them.

Rommel's Operation Sonnenblume ('Sunflower') had pushed General Streich's 5th Leichte (Light) Division up to the Tobruk perimeter. Rommel attached the greatest importance to the capture of Tobruk, mainly for its excellent harbour but also because the garrison there could – perhaps – cut his lines of communication. The first German attack on 11 April on the south-west, along the track to Hill Point 209, fizzled out. Lieutenant Bouverie-Brine of 'B' Squadron wrote:

10 April first scramble. I was sent to Derna Road with my troop of light tanks to protect HQ 9th Aus Div. 11 April 5.30pm B Squadron ordered into action against 30 German tanks attacking astride El Adem Road. On contact we knocked out one German Mk III and an

Italian light tank and they then withdrew. Very soon after 12 German Mk IVs appeared from our north, evidently also withdrawing. In this skirmish we got two of them but lost two A-10 cruisers. Our squadron leader Major George Hynes was unscathed but his driver Trooper Knapton was killed and Troopers Bryant, Ash and Jamieson were severely burnt. The crew of the other cruiser commanded by Lieutenant Cecil Bangham was saved.

Major Leakey recalled:

At dawn [10 April] we were told that several enemy tanks had broken through at a place called Acroma. They were little Italian two-man tanks SV33/L35s called 'Carrolancia-Flamme' which towed trailers with flame fuel. We soon disposed of them. We then moved east to the Tobruk–El Adem road. Enemy tanks were closing in on the perimeter and the Australians in this area had no anti-tank guns.

Leakey's 'C' Squadron fought against the German tanks, using the 1 RTR light tanks to distract the enemy: 'We opened fire on them when they were within 800 yards of us. We were disturbed to see our 2-pdr solid shots bouncing off their armour.' At the end of the action 'C' Squadron had lost three tanks brewed up for the loss of only one German tank. The Luftwaffe sent over bombers every day and most nights. Trooper Lionel Bowden of 1 RTR was appointed anti-aircraft machine-gunner on HMT *Bamora* in Tobruk harbour. He won the Military Medal for firing continuously at the Stuka dive-bombers. The ship was hit three times and Bowden was badly wounded. Sergeant William Cornish was also awarded the MM. A tank

Tobruk, 1941. Dick Edwards, Dusty Miller, James Bouverie-Brine, Crafty Crouch and Joe Sassoon. (*James Bouverie-Brine*)

1 RTR group in Tobruk. (*James Bouverie-Brine*)

commander near a minefield, he was hit by shellfire. Although wounded three times, he walked calmly in front of the tank (itself hit ten times) to guide it through the minefield.

Bertie Rendell, now a sergeant, wrote:

> Tobruk was entered 6 April, and halted at the Blue Line. The perimeter was defended by infantry, 25-pdrs, a few heavies and 1 RTR in tanks. The harbour was the main base. At times we extended the perimeter at great speed! It really was a siege, we drank distilled sea water for a long time. Now and again a tanker came up at low tide to get some water into Tobruk, then millions of gallons were put into army water tanks. Tobruk had been a very beautiful town – it was all snow white – it had everything, an Italian hospital. We had dive-bombers coming and you could count 50 up there. If you saw under 30 there was something wrong! They would come in at least three times a day and sometimes at night. They would climb and climb and come down perpendicular on whatever they wanted to hit. Bully beef was the main meal; barrels of sea water were brought up to all regiments, distilled by boiling over a diesel fire.

In skirmishes Rendell lost two more tanks. One driver was replaced by 'Piggy' Parker, aged just seventeen – he was killed by a sniper two months later, driving a tank. At mealtimes the crews were visited by jerboa desert rats. Sangers (shelters) made of boulders and stones were built adjacent to the tanks defending the Blue Line. In addition to acting as 1 RTR's Intelligence Officer, Captain John Wollaston was also the regimental navigator and OC Headquarters Troop. He noted:

Tobruk was a small town on a small hill overlooking a large harbour in the vast desert. The Italians had fortified it by putting a barbed wire fence from four miles east of the harbour out into the desert, then westward and back to the sea. They dug anti-tank ditches outside the fence and platoon posts inside. These consisted of underground accommodation for a platoon and included an air raid shelter. Passages led to weapon pits around the living quarters. These posts were situated next to the wire about every thousand yards. Also a second line about one thousand yards to the rear covered off the intervals. RHQ Troop was armed with four A-9 cruiser tanks, with main turret and a one-man MG turret on each side of the driver – issued from the Tobruk Base Workshops.

Everyone praised the formidable fire (direct anti-tank or indirect HE) laid down by Captain Geoffrey Goschen, the RHA FOO for Chestnut, Rocket and E Troops, 1 RHA.

Rommel personally commanded a major onslaught on 14 April, with Lieutenant-Colonel Ponath's infantry of 5th Leichte Division backed by Olbrich's 5th Panzer Regiment with thirty-nine panzers. A very heavy barrage fell on Brigadier Murray's 20th Australian Brigade at 0430 hours, followed by mass Stuka dive-bombing. Posts 31, 32 and 33 west of the El Adem road were the initial German objectives, but 1 RHA anti-tank portees (guns mounted on trucks), plus the 3rd Anti-aircraft/Anti-tank Regiment, enfiladed the attack. As the panzers retreated, 1 RTR tanks intercepted them. Lieutenant Bouverie-Brine of 'B' Squadron recorded:

Matilda tanks and troops below a ridge during the siege of Tobruk. (*James Bouverie-Brine*)

14 April moved out at 5.15am to the Bardia road where 16 enemy tanks had broken in. Arrived at 6am where we met C Squadron and were in action at once. After a lively exchange of fire the enemy withdrew, leaving 5 burnt-out tanks. We lost one light tank [that of Second Lieutenant B.E. Leakey, cousin of Rea Leakey] and C Squadron lost an A-10 and an A-9, having Sergeant Hulme and three crew killed. B Squadron got on the west side of a gulley and could not get into range.

'C' Squadron was commanded by Major Walter Benzie, with four cruiser tanks and eight light tanks. Benzie was quite short, with fair hair, a small ragged moustache, a red nose and an ugly face, but he had 'the guts of a lion'. When Benzie's own tank was hit and set alight, he baled out and ran to Captain Rea Leakey's tank to transfer his pennant to it. As he climbed up a shell hit and penetrated the engine. Lieutenant J.G. Plaistowe was watching this drama from his light tank. Captain Leakey, unaware that his tank could not now move, kept ordering his driver to advance. Hynes thought it was extremely funny! But then Leakey's gunner Trooper Milligan was killed by a direct hit from a shell. The first sub-turret gunner was also dead, his clothing burning fiercely. Leakey saw Sergeant Hulme emerge from the turret of his tank after a group of German infantry had apparently surrendered. He was shot at close quarters with 'seven bullets in his heart', but the Australians 'saw red and put three long bayonets into the German's stomach'. That day about nineteen German panzers were knocked out and about 500 infantry killed or wounded. In addition, some 200 members of the Tobruk garrison who had been made prisoner were released.

On 24 April Lieutenant-Colonel 'Buster' Brown arrived by air to take over command from Lieutenant-Colonel James Culverwell, whose health had suffered from the difficult and harsh living conditions.

Captain John Wollaston acquired the diary of a captured German tank captain. 'He was amazed at the [British] anti-tank fire, mentioned the 14 [1 RTR] tanks coming into action. German losses were 17 lost out of 38 tanks that went into the battle. Two German tank officers were killed, seven wounded. The German panzers all carried infantry on top into action.' The aerial dogfight during the day resulted in nineteen Stukas shot down for the loss of two Hurricanes. Lieutenant Bouverie-Brine in his diary noted: '29 April 6pm attacked by 14 JU87 [Stuka] dive-bombers. Hair-raising to say the least, but when it was all over and the last cloud of dust had rolled away, we could find no damage.'

On 30 April Rea Leakey handed over command of 'C' Squadron to Major Walter Benzie, who was several years his senior in rank. Leakey stayed as squadron second-in-command. On the same day Rommel launched another major attack and broke through the outer defences near the Acroma road. RHQ Squadron 1 RTR were then east of Pilastrino, with 'B' Squadron to the west and 'C' Squadron covering the El Adem crossroads. Rea Leakey noticed that the RAF had been swept from the skies; the Luftwaffe were now based at El Adem aerodrome only 10 miles to the south. Lieutenant Bouverie-Brine's diary recorded:

30 April/1 May. Major attack by Germans on SE perimeter: an infantry assault had penetrated up to 3 miles by dark. At 7am B Squadron advanced, joined up with C Squadron on the way and after much jockeying for position put in an attack at 12 noon. B Squadron commander (George Hynes) was soon hit and his A-10 cruiser went up in flames, killing two of his crew and burning him. Sergeant Cornish was next receiving 5 hits, wounding him and killing Corporals Leehan and Pembury. This cruiser was recovered, an important point as 1 RTR was down to a total of 15 tanks. Another attack at 2pm proved equally disastrous. The CO's tank [Lieutenant-Colonel Brown] and his IO's [Captain Wollaston] tank [were] KO'd followed by three I [Matilda] tanks of 7 RTR. We had no further personnel losses but 7 RTR lost 3 men, and several wounded.

Major Hynes had watched the panzers advancing into a British minefield where six had their tracks blown off. Hynes's driver Lance-Corporal John McConnachie, a Canadian, won the Military Medal. He ran 150 yards to secure first aid for the wounded, then twice repaired broken tank tracks, all the time under fire. Major Hynes's burned-out tank up on the ridge became a landmark known as 'George's Tank' or 'George's Ridge'. Hynes himself, badly burned, went into Tobruk hospital which Stukas later bombed, killing thirty-six Italian and German wounded.

Hynes spent eight weeks recuperating in Cairo. He returned on a Royal Navy destroyer which was attacked by bombers and a U-boat. The U-boat was sunk. HMS *Waterhen*, badly damaged, was towed towards Tobruk, but turned turtle and sank. George Hynes survived this incident and rejoined 1 RTR on 1 July as second-in-command. Lieutenant Bouverie-Brine was in temporary command of 'B' Squadron, with three cruisers and six light tanks, but was soon joined by Lieutenant Freddy Plaistowe with two cruisers 'renovated' by the Tobruk workshops. Sergeant 'Dodger' Green was in command of 'B' Squadron's Light Aid Detachment, and was 'one of the bravest and most competent of mechanics. Throughout the siege and afterwards he followed the squadron on every sortie in his unarmoured 15-cwt LAD wagon'. Lieutenant Bouverie-Brine put him up for a MM but without success. Captain Rea Leakey recalled:

> As the sun was setting [on 1 May] the German attack was launched. They looked east while we looked west into the sun. We could see little through the dust and smoke but at least we stopped the enemy tanks closing in on the Australian pill-boxes. When darkness fell we were of little use and pulled back a mile. All that night the attack raged and the Germans captured 4 miles of the perimeter. There was no second line of defence. Every man in the garrison who could be spared was now brought up, given a spade to dig with and a rifle to shoot with. Cooks, clerks, lorry drivers, even skilled mechanics were pushed into the line, and the line held but only just. All that day we moved about from place to place and fought back enemy tanks that were trying to probe forward.

Rommel's forces had taken 15 of the 130 defensive posts, 11 in the outer ring and 4 in the inner, and had gained the vital Hill Point 208. But of the 81 panzers that started on 1 May only 35 were battleworthy next morning. For four days and nights the battle raged and it cost the Axis troops 53 officers and 1,187 men killed or wounded.

★ ★ ★

In mid-May the resourceful Tobruk tank repair workshops disgorged a new type of cruiser tank – twelve of them – left behind by the unfortunate armoured brigade torn apart in Rommel's drive eastwards. These Mk III cruiser tanks, known as A-13s, had a crew of four, weighed 14 tons, were armed with 2-pdr gun and a .303 Vickers machine-gun, and were powered by a Nuffield Liberty 340hp engine. Major Benzie's squadron found them fast but mechanically unsound and they were constantly breaking down. Benzie and Leakey became firm friends. Leakey said: 'In some ways he [Benzie] almost courted death and he certainly did not know what the word "fear" meant. He had an infectious laugh. He never lost his temper. The men almost worshipped him.' During May there were small tank actions every two or three days and 1 RTR made raids with, usually, four tanks. Major Benzie went round the various Australian battalions holding the perimeter offering them a tank raid. One took place on 13 May against Italians holding road-blocks on Bardia road and also against the Wadi Belgassem. To support Wavell's Operation Brevity, a feint attack was made on 15 May to entice Rommel's armour away from the frontier posts held by the Afrika Korps. Benzie and Leakey's squadron advanced to Fig Tree, and separately Lieutenant Geddes with three troops of cruisers crossed Pilastrino road towards Wadi Giaida. Although they flaunted themselves, there were no takers and no casualties. On 30 May Leakey with Major Goschen of 1 RHA, with three cruisers and two light tanks, had a brisk battle with ten Panzers 6,000 yards south of the perimeter.

Major-General Morshead (known as 'Ming the Merciless') was a tough, able and determined garrison commander and much credit must go to him for masterminding his large mixed forces. Petrol supplies via the Royal Navy were so much reduced that tanks had to be 'grounded'. Benzie and Leakey, bored stiff, became 'honorary corporals' and joined the Australian infantry. One of the hazards of inactivity was the number of stupid accidents caused by bored troops 'playing' with hand grenades. Bouverie-Brine noted this happened on 10 June and 26 August. His new OC, Major Jimmy Cruickshank, arrived on 20 July and left on 26 September, and Bouverie-Brine took command of 'B' Squadron as a major. Brigadier Reggie Keller, who had commanded 3 RTR in the heroic defeats in Calais and Greece, became OC Tobruk tanks. The splendid 9th Australian Division was replaced by the 70th British Division and the Polish Carpathian Brigade. For the time being, after suffering two bloody noses, Rommel seemed content for Tobruk to be invested (although it was still being supplied by courageous Royal Navy night convoys). No fewer than 15,000 men were brought in and taken out by the Navy. The 32nd Army Tank Brigade was formed from mid-September under Brigadier A.C. Willison DSO, MC (nicknamed 'Ant'). It consisted of 1 RTR (with 28 assorted cruisers and 34 light tanks); 'D' Squadron 7 RTR and 4 RTR (with 69 Matildas between

Tanks used in defence of the Tobruk perimeter were either dug-in or otherwise protected from air attack. This A-9 cruiser is partly surrounded by a low stone breastwork. The object was to maintain them and their crews well forward so that they could respond quickly to sudden attacks. (*Tank Museum 2258/D3*)

them); and 'C' Squadron, Kings Dragoon Guards. The brigade had a total strength of 166 AFVs. The principal role of 4 RTR was to engage and destroy enemy AFVs. 1 RTR on the outer flank would cut off retreating AFVs while 7 RTR was held in reserve. 'A' Squadron 1 RTR was reunited with the rest of the regiment courtesy of the Royal Navy's overnight convoys.

General Auchinleck succeeded Wavell, and after the failure of Operations Brevity and Battleaxe it was hoped that 'Crusader' would succeed. After several furious tank battles around Sidi Rezegh, the 'end game' for the Eighth Army was to link up with the Tobruk garrison and force the Afrika Korps westwards. General Scobie, the garrison commander after 'Ming the Merciless', had left with his division for the Delta, had drawn up comprehensive plans for the break-out. The key defence posts to be captured were called Wolf, Tiger, Lion, Tugun, Jack, Jill, Butch, Walter, Freddy, etc. However, the Axis troops surrounding Tobruk had been underestimated. Instead of meeting the Italian Bologna Division, they encountered three divisions backed by 210 guns. Captain John Wollaston recalled: 'At our break-out at the end of November the only Australians left in Tobruk were the 2/13th Battalion of infantry who joined the two brigades, one tanks and one infantry. We found we were fighting crack Engineer Assault units getting ready to capture Tobruk.'

The break-out plan involved an advance on Wolf, via Jill and Tiger, on the left flank, and via Butch and Jack on the right to Tugun. The eventual objective was to meet up with the advance units of the Eighth Army at El Duda, 7 miles south-east of Tobruk. Preparations were made with speed and secrecy. Ammunition dumps were formed and camouflaged. Six timber bridges were made to allow the tanks to cross the anti-tank ditch. The routes were marked by screened lights and white tapes. The Polish brigade was to attack to the west of the perimeter to keep the enemy guessing while the real break-out took place to the east. At 0445 hours on 21 November the attack started between R67, R68, R69 and R71. Captain Bouverie-Brine recalled:

> We moved from our FAA by the tower and crossed the start line at 0710, 20 minutes late. No guides and no features to steer by, so two squadrons and RHQ went out of the perimeter through the *same* gap. C Squadron and a Matilda got stuck on the minefield. We were held up for 2 hours. East of Tiger Lieutenant Dick Edwards in the lead tank was shot in the head (and died on 23rd). Corporal Walpole and Trooper Winforth were seriously wounded when their tank was blown up on an Italian box mine. 10 minutes later my tank got a direct hit from an HE shell; wrecked the tank as it burst the petrol tank in the rear, jammed the guns. Got into Sergeant Gartery's tank: at 12 we went to help A and C Squadrons at Freddy. When an 88mm anti-tank gun came into action, we withdrew and eventually returned to the FAA.

Captain F.G. Plaistowe's tank was hit by an 88mm shell which killed his driver, but his gunner quickly knocked out the 88mm gun. Plaistowe and the two survivors moved to a light tank, and scrambled on the back when it, in turn, was destroyed by an 88mm shell, killing all the crew.

Walter Benzie's 'C' Squadron led the advance into a minefield. Four tanks were disabled and came under fire. Trooper Clarke was killed by a sniper, as was Trooper Spencer. Sergeant Ashewell's and Sergeant Frost's tank crews baled out and were captured but Lieutenant Ellison and Sergeant Rendell got their crews away to safety, rescued by the 2nd Queens Infantry and by Lieutenant Farmer of 1 RTR who picked up five survivors. 'A' Squadron soon arrived on the scene and Lieutenant Young's troop opened BESA machine-gun fire on the enemy infantry in their sangers. Sergeant Shields killed several machine-gun crews. 'A' Squadron then rallied north-west of Jill, thus missing the deadly minefield. At 0905 hours the CO, Lieutenant-Colonel 'Buster' Brown, ordered 'A' Squadron north of Tiger but it came under heavy fire; Trooper Beck was killed, Major Sir F. Coates (OC

Squadron) and Corporal Watts were hit and wounded. Sergeant-Major Alexander rescued his OC and Captain Plaistowe took command. Brought up by KDG armoured cars, Royal Engineers arrived to clear the minefield, and under fire grubbed up enough mines for the surviving cruisers to get through.

Brigadier Willison later wrote: 'A final try had to be made and the two following orders were issued: "To 4 RTR, employ your reserve squadron, you will capture Tiger position" and "To 1 RTR, swing wider, you must break through". The response was immediate. It was inspiring to see the cruiser squadron 1 RTR led by their fearless commander Major Benzie rushing forward.' C Squadron with seven surviving cruisers led the way, followed by 'A' Squadron, RHQ Squadron and 'B' Squadron. Once through the minefield, they turned south-east for Tiger followed by 4 RTR and the survivors of a Black Watch battalion piped into battle. Tiger was eventually captured together with 12 field guns, 30 Spandaus, several flame-throwers and 500 prisoners. 1 RTR bypassed Tiger and 'A' Squadron took on Freddie. Captain Plaistowe and Troopers Billings, Clark and Williams were wounded. Lieutenant Richards took over command of 'A' Squadron.

Benzie's 'C' Squadron was under heavy fire from Freddie and the major was hit and wounded. Sergeant Turner's tank brewed up and the crew baled out. Lieutenant Hayter's tank was hit four times and the crew were rescued by Lieutenant Dawson's tank. 1 RTR then moved away from Freddie, as 'A' Squadron following 'C' Squadron took more casualties. Two more tanks were hit. In one, Sergeant Corbett and Troopers Crighton and Ratcliffe were killed and Troopers Bracey and Lynch wounded. In the other Sergeant Burgess was killed and Troopers Roberts and Mottram were wounded. At 1440 hours Brigadier Willison reported to General Scobie: 'Tank state is 26 Is [Matildas], 12 armoured cars, 6 cruisers and 6 lights [of 1 RTR].' With this reduced strength Operation Plum, intended to get to El Duda, had to be cancelled, but Tugun's Italian garrison, 185-strong, was taken prisoner. The British held the battlefield and had excellent tank recovery units to restore numbers.

At the end of the 21st only 40 out of 158 AFVs were battleworthy, but Tiger, Jack, Tugun and Jill had all been captured and an advance of 4 miles made on a 2-mile front. In addition, over a thousand prisoners, mainly Germans, had been taken. Nevertheless it was a disastrous day for 1 RTR. The regiment had lost 11 cruisers and 7 light tanks, and had at least 8 men killed and 20 wounded.

By D+1 (22 November) Captain Price's RAOC recovery team, which had worked through the night, had managed to increase 1 RTR's strength to 8 cruisers and 13 lights. 'A' and 'B' Squadrons were merged under Major Bouverie-Brine, but were not in action. By nightfall strength was up to 9 cruisers and 20 lights. On D+2 (23 November) Bouverie-Brine 'moved outside perimeter at 0600 to safeguard the right flank of the attack on Dalby Square, advancing west from Tiger. My two cruiser troops had captured

Tiger, with 85 PoWs, 12 105mm field guns and 8 bottles of Chianti. I had one for lunch.' Later three Italian CV3 light tanks were knocked out at Bir Gheroa. 'I could see the frontier force fighting at Sidi Rezegh.' The corridor was now 5 miles deep and 4 miles wide and 1 RTR were up to 13 cruisers and 22 lights. D+3 (24 November) was a full day of rest and maintenance. On D+4 (25 November) Lieutenant 'Dusty' Miller scrounged whisky and cigarettes from the NAAFI and distributed them to the tank crews. On D+5 (26 November) Operation Plum, the advance on El Duda, was reinstated. Bouverie-Brine's diary recalled:

Today the 32nd Army Tank Brigade decided to take the El Duda feature on the El Adem encampment and cut the Tobruk by-pass. We left the FAA at 0415, assembled north of Lion at 6am and at 9am the attack started. 4 RTR and 7 RTR 'I' tanks went first in waves and we brought up the rear with the KDG Marmon Harrington armoured cars. There was no immediate opposition but we were shelled to hell. After we had taken El Duda we had to sit on it like coconuts in a shy and we were sniped by a 210mm and 75 Battery over open sights. This 210 knocked out a light tank and a cruiser and killed Lieuts Bill Yeo [the popular adjutant] and Binks Richards, and wounded 4 ORs. Two Italian staff cars tried to race through on the road and were shot up. The RAF bombed our infantry coming up in lorries to consolidate; they killed 20, wounded 30 [and] wrecked 2 lorries and a Bren-carrier. They caused more damage than the Jerrys. Leaguered the night on N slope of Duda.

After various adventures Lieutenant Jeffrey Hilltout rejoined 1 RTR in Tobruk. He wrote:

The break-out was well advanced. I led my troop, spotted a lone tank moving slowly and erratically through the dust and smoke. I ordered my driver to advance and halted beside this tank. I jumped down and climbed on to it. Inside I saw Bill Yeo with a hole behind his left ear and slumped in the turret. He was quite dead. His driver was in shock.

On D+6 (27 November) 1 RTR left El Duda to protect the corridor flanks. Bill Yeo's father, who was CO 44 RTR, arrived in Tobruk and 'was broken-hearted when he heard the news. Bill is an awful loss. I have known him for 2½ years and he was a good adjutant,' wrote Bouverie-Brine. 1 RTR tank strength was now down to 9 lights and 6 cruisers. On D+7 (28 November) there was an attack on the Walter and Freddy strongpoints. Captain B.C. Forster led 'C' Squadron towards Sidi Rezegh on a recce. At 1532 hours 1 RTR cruisers went off to assist 7 RTR.

Lieutenant Geddes and Major George Hynes came across a bomb, which Hynes picked up. It exploded, wounding both officers. All three squadron COs had become casualties in the corridor. Bouverie-Brine and Lieutenant Steve Gane saw four Italian anti-tank guns and charged at them shooting hard, at which some 250 Italians rose from the ground and surrendered. On D+8 (29 November) 15 Panzer Division with 100 tanks plus 60 small Italian tanks made a determined counter-attack. By dusk they had achieved a major penetration but a magnificent counter-attack was launched by 4 RTR, supported by Australians, New Zealanders, RHA guns and British infantry. Battle Group 1 was broken and mainly captured, while Battle

Group 2 was pushed back about 1,000 metres. By D+9 (30 November) 1 RTR were down to 3 cruisers and 3 lights, based around the central positions Jill and Tiger. Padre Ogilvy held a short service in a trench under shellfire. By the next day the Tobruk workshops had again worked wonders and tank strength had increased to 12 cruisers and 13 lights, and 1 RTR was quickly back in action, wiping out a Zug B force of 130 enemy infantry, with anti-tank guns and flamethrowers, trying to seize Jill. Captain Basil Forster's light tank was blown up on a mine, and his driver Trooper Cameron had his left leg blown off. Steve Gane and Sergeant Mears engaged in a fierce action with three 28mm anti-tank guns guarded by 100 German sappers. Before they were silenced Corporal Mears was wounded, as was Corporal Higgins. On 2 December Bouverie-Brine shared a pit with Lieutenant Tony Geneve, lashed by heavy rain and an icy-cold wind. But a NAAFI issue of two tins of beer and 100 cigarettes per man and a half-bottle of whisky per officer helped them survive. On 4 December Rommel ordered one last attack on El Duda. 1 RTR and 4 RTR defended Leopard against the Mickle battlegroup near Trigh Capuzzo.

A German 88mm gun knocked out at least twelve Matilda tanks but most were repairable. Then Rommel called it a day. On 6 December Lieutenant-Colonel 'Buster' Brown sent out 1 RTR to beat up the enemy south-east of El Duda. At 1500 hours 'B' Squadron moved up to the escarpment, and remained west of Bel Hamed. 'C' Squadron with its fast A-13 cruisers went to Sidi Rezegh and found it free of enemy. Bouverie-Brine wrote:

> 7 December. Wonderful day. Movement and new scenery for the first time for eight months. Padre Quinn held a field service at 10am. B Squadron moved to Gambut with a troop of 1 RHA, two companies of KORR. I put Steve Gane i/c the six cruisers on an encampment 3 miles south, Captain Basil Forster's light troop on an encampment two miles north and Sergeant Gartery's troop on the road. We arrived at Gambut at 4 and linked up with South African armoured cars on the aerodrome, with 39 wrecked German aircraft.

It looked as though the siege was over but 1 RTR continued in action. On the 8th Bouverie-Brine and SSM Alexander travelled through an Italian box minefield: 'Our tracks missed every mine. God must be looking after me.' The next day an Italian canteen dump produced for every man eight bars of chocolate, a bottle of Ricoaro water and tin of sardines. Each tank and lorry crew got a tin of jam. Lieutenant Hilltout and Captain Basil Forster (and many others) suffered badly from desert sores. Hilltout recalled: 'We had no green vegetables, and quite small cuts failed to heal and spread into larger wounds. To counter this deficiency in our blood we received ascorbic acid tablets which helped but were no substitute for sprouts, beans or garden peas. To relieve the monotony [during the siege] we put on concerts, anyone with a talent to entertain taking part followed by a party, enlivened with the rum ration brought by the Navy and hoarded for these occasions.'

'B' Squadron were heavily dive-bombed on the 12th and Corporal Hook was wounded. Major Jimmy Cruickshank and Captain Derek Thom rejoined the regiment. Bouverie-Brine's tank ran over a thermos bomb which blew a track off, damaging a bogey and the jockey roller. He then destroyed twelve other bombs with fire from his German rifle. No wonder he felt dizzy after the concussion and had awful dreams at night. On the 14th he wrote:

> Near Point 204 we were shelled all day and five shells landed within yards of me, at 1.15 we were attacked by 12 German Mk III tanks. For fifteen minutes 50mm shells and bullets flew everywhere. My tank was hit and had its L track blown off for the second time in a month. I ordered Steve [Lieutenant Gane] to go west and make a demo in their rear. It worked as the enemy tanks withdrew at once leaving three knocked out. Unfortunately when returning Steve went too far and both tanks 7200 and 7199 under Second Lieutenant Miller and Sergeant Hughes ran into the enemy area and were captured. Withdrawing from Pt 204 was most unpleasant. We left at 4, as a terrific Stuka raid came on. We had 14 lorries in the convoy and this drew shellfire and MG fire from everywhere. Miraculously nothing was hit. 1 RTR now consists of 10 lights and 1 cruiser. In the evening of 16th the CO Lieutenant-Colonel Brown ordered that all remaining cruisers should be handed over for a probable return to Cairo. Got a lump in my throat when I heard this.

The two indomitable honorary Australian infantrymen 'Corporals' Walter Benzie and Rea Leakey survived, the latter going to a staff course in Cairo, then to 3 RTR.

★   ★   ★

There were many unsung heroes of this action: the indefatigable RAMC personnel, who kept alive, if they could, not only Australian and British casualties but Italians and Germans as well; the South African W/T operator Lance-Corporal Holmes, operating his set in the depths of Bouverie-Brine's tank; Signalman Frank Harrison (who subsequently wrote the book *Tobruk – The Story of a Great Siege Remembered*); Geoff Knights, an ambulance driver/operator, who recalled that the 'enemy counter-barrage gave us a real headache – our T group (ambulance, staff car, fitters lorry, signals truck and ammo and petrol 3-tonners) lost most of its vehicles'; and young Captain William Yeo, the erudite adjutant whose influence was considerable. Sergeant Allan Appleby won the Distinguished Conduct Medal as acting troop commander. Two of his tanks lost their tracks in a minefield and Appleby used the wrecked tanks as machine-gun pill-boxes to fend off infantry attacks, then repaired the tracks while under fire. By nightfall his troop was battleworthy again. Sergeant G. Devlin was captured on 21 June and was sent via Benghazi to Munich for interrogation, and then to Italy via Tutorano, Altamura and Carpi to Campo 73 Sulmona. He made two unsuccessful attempts to escape before Italy surrendered. He conducted three convoys of Allied prisoners of war to safety and he too was awarded the Distinguished Conduct Medal. And of course the gallant Royal Navy, which suffered very badly as they struggled to keep the Tobruk garrison supplied with food, ammunition and rum for eight long months.

CHAPTER SIX

The Battles for Sidi Rezegh

Christmas Eve 1941 was spent outside Alexandria. Lieutenant-Colonel Brown DSO still commanded and Captain J.A. Sassoon became adjutant, with E.C. Foote still Quartermaster and W. Fletcher the RSM. A period of rest and re-equipment outside Cairo followed. Jeffrey Hilltout recalled 'the luxuries of hot baths, cool sheets and ice-cold beer'. Early in the new year the Axis garrison at Halfaya surrendered. Operation Crusader had cost the Axis 300 tanks and the British 278. It was remarkable how 1 RTR LAD and the workshops were able to 'patch up' tank casualties. But if Rommel had retreated he had not yet been beaten, and he renewed his attacks on 21 January, breaking through the outpost line at El Agheila, pushing through Msus and recapturing Benghazi on the 29th. The Eighth Army stabilised its defensive line at Gazala on 5 February, while friend and foe spent four months building up their forces, integrating reinforcements and training with new equipment. Major Bouverie-Brine wrote:

> Our next tanks turned out to be one squadron of Honeys [the American Stuart M3A1 light tank] and three squadrons of Grants [the American medium Mk 3]. We had already learned that light tanks were valueless except in a reconnaissance role (which we were not) because they were too vulnerable and their armament, a 37mm gun, was outclassed by every German tank gun. The Grant was mobile artillery. Its main armament was a short-barrelled 75mm gun mounted in a sub-turret alongside the driver with an effective traverse of only 30 degrees; this meant that the whole tank had to be turned to face a target outside this limit. Another weakness was that the tank commander's eye-level was some 8 feet above that of the gunner. No advantage could be taken of slopes or mounds because the whole tank had to be exposed before the gunner could see what his commander was indicating.

The Grant tank with its 9-cylinder radial aeroplane engine, powered by high-octane petrol, tended to catch fire very easily. Nevertheless from 1,000 yards (a fairly typical range) the Grants could penetrate the frontal armour of all the German tanks they fired at, including the panzer Mk IIIs and Mk IVs. The other British tanks could penetrate only the smaller target of the turret front. Altogether 250 Grants had arrived in Egypt.

1 RTR spent January at Mustapha Barracks in Sidi Bishr (near Alexandria), tankless but with a strength of 17 officers and 406 men. In February they were on garrison duties and their strength had risen to 23 officers and 424 ORs. Lectures were given on internal security; the anti-paratroop role; camouflage; lessons learned from the 'first 14 days of the Libyan campaign in November 1941' and signal security. By 12 April the

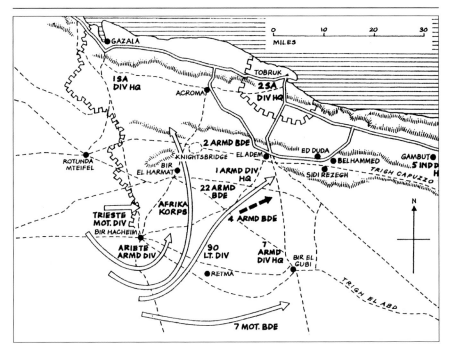

The Battle of Gazala, May–June 1942.

regiment was in Cowley camp, Cairo; its strength had risen to 30 officers and 600 ORs, and its 'new' tanks were 24 Grant cruisers and 20 Stuart lights. May was spent on exercises and calibrating guns in the desert in the El Adem area. At the end of the month movement orders were received and, via Amiriya, El Duda, Matruh, Sidi Barrani and Fort Capuzzo, 1 RTR moved towards Bardia along the coast road. 'A' Squadron under Major A.G. Cruickshank had 16 Stuarts, 'B' Squadron under Major Bouverie-Brine 1 Stuart and 10 Grants, 'C' Squadron under Major Walter Benzie 1 Stuart and 11 Grants. RHQ Squadron had 2 Stuarts and 2 Grants under Captain Sassoon.

Lieutenant-General Ritchie, GOC Eighth Army, faced a very experienced enemy. Rommel's Panzerarmee Afrika bypassed the southern end of the Gazala line at Bir Hacheim (26–27 May) and a few days later overwhelmed the 150th Brigade and the 1st Army Tank Brigade. On 5 June 10th Indian Infantry Brigade was overrun and the French Foreign Legion under siege at Bir Hacheim (6–10th) and around 'Knightsbridge' track junction (11–13th). British tank losses were severe.

On their way to El Duda on 1 June, 1 RTR were bombed. A petrol lorry was hit and four troopers were killed. Nevertheless a war correspondent with a ciné camera was present at 0700 hours when Sergeant Page lost his Stuart on a minefield. Under command of the 22nd Armoured Brigade

1 RTR were at Bir Bellefa by the 3rd. Within a couple of days the regiment was part of 22nd, 23rd and 4th Armoured Brigade. Poor Second Lieutenant Cameron was the liaison officer with 7th Armoured Division. On the 5th the adjutant's Stuart T37878 was hit by anti-tank fire; it burst into flames and two ORs were killed. Sergeant Whiteland's Stuart T37953 was also hit and abandoned. Sergeant Rendell, in his first action with a new General Lee/Grant cruiser, 'hit by a shell [on the] cupola, spun like a top and fell to the bottom of the tank. We had a bad time, the tank KO'd but later recovered.'

Confused fighting continued in the Knightsbridge area, along the Hacheim track and around Trig Point 171. By the 8th two more Stuarts had been wrecked – T24749 with Lieutenant A.T. Hughes killed and Lieutenant Clarke's T24795 destroyed. Forty-nine enemy tanks were spotted west of Knightsbridge box and during an evening battle the regiment accounted for two tanks, a field gun and two ammunition lorries. The battles on the 10th were disastrous. 1 RTR started the day with 14 Stuarts and 16 Grants, and ended it with 12 Stuarts and 2 Grants. As part of the 4th Armoured Brigade (with 6 RTR), the regiment advanced at 0630 hours as left flank protection for 6 RTR, to attack an enemy concentration around Bir el Aslagh with 'A' Squadron, 'C' Squadron, RHQ, 'B' Squadron and 'A' Echelon. Bitter fighting went on all day. There are interesting accounts by Major A.G. Cruickshank of 'A' Squadron, Major Bouverie-Brine of 'B' Squadron, Major Benzie of 'C' Squadron and the Intelligence Officer Lieutenant John Wollaston. By the end of June 2 officers, Major Walter Benzie and Lieutenant Hughes, and 12 ORs had been killed; a further 6 officers and 28 ORs were wounded, and 1 officer and 23 ORs were missing or prisoners – a total of 72. The RMO Captain F.J. Wainman RAMC and the second-in-command Major F.W.D. Sturdee made heroic efforts to tend or rescue the wounded and the dying. There did not seem to be much on the credit side – three tanks hit and destroyed, three anti-tank guns silenced and two lorry-loads of infantry hit and dispersed.

The gallant hero of Tobruk, Walter Benzie's tank T24235 was hit at 1100 hours on 12 June; it caught fire and he was killed. Captain D. Thom, Sergeant Kirkpatrick, Sergeant Beeden, Sergeant Weller and Second Lieutenant Hayter all had their tanks hit and destroyed. Major Bouverie-Brine saw four of his Grants go up in smoke – those of Captain E.P.H. Gane, Lieutenant Sproull, Sergeant Horry and Sergeant Shinnis. Major Loder-Simonds of 1 RHA had three FOOs in 'A' Squadron's area and they brought down excellent defensive fire – both anti-tank and indirect – but it was not enough.

There had been several reports of the Axis strength up in front. At 1000 hours on the 9th '55 enemy tanks reported approaching from west'; at 1810 hours 'Numerous reports from 'A' Squadron confirm much activity of tanks, armoured cars, MT and men in area Bir el Aslagh'; and at 1700 'Reports confirm 50 enemy AFVs lined up ready to advance or meet an attack by us'.

On 10 June '1106 Commanding Officer warns regiment of A/T guns in area of Barrel 230' and at 1200 hours 'Information received enemy are using captured 25-pdrs and using tanks as OPs'.

On 11 June Major E.C. Mitford MC took command. Amid heavy shelling a YMCA canteen arrived at 1600 hours and three Grants arrived with American crews! The War Diary reported on 13 June a typical action:

> Grants advanced and engaged enemy. Visibility very poor due to severe dust storm. Enemy tanks reported advancing along bottom of escarpment supported by heavy artillery fire. 'A' Squadron contacted own infantry who appeared to be very confused and somewhat shaken. The whole line withdrew slightly east. 'A' Squadron tried to continue line to south facing west but were beaten off by heavy A/T fire. Sergeant Whitlam was hit. The MO arrived quickly on the scene. Sergeant McGregor drove the tank out of action.
>
> 15 June. 1 RTR arrived on Tobruk perimeter. Lieutenant D. Munson's tank blown up on a minefield.

Units had to be amalgamated and reformed because of the heavy losses. Five battleworthy tanks were handed over to 7 RTR, so tank strength on the 16th was down to 11. Spare tank crews were sent to 4th Armoured Brigade HQ. On the 18th 'A' Squadron handed over 9 Stuarts to 6 RTR and three days later 10 'B' Echelon vehicles to 4th Armoured Brigade HQ (which had been ambushed and just about destroyed in a night action). But on the 25th 118 ORs were received from TDR and the Sherwood Rangers handed over 36 Stuarts (RHQ 4, 'A' and 'B' Squadrons 16 each). For nearly a week 1 RTR had not been a fighting regiment; now it was once again, as two days later 'C' Squadron with 12 Grants rejoined the regiment. But the next day 'C' Squadron took their Grants away again, having been attached to 6 RTR. They changed places with 'A' Squadron 6 RTR, whose 17 Stuarts brought the total strength of 1 RTR up to 53 Stuarts. The next day 'A' Squadron 6 RTR returned to *their* regiment! The War Diary again: 'We are now a column of two Stuart squadrons, one battery RHA, one troop A/Tk guns and 'A' Company of KRRC . . . 22 enemy tanks approached us from NE. Regiment engaged . . . Midnight attacked in leaguer.'

One of the miracles of desert warfare was how the RASC (or the regimental equivalent) managed to get POL (petrol, oil and lubricant), ammunition, food and water (and sometimes mail) to the exhausted squadrons in night leaguer. On 1 July this was not the case. 1 RTR was grounded with no petrol and no ammunition. The War Diary noted:

> 1235. Information received that 8 enemy tanks are moving east at 877290. Also two concentrations of 38 and 28 tanks at 875281. 1445. Meanwhile the tanks stand immobilised. CO has gone to Bde, as LO and RIO have been looking for it for 3 hours . . . Now under command 22 Armd Bde ordered to assist 4 CLY on their left.

In due course POL and ammunition were delivered!

Every day during what became known as the battle of the Cauldron 1 RTR suffered casualties. On 1 July 'A' Squadron lost T37734 (Lance-Corporal Pulleyblanc) and T37942 (Sergeant Horsfield), while on 2 July

1 RTR A-9 cruiser tank inspection. (*James Bouverie-Brine*)

T37933 (Sergeant Horsfield again) was hit by anti-tank fire and abandoned, T37842 (Corporal Hook) was also hit but recovered, and T37340 (Lieutenant Smethurst) was hit on the track by an HE shell. On 3 July T37357 (Corporal White) was hit by anti-tank fire in its gun-mounting. And so it went on. Sometimes the crew were lucky, sometimes they were not. On the 2nd there were 19 casualties, but only 6 on the 3rd. Command of the regiment changed hands with alarming rapidity. On 4 July Captain Basil Forster of 'B' Squadron was in command of *all* tanks in the regiment except RHQ's. Lieutenant-Colonel Teddy Mitford and Major Sturdee, as second-in-command with RHQ's four Stuarts, left to command 6 RTR. Then Sturdee of 1 RTR was made CO (but went on leave on the 10th) and Lieutenant-Colonel G.C. Webb MBE took command.

The CO gave a lecture on the 12th:

> There are three possibilities. (1) B Squadron returns from 7th Motor Bde to 1 RTR, then 1 RTR goes back for complete refit. (2) As at present go further back, nucleus of a new 1 RTR, leaving behind all tank crews, and transport will be driven to reinforce other units. (3) RHQ, A and C Squadrons with Stuarts join B Squadron operating in desert south of El Alamein. The CO hoped for solution No 3 as B Squadron in desert cannot be relieved.

Reinforcements arrived to fill the gaps. On 12 July Lieutenant Mears and Second Lieutenant Cameron joined with 47 ORs and Major J.A. Hotham became OC 'C' Squadron. Three days later Lieutenant Myers, Lieutenant Campbell, Second Lieutenant Cutting and Second Lieutenant Reynolds also joined. Captain Sassoon the adjutant was wounded in Tobruk and was succeeded by G.J.W. Pedraza; when he was promoted to major, Captain D.L. Murison became adjutant. Lieutenant Vaughan Williams MSM and 22 ORs joined the regiment on 17 July. When the unfortunate Major Hotham was killed in action on the 27th, he was replaced as OC 'A' Squadron by Major C.A. Holliman. The GOC 7th Armoured Division congratulated Major Forster's actions with 'B' Squadron in 7th Motor Bde Group. Troop Sergeant T. ('Conky') Harland was awarded the Distinguished Conduct Medal in July for bravery in the Gazala fighting. Geoff Knights was a 37mm gunner in a Grant during the Taga plateau battle. He recalled:

> Our troop came face to face with about a dozen Italian tanks. About to open fire on these 'sitting ducks' I was frustrated by an AP shell shattering my periscope. The remains were jammed in the protective shield, so no replacement could be fitted. Then my gun mantle was also jammed by a shot that half penetrated and stopped all elevation and traverse. The same thing happened to the 75mm, so that was that. We were pulled out but the Italians never followed up. Our Grant had received 25 to 30 direct hits but nothing penetrated.

Major Bouverie-Brine wrote:

> In April 1942 1 RTR returned to the desert in the El Adem area. I was in full command of B Squadron as George Hynes had been wounded in the leg by a shell splinter on El Duda. We did not know it at the time but this was in fact the beginning of the withdrawal to Alamein. To me it seemed a continuous period of longstop and hole-plugging actions punctuated by a series of hasty reorganisations in efforts to save other groups, including at one time the 1st Free French Brigade. My three and a half years with 1 RTR ended in mid-June 1942 when we were sent in to attack a German 'tank formation'. This turned out to be the main body of 21 Panzer Division and our action turned into a mini disaster as tank after tank was lost (petrol engines caught fire easily). By the time the regiment withdrew, B Squadron had lost six tanks (with crews in four cases) including my own which received a direct hit from an A/T shell which did not penetrate but jammed the gun turret. After this the regiment had less than 20 tanks left and virtually reduced itself to one active [composite] squadron until it reached Alamein.

Bouverie-Brine later went to 50 RTR and continued the desert war to Tunis.

Sergeant Rendell made the same point! 'My General Grant was hit by a shell which dropped inside the gearbox, when we were running away from Knightsbridge. It was all flames. We got on the macadam road to Bardia.'

There were more actions and more casualties on the 22nd (six), the 23rd (five) and the 27th (eight, including Major J.A. Hotham killed). Eventually the survivors reached Amiriya Metropolis camp via the Alexandria–Matruh road.

In June and July 1 RTR casualties totalled 13 officers and 120 ORs. Of those, 4 officers and 24 ORs were killed in action or died of wounds; 8 officers and 61 ORs were wounded; and 1 officer and 35 ORs were missing.

General Sir Claude Auchinleck sent a special order after the battle. 'You have fought hard and continuously for over a month. No troops could have fought better. You have had heavy losses. . . . We're fighting the battle of Egypt in which the enemy must be destroyed. . . . He must be attacked and buried wherever you find him. The battle is not yet over and will not be over until we have defeated him and defeat him we will.' Tobruk had surrendered on 20 June with South Africans, Guards, Indians and 4 RTR and 7 RTR going into the bag. It was a terrible blow to the desert army's morale. After the first eight-month siege in which 1 RTR had played a vital role, Tobruk had been considered to be impregnable.

★ ★ ★

Back near Alexandria 1 RTR regrouped with some new faces. Lieutenant-Colonel Webb commanded, with Major C.A. Holliman OC 'A' Squadron, Major J.M. Pink OC 'B' Squadron and Captain Coulson OC 'C' Squadron. The strength was 17 officers and 236 ORs with the unit, a further 9 officers and 287 ORs detached and 8 officers and 42 ORs attached. Tank strength was 22 Grants and 22 Stuarts. 'B' and 'C' were the cruiser squadrons and 'A' the Stuart squadron. Brigadier 'Pip' Roberts commanded 22nd Armoured Brigade of which 1 RTR was a part, and inspected them on 3 August. Two days later Major-General Renton, GOC 7th Armoured Division, visited. Two exercises were carried out entitled Partridge and Snipe. Pheasant and Grouse followed on the 7th and 12th, codenamed 'Twelve August' and 'Second Phase' in preparation for – predictably – Operation Gamebirds.

CHAPTER SEVEN

Operations Gamebirds, Lightfoot and Supercharge

The great commanders in the desert came and went. O'Connor had been captured and Wavell, Ritchie and Cunningham replaced, and now the 'Auk' was about to be succeeded by General Alexander. After the débâcle of Operations Aberdeen and Splendour (Gazala and Sidi Rezegh), Winston Churchill and the CIGS General Alan Brooke visited the Delta to resolve the crisis with the Afrika Korps knocking on the doorstep. Brigadier 'Pip' Roberts commanding 22nd Armoured Brigade (1 RTR, 5 RTR and 4 CLY) met in mid-August 'a little man with white knobbly knees, an Australian bush hat and no badges of rank, whom I took to be a newly arrived correspondent'. In fact Lieutenant-General Bernard Montgomery had arrived. Appointed by General Alexander, he was to become one of the two most brilliant generals in the British Army in the Second World War. 'Monty' was the replacement for the dashing General 'Strafer' Gott, who had been tragically killed in an aircraft accident. The first thing Monty did – after making himself personally known to the majority of the Eighth Army – was to plan a defensive battle at Alam Halfa ridge (10 miles south-east of Alamein) in the defence line stretching 30 miles south-west down to the impassable Qattara Depression. Codenamed Pepsodent, this battle marked the start of Operation Gamebirds.

On 15 August 1 RTR took up battle positions, with 5 RTR in the left rear and 4 CLY in the right rear, on Pt 887269. Monty visited the regiment early on the 16th, and four days later Churchill reviewed the two Grant squadrons, 'C' and 'B', in their hull-down positions. On the 21st Squadron Leader Judd RAF lectured all the tank commanders on the close-support bombing to take place by Kittyhawks.

Major Basil Forster, now second-in-command, wrote his report of 1 RTR's part in Gamebirds on 31 August:

At about 5pm the head of a large column of tanks was sighted by the 1st RTR moving north-eastward across its front. They were about 2,000 yards from our tanks and not a shot was fired from the brigade position. The wind deadened the noise of their engines and they came on in silence. Our tanks, where possible, were turret down with the commanders standing on the turrets. At 1730 the column was still moving up though its head had stopped in suspicion . . . one tank, elbowed out of the mass and more northerly than the others, approached the exact position behind which was Major Pink's tank. He had no alternative but to advance to a

An M3 Stuart light tank near Mt Himeimat. (*Imperial War Museum – BM 17696*)

German tanks and lorries on fire on the battlefield. (*George Forty*)

hull-down position or be caught behind his bank. But before he could get on to his prepared platform the other tank had seen him and stopped. The two tanks were at too steep an angle for their guns to bear and both tank commanders looked at each other at a range of under 30 yards. After what seemed a very long time the German tank reversed and rejoined the stream.

At 1800 hours the whole column was halted with about fifty tanks directly opposite the regiment at a range of 1,500 yards, and an intense fire was brought to bear on the squadron of 4 CLY, who were positioned between the regiment and the 5 RTR tanks on the left. At 1810 hours brigade ordered fire to be opened and all tanks adopted the hull-down positions and started firing. The clouds of dust resulting from the muzzle blast made observation extremely difficult. At 1930 hours the enemy broke off the engagement leaving thirteen tanks behind, opposite the regimental position. Our casualties had been nil as the enemy's fire had been mostly AP with very little HE landing on the position.

It had been a long, nerve-wracking day. One felt that at any time the regiment's position could have been overrun by sheer weight of numbers . . . This was most probably not so though. Each tank was in a well-recced position and had every opportunity of bringing accurate fire to bear . . . As it turned out no massed assault had to be dealt with and we were enabled to have tanks all along the line moving up at odd intervals to fire a few rounds and then reverse back while another tank left or took up the fight.

Despite minefields, immense RAF bombing and massed British artillery, the German 90th Light, 15 and 21 Panzer Divisions had made a very determined hook attack in the south of the Alamein line. On the 22nd Armoured Brigade front 1 KRRC and 4 CLY were fully engaged and severely damaged the Axis forces in front of them. Fighting continued until 7 September with RAF bombing raids by Bostons, Baltimores and Mitchells

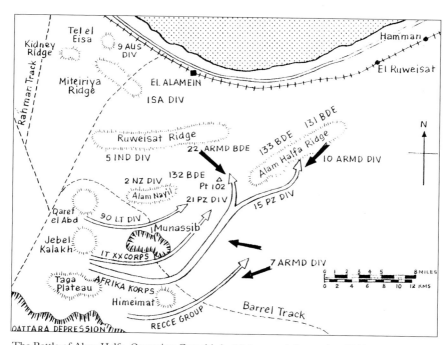

The Battle of Alam Halfa, Operation Gamebirds, 30 August–1 September 1942.

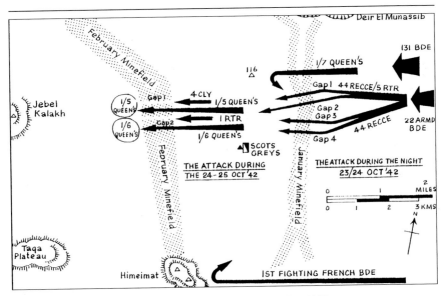

XIII Corps attacks during the battle of El Alamein, 23–5 October 1942.

south of 1 RTR in the Ragil area. On the 2nd 120 enemy tanks were identified ahead. The next day Sergeant MacGregor with 3 Troop, 'A' Squadron, reconnoitred Deir el Tarfa; they met strong anti-tank fire and lost two Stuarts, T30219 (Sergeant Wragg) and T28014. Corporal Anderson claimed two enemy 50mm anti-tank guns destroyed, and Lieutenant Cutting of 8 Troop another. 'A' Squadron sent out daily reconnaissance patrols for the next week. Sergeant Robert MacGregor won the Distinguished Conduct Medal on one of these patrols.

Lieutenant-Colonel Webb left to become AQMG of X Corps and a week later Lieutenant-Colonel Teddy Mitford MC returned as CO. Visits were made by various 'Brass Hats' – Major-General John Harding GOC 7th Armoured Division on the 16th, Brigadier 'Pip' Roberts four days later and Monty himself, who came to watch the regiment on exercises on the 24th. Sand-table exercises followed under XIII Corps and Exercise Camel on 1 October was a night 'attack' by the brigade. Major Pink was posted to XIII Corps HQ and Captain N.G. Crouch was promoted OC 'C' Squadron.

Monty had taken infinite trouble over the planning of Operation Lightfoot, a long, attritional battle by the whole of the Eighth Army intended to clear the Axis forces out of Egypt. 7th Armoured Division would start in the south with a possible breakthrough by night on the 23rd. Two large minefields codenamed January and February had to be cleared and gapped initially by Royal Engineers and the newly joined 131st Queens Infantry Brigade. But first the 22nd Armoured Brigade had to pass through prepared gaps in the British minefields called Nuts and May. The minefield task force composed 44th Division Recce Regiment plus carrier platoons, six Scorpion mine-clearance tanks, a squadron of Greys, two companies of 60th Rifles and finally 4th Field Squadron RE (for mine clearance if the Scorpions failed to beat and flail the mines ahead of them). Four gaps were to be made in January and February with 5 RTR using the two northern routes and 1 RTR the two southern routes. H-hour for Lightfoot was 2140 hours on the 23rd. The two southern gaps were difficult to traverse because of the soft sand and the Scorpions overheated and broke down. 1 RTR moved to pass through January at 0100 hours on the 25th but its tanks were held up by the long column ahead; at 0400 hours 'A' Squadron moved ahead as the Royal Engineers cleared a path but the leading tank blew up on an uncleared mine. Enemy shelling was vicious from both flanks (despite Monty's 1,000-gun barrage). Three more Stuarts went up on mines, resulting in five casualties, and the regiment moved back through the January minefield to a lying-up area. Brigadier 'Pip' Roberts was on the spot and recalled: 'The initial impression was of complete chaos – vehicles, tanks and carriers facing in different directions, some still burning, some at curious angles and enemy shells arriving fairly steadily.' Meanwhile 1 RB and 1 RTR had got through the minefield and were within 3,000 yards of Himeimat, a long high ridge on the southern end of the Alamein defence line.

'Pip' Roberts had been told by Monty to keep his brigade more or less intact for the final breakthrough when Lightfoot was over and Supercharge – the planned breakout – came into effect.

The main Alamein battle now took place in the centre and north. On the 29th 1 RTR moved through the gaps in the Nuts and June minefields and later on passed through May and Barrel. 7th Armoured Division moved north and on 1 November crossed the railway at El Himaiyima station and the next day reached Alamein station. On 4 November 21 Panzer Division, moving west in retreat on the desert route, took a short cut to 'Charing Cross'. The regiment had several brisk little actions, destroying four of Rommel's valuable 88mm anti-tank guns. Two days later 1 RTR were in action all day around Bir El Himaiyima, knocking out five of the fifteen battered panzers destroyed by 22nd Armoured Brigade on that day.

The War Diary noted that in heavy rain fifty vehicles were destroyed, half of which were tanks taken on by the two Grant squadrons, which knocked out five tanks, two 88mm anti-tank guns and five lorries but lost two Grants with seven casualties. 1 RTR crossed the frontier wire at 1600 hours on the 10th, having covered 160 miles in three days.

Peter Roach was the wireless operator/gun loader in an RHQ Stuart. His tank commander was Harry, a regular soldier who had spent two years fighting up and down the desert. 'Dingo' was the tank driver and Eddy the gunner; Eddy had spent a year in desert war. Harry was also the regimental navigator. With a sun compass the converse of a sundial, if he knew the time then he knew the direction – but he didn't have a watch! In his book *8.15 to War* Roach wrote:

We made contact with the enemy. The wireless was chattering and the tanks set off on a mad scramble, bouncing and pitching steeply down. There were anguished calls from the Colonel [Mitford] for smoke, shooting, bangs and uproar. Slowly order reigned and we were halted. We had come down the escarpment on to the coast road beside one of the Italian Albergos and run into a German 'party' drawing out. The colonel's tank stalled in surprise, the 2i/c hit a mine and so did the MO in his scout-car. A 3-ton truck went up on a mine. We were then violently strafed by some RAF Kittyhawks. We flung ourselves down as a roar of flame burst from their shells. Then all was peace again.

The tanks taking part in the hot pursuit that was Supercharge reached Tobruk on the 13th and the brigade halted near El Adem for a week to refit. During this time thirty Grants and, *mirabile dictu*, new Shermans arrived. These American tanks were produced in tens of thousands and first saw action at El Alamein. Weighing in at 30 tons, carrying a crew of 5 and armed with a 75mm gun plus two Browning machine-guns, the Sherman was powered by a Continental 9-cylinder radial 400bhp engine, with a top speed of at least 24mph. In late 1942 it was a vast improvement on the Grants, Stuarts and Crusaders. Peter Roach agreed: '1 RTR re-equipped – the two heavy squadrons with Sherman tanks. For the first time we had parity with the Panzer units so long dominant. A stupendous boost to our morale. We set off on tank transporters in high spirits towards El Agheila.' 1 RTR now had 14 Shermans, 5 Grants and 19 Stuarts, plus 5 to come. But of course the remaining German 88mm anti-tank guns could easily destroy Shermans.

In fact the Shermans had been officially hijacked from the 10th Hussars, who were predictably rather cross! On the 20th 1 RTR reached Antelat and the next day were in Agedabia, having travelled 230 miles in three days. Agedabia had been held by the German 90th Light Division. Brigadier 'Pip' Roberts was, however, unimpressed by the 1 RTR gunners who fired at Italian M-13 tanks emerging from Agedabia. Major Crouch OC 'C' Squadron was engaged all day on the 22nd. Sergeant Place's tank lost a track and Sergeant McConnachie MM received a direct hit on his tank, T144986. Lieutenant J. Mears engaged six six-wheeled armoured cars and three Mk III tanks, destroying one.

1 RTR casualties in November had been high. Captain Gane MC, Sergeant Horsfield, Corporal Wheeler, and Troopers Carter, Denny, Nicholson, Jury, Bransdown, Robbins and Brassley were all killed in action. Captain Sproull, Lieutenants Elgar, Lawrence and Cameron and 18 ORs had been wounded, and four men were missing. On 1 December 1 RTR handed over 12 Shermans, 3 Grants and 12 Stuarts to the Royal Scots Greys. Peter Roach again:

We unloaded the tanks and handed them over to alien faces [Greys]. Back to a camp a few miles west of Tobruk, a patch of scrubby desert near the sea [Zt Mrassas]. Christmas Day came – huge feed, game of rugger . . . The advance was earned by the blood of those in front – by the patient infantry, the true heroes of any army, always there whenever things became difficult. They moved on until they were wounded or killed, going back in for a period and then out for a short rest and in again knowing that only luck would spare them.

The Queens Brigade was indeed superb and proved a magnificent partner to 22nd Armoured Brigade in 7th Armoured Division.

★   ★   ★

In the New Year (1943) 1 RTR re-equipped with a mix of Shermans, Grants and Crusaders (no Stuarts) moved ever westwards via Sollum, Tobruk, Buerat and Misurata. On 27 January Lieutenant-Colonel Teddy Mitford became second-in-command to 'Pip' Roberts of the 22nd Armoured Brigade, and Lieutenant-Colonel R.F.K. Belchem OBE took command. Leave was granted into Tripoli and when Winston Churchill flew in for a grand victory parade 1 RTR supplied two officers and sixty ORs.

Major Basil Forster was second-in-command, while the squadron OCs were Majors Holliman, Sassoon, Pedraza and Crouch, supported by Captains Bailey, Murison (adjutant), Campbell, Sproull, Stait-Gardner, Oliver, Young and Withers. 1 RTR strength was then 30 officers and 463 ORs with 21 Crusaders, 27 Shermans and Grants and 6 scout-cars. On 4 February Churchill inspected 1 RTR in the Corso Italo Balbo and said: 'Let me thank you and let me then assure you that your fellow countrymen regard your works with the greatest admiration and gratitude and that after the war is over it will be quite sufficient for any man when he is asked "What did you do?" to reply "I marched with the Eighth Army". That must be a source of sober pride which you are all entitled to feel.'

Awards for Gamebirds and Lightfoot were made at this time, with Military Medals being awarded to Corporal J. Anderson, Sergeant R. MacGregor DCM, Trooper R. Spedding and Sergeant H.W. Jones.

Early in February the new Dingo troop under Captain B.S. Young formed three two-car patrols and on the 11th made a recce into Tunisia. Meanwhile 1 RTR at Zuoria had a demonstration of the use of smoke for close defence by Crusader CS tanks and attended lectures on anti-tank and anti-personnel mines – a great problem as Rommel's retreating troops were unfortunately brilliant at mining and setting booby-traps. There were also lectures about the new German Mk VI Tiger tank about to appear in Tunisia. On 9 February Monty addressed all XXX Corps officers. On the 14th the regiment moved into the Fort Sidi Toui area in Tunisia and the next day went on to Taghelmit. The CO held a TEWT attended by Brigadier 'Looney' Hinde and Colonel Mitford, and a new padre joined, the Revd J. Wallace CF. The Sherman stabilisers were tried out successfully on the ranges at Nefatia. The strength was now 20 Crusaders, 10 Grants and 16 Shermans. On the 20th the brigade made a flank attack west of the Tadjera hills blocking the approaches to the Mareth line. The dawn advance saw 5 RTR leading, with 1 RTR on the right and 4 CLY on the left. A brilliant action was fought by Lieutenant-Colonel 'Fearless' Hutton's 5 RTR, while 1 RTR came under fire.

One 1 RTR veteran wrote about life in the Western Desert:

Who will ever forget those dark, perishing cold desert nights? Sleeping beside your own vehicle with everything packed in case of a move at a moment's notice. Covered by the tank sheet, with only your head exposed, you would hear the wind whistling through track plates, you could feel the icy dampness settling on your face and you would subconsciously hear the slow pacing of the sentry-go. Maybe you would have kipped-down for only two hours when suddenly a rude shake would bring you to life. It was the sentry to tell you it was time to do your turn or to tell you that the Squadron Commander wished to see you immediately. And whilst you were sitting up and putting your boots on, you would see, over the horizon, coloured Very lights being put up by the German patrol. Sleep, hot food and mail meant everything towards maintaining morale. 'Miranda' was our codeword for 'brew-up' and as we stood round the brew-can in greatcoats, scarves, woollen gloves and balaclavas, waiting for the precious water to boil, we would exchange news about home, smoke cigarettes, and the Tank Commander would place himself so as to hear messages that might come over the W/T. Usually the head-sets for this purpose would be hanging down the side of the hull. 'Mirandas' were not always so successful. On many occasions Jerry demanded attention before 'Miranda' was completed, in which case the water was hurriedly poured back into the container and saved for another time. But on all occasions we kept a tin of bully, butter and issue biscuits on top of the wireless set and the operator would make himself responsible for supplying the rest of the crew as we went along.

On occasions Sergeant Doyle of 'C' Squadron bartered with the Bedouin, and in return for tea and biscuits he acquired a young goat, a pied puppy, a cockerel and various other waifs and strays to add to the squadron's collection of chameleons, snakes, lizards, jerboas and other desert creatures. He also acquired a scraggy hen called Biddy in partnership with 'Piggy' Parker. Although the miserable fowl was fed daily with crushed biscuits mixed with tinned beans, she never laid any eggs!

On 6 March the curious battle of Medenine was fought. Curious, because Rommel had secured an excellent defensive position on the Matmata mountains south of the main Mareth line. He decided to launch his 15, 21 and 10 Panzer Divisions down from the hills on to the most powerful anti-tank screen the Eighth Army had yet assembled. The main attack fell on 7th Armoured Division, and the Queens Brigade bore the brunt of it with their 6-pdr anti-tank guns. From their Wellington position 'C' Squadron helped fend off two enemy thrusts; they engaged and hit, possibly destroying, 10 tanks, 2 ammunition lorries, 2 half-tracks, a staff car and a 50mm anti-tank gun! 'A' Squadron was also engaged in the battle. Troopers H. Bressloff and H. Scott were both subsequently awarded Military Medals. Scott, a 75mm Sherman gun-layer, accounted for at least three enemy tanks and two ammunition lorries.

After suffering heavy losses – at least sixty tanks were knocked out and infantry casualties were equally high – Rommel withdrew his forces behind the Mareth line. Tired and ill, he flew back to Germany on sick leave before the major battle for the Mareth line, which started on 21 March. Now 50th Tyne Tees and the 4th Indian Divisions bore the heavy losses of the first three days of intensive fighting. 7th Armoured Division was in support of the 50th Tyne Tees and 51st Highland Divisions but only received incoming fire. The left flanking attack by X Corps was a brilliant success and 22nd Armoured Brigade advanced carefully and slowly northwards through the Mareth line – littered with mines everywhere – towards the Italian General Messe's forces gathered at the Wadi Akarit line, 10 miles north of Gabes. Monty had deployed a night attack with three infantry divisions to smash the Axis defences. The hot pursuit continued through the Gabes gap, north of Wadi Akarit. On 8 and 9 April 1 RTR had a field day east of Agareb. They came out on the flank of a surprised enemy who retreated at full speed. But five enemy lorries in the middle of the column were set on fire, compelling the rest to halt. Eight enemy tanks tried to come to the column's rescue but 1 RTR then knocked out two Panzer Mk IIIs while another tank destroyed 9 guns, 3 staff cars, 7 half-tracks and 29 MTs and took 44 prisoners. Sergeants A.W. Davies, H. Lincoln, G. Horne, K.J. Dunnett and Thomas Harland and Trooper N. Jenkins were all awarded Military Medals.

In three days of pursuit 1 RTR captured 6 tanks, 16 guns and 58 vehicles and took 749 prisoners. The CO, Lieutenant-Colonel R.F.K. Belchem, was awarded the Distinguished Service Order, while Major G.J.W. Pedraza and Captain G.T. Withers received the Military Cross. Belchem left on 16 April for a staff job with Eighth Army and Monty celebrated his series of victories with a big parade in Sousse.

CHAPTER EIGHT

First Tank Group into Tunis

Lieutenant-Colonel R.M.P. Carver DSO, MC, who had been a young subaltern in 1939, took command on 15 April. He already knew Major Gus Holliman OC 'A' Squadron (Crusader/Light) well. Captain David Murison was adjutant and Lieutenant John Rogers IO, while Major G.J.W. Pedraza was OC 'B' Squadron and Major James Pink was second-in-command. Before he died Field Marshal Lord Michael Carver gave permission for his campaign notes to be included in this history:

Two days after I had assumed command we moved forward to the area south-west of Enfidaville, which X Corps was planning to attack with the New Zealand Division, 4th Indian Division pushing into the hills on their left, and 7th Armoured Division probing forward between them and the French 19 Corps under First Army in the hills to the west. It was ideal as a breaking-in period for me. We were engaged in active operations, but not very intensively. I was able to pick up the wireless procedures and general habits of the regiment, accustom myself to the way in which it went about its life, and get to know all and sundry, while they could take stock of me. I knew a number of the senior non-commissioned officers who had served with the regiment ever since we had arrived in Egypt. The only officers from that time were Gus Holliman and the second-in-command, James Pink. I found, as I had expected, that the general level of efficiency was high. Things were done quickly, efficiently and with the minimum of fuss. I soon found myself at home presiding over the 'regimental net', the wireless frequency to which all the tanks of the regiment were tuned in. Sergeant Brown, the commanding officer's operator, ruled it with a rod of iron. The New Zealanders and 4th Indian [Division] had a tough fight to capture Enfidaville and the hills to the west. My twenty-eighth birthday passed as we felt our way gingerly towards the foothills on the left of the Indians. Eighth Army's next objective was Hammamet, 20 miles further up the coast, and it was clear that some stiff fighting confronted us in much more difficult country than that which we had faced hitherto.

We were therefore relieved when, on 30 April, we were suddenly told to move back, load on to transporters, and be switched to join First Army, which had now captured the key town of Medjez el Bab, only 40 miles south-west of Tunis. Both 7th Armoured and 4th Indian Divisions were to join 9 Corps, to command which Horrocks had been transferred from X Corps, its commander, my old Company commander John Crocker, having been wounded at a demonstration of a new infantry anti-tank weapon, the PIAT (Projector Infantry Anti-Tank). We set off on a 300-mile journey, starting on the night of 30 April and finishing at Le Krib on 2 May. From there I went forward with my squadron commanders to have a look at the ground east of Medjez el Bab, while we received a few more Sherman tanks from First Army sources and my resourceful technical adjutant, Captain Bailey, drove to the Kasserine Pass with his flame-cutter, opened up the American Army Shermans abandoned on the minefield there, and acquired an invaluable supply of spare parts, notably the injectors for our diesel-engined Shermans, which were as rare as rubies.

The plan was for 9 Corps to launch an attack astride the road from Medjez el Bab to Tunis, with 4th Indian Division on the left north of the road and 4th British on the right, to capture the high ground a few miles beyond the line, 10 miles beyond Medjez el Bab, which 5 Corps had reached at the end of April. 7th Armoured Division on the left and 6th Armoured on the right were then to pass through the infantry divisions and drive forward to

EIGHTH ARMY

Personal Message from the Army Commander

(TO BE READ OUT TO ALL TROOPS)

1. On 20th March, in a personal message before we began the battle of Mareth, I told you that the Eighth Army would do three things:—

   1. Deal with the enemy in the Mareth position.

   That was done between 21st and 28th March and we took 8,000 prisoners.

   2. Burst through the Gabes Gap.

   That was done on 6h April. The enemy was so unwise as to stand to fight us on the Akarit position. He received a tremendous hammering and we took another 7,000 prisoners.

   3. Drive Northwards on Sfax, Sousse and finally Tunis.

   That is now in process of being done; and if we collect in the prisoners at the present rate the enemy will soon have no infantry left to hold his position.

2. I also told you that if each one of us did his duty and pulled his full weight, then nothing could stop us. And nothing has stopped us.

   You have given our families at home, and in fact the whole world, good news, and plenty of it, every day.

3. I want now to express to you, my soldiers, whatever may be your rank or employment, my grateful thanks for the way in which you have responded to my calls on you and my admiration for your wonderful fighting qualities.

   I doubt if our Empire has ever, possessed such a magnificent fighting machine as the Eighth Army; you have made its name a household word all over the world.

   I thank each one of you for what you have done.

   I am very proud of my Eighth Army.

4. On your behalf, I have sent a message of appreciation to the Western Desert Air Force. The brave and brilliant work of the squadrons and the devotion to duty of all the pilots have made our victories possible in such a short time.

   We are all one entity—the Eighth Army and the Western Desert Air Force—together constituting one magnificent fighting machine.

5. And now let us get on with the third task.

   Let us make the enemy face up to, and endure, a first-class DUNKIRK on the beaches of TUNIS.

6. The triumphant cry now is:

FORWARD TO TUNIS! DRIVE THE ENEMY INTO THE SEA!

8th April, 1943.

B. L. Montgomery,
General, Eighth Army.

the hills overlooking Tunis itself, preventing the Germans under von Arnim from forming yet another defensive line. The attack was to be launched at dawn on 6 May. Jim Hutton's 5th Royal Tanks was to lead 22nd Armoured Brigade in the centre, with Arthur Cranley's 4th County of London Yeomanry on the left and ourselves on the right. We moved forward at 5.15am, my regimental headquarters in the lead. I had attached the reconnaissance troop (three Daimler scout-cars) to the leading battalion of the brigade of the 4th Indian Division through whom we were due to pass. As the Indians made good progress from one objective to another, we moved forward behind them and at 11am we were ordered to pass through them on their final objective. Apart from some shelling, this posed no problem as there were no mines about.

We were operating in country very different from the desert, open rolling hills reminiscent of the fringes of Salisbury Plain. Instead of following a geometrical pattern of movement, we could move from feature to feature. This was a help to me, as everyone else was as new to the conditions as I was. I had always had a 'keen eye for ground' and had no difficulty in giving my squadrons definite objectives and devising a plan combining fire and movement, with the squadrons, the battery of 5th Royal Horse Artillery and the company of 1st Battalion The Rifle Brigade so disposed that I had something in hand to meet the unexpected. As Gus Holliman's Crusader squadron probed its way forward to the ridge west of Furna and then on towards the village of Massicualt, I could see that 'Pip' Roberts' 26th Armoured Brigade of 6th Armoured Division on our right was both lagging behind and veering away to the east, opening up a gap between us which would leave the high ground south of the road (Sidi Abdel Krim) untouched. If the enemy held it, our right flank would be very vulnerable as we advanced. I therefore ordered Norman Crouch's C Squadron to move south of the main road and occupy it. As they did so, an 88mm anti-tank gun fired on them and hit Major Crouch's tank, seriously wounding him. His second-in-command, Colin Sproull, quickly brought effective fire to bear on the gun, which was knocked out; the high ground was occupied and the advance resumed. It was my first experience of a friend being seriously wounded as a direct result of an order I had given, an unpleasant feeling. Nevertheless I had no doubt that my order had been correct.

We spent the night in a leaguer a few miles beyond Massicualt. I sent 'C' Company of 1st Rifle Brigade and the troop of the Royal Engineers, attached to us, forward to the bridge over the Wadi Chafrou a few miles further on to make certain that the enemy did not destroy it during the night. Apart from anxiety about Norman Crouch, I was pleased with the day's operation, and I felt that we had done well. My main concern was that Gus Holliman's Crusaders were showing signs of their age. His numbers had fallen from eleven to seven in one day, all due to mechanical faults. 'Pedro' Pedraza's B Squadron had 12 Shermans and Colin Sproull's C Squadron 14. At 4.45am we started off again and, as I expected, found that the enemy was covering the Wadi Chafrou and an irrigation ditch which ran parallel to it, with fire from tanks and anti-tank guns supported by artillery. The tactics I had employed the previous day proved effective, the deliberate fire of tanks and our own supporting guns methodically eliminating the opposition or forcing it to move, while Holliman's Crusaders worked round the western flank near St Cyprien. Two incidents enlivened the morning. In order to get a better view of the area beyond the wadi, I moved my tank up to the side of a small farmhouse, where I hoped to be unobserved. However, just as I drew up beside the back door, an anti-tank gun fired at us, the shot fortunately bouncing off the front plate. I saw where it had fired from, and instantly ordered '75mm/HE action'. My tank was a Grant in which the 75mm gun was in a sponson. It was almost unheard of for the commanding officer's tank to fire its main armament, and the sponson had become the home of a white rabbit called Tripoli, which the crew had acquired there. They had intended to eat it when they arrived at Tunis, but by now it had become a well-loved pet. After a pause, instead of the expected reply '75mm loaded', the plaintive voice of the gunner came over the internal communication system 'What about Tripoli?' My retort was sharp and showed no concern for the rabbit's nerves. The gun having fired, I ordered the driver to reverse, only to find myself, with my head outside the turret, entangled in the washing-line, watched by the terrified farmer's wife from the kitchen window. Not long after this we were alarmed to find ourselves being attacked from the rear by infantry, supported by mortars and machine-guns. I soon realised the cause of this. About an hour previously B Squadron had been troubled by snipers firing at tank commanders from farm buildings on their right. 'A' Company of the Welsh Guards from 26th Armoured Brigade was near us at the time, apparently doing nothing, and I had asked their commander if he could send some of his men into the

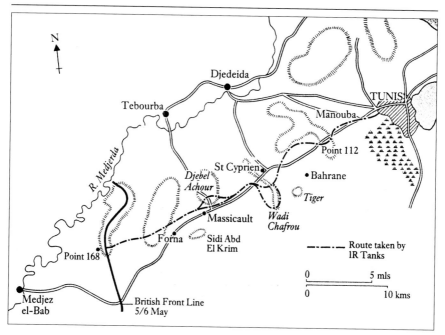

The approach to Tunis, May 1943.

buildings to flush the snipers out. When he told me that it would take him three-quarters of an hour to organise, I told him to forget it. However, he must have misunderstood me, and set about organising a formal attack in the best School of Infantry style. Unfortunately we were by then on the objective, and I told Colin Sproull to threaten them with a counter-attack if they did not desist immediately. The only casualty to us was one officer slightly wounded in the back. It was not the first time that we had been attacked by our own side. We had been heavily bombed by three squadrons of our own bombers the previous day. It had produced a lot of noise and had made us very angry, but the only damage inflicted was to the impedimenta we carried outside the tanks, bedding rolls, cooking equipment and the like.

As soon as we were across the wadi, we came under fire from a Tiger tank, the first we had encountered, and one or two 88mm anti-tank guns, and we could see enemy tanks and anti-tank guns out of range. The ground south of the road was flat and open, although farm buildings and orchards provided cover. North of the road there was more incidence in the ground, and I decided to make use of it to advance by bounds and thus outflank the enemy straight ahead of us. In leading his Crusaders in this direction, Gus Holliman's tank was knocked out by the Tiger, he and his crew fortunately escaping without injury, as the shot had hit the engine compartment. Our tactics were successful and culminated in a shoot by B Squadron against a company of Company of enemy tanks engaged in refuelling near the crest of the ridge, beyond which the ground fell away towards Tunis, only 5 miles away. We pressed on down the road to the village of Manouba, 3 miles from the outskirts of the city itself. German vehicles kept appearing from every direction, and we soon had a large and varied collection of prisoners, including a paymaster with a copious supply of cash. Armoured cars of the 11th Hussars advanced towards the city, and I sent the motor company and a troop of tanks to help them, when they met opposition on the outskirts. These were later relieved by the Queens of 131st Brigade.

We were not to enter Tunis itself. Our task for 8 May was to secure the high ground about 6 miles away on the road to Bizerta, in order to prevent the enemy, pressed back by the Americans north of the River Medjerda, from entering Tunis from that direction. We were now in much closer country than any we had yet experienced, and could no longer move in our extended formation across country. For the first time in the war we had to move in line or double-line ahead, following roads or tracks. We met no opposition, although continuing to collect large numbers of prisoners. At 8am we were ordered to advance and capture the bridge over the River Medjerda at Protville, 6 miles further on. This was protected by a ridge of high ground, overlooking a flat plain intersected by irrigation ditches and a wadi, a marshy area to the east and the river to the west preventing us from outflanking it. I asked, without success, for air support, and while we were methodically attempting to suppress the enemy fire, which included an 88mm, there was a large explosion, clearly the demolition of the bridge, and we were able to get forward to the ridge ourselves. From it we could see the enemy on the far side of the river withdrawing towards Porto Farina, but they were out of range of our tank guns. CC Battery 5th RHA enjoyed themselves, while the reconnaissance troop searched for a way to cross the river. I decided to join them and went forward in my scout-car in the thick corn, going down to the river bank on foot with Corporal Roach when the scout-car could get no further. It was clear to me that we could not get tanks across. On our way back to the scout-car we were fired on with a machine-gun by one of my own tanks. Fortunately the bullets went over our heads and the firing did not last long, but James Pink got the rough edge of my tongue when we reached the wireless set in the scout-car. We stayed there until the following morning, 9 May, when we could see American troops advancing on the far side of the river and were ourselves relieved by the 1st/5th Queens of 131st Brigade. We had fired our last shot in anger in Africa after three years of desert fighting, little realising how much more there was still to do in Italy and north-west Europe.

Corporal Peter Roach, the CO's driver, wrote:

The North African war was over and we each had half a bottle of beer with which to celebrate; not much, but we had the joy. The next day we began to move back and parked on the edge of Tunis to enjoy the fruits of our victory. Rather like children we set out simply to look and enjoy the sights and sounds of what was practically a European city: streets and houses and cafés, girls in dresses, housewives and their husbands, and, to the fathers among us, the joy of seeing children. Quite happily we meandered through the town, asking nothing but to feast quietly on this sight. The town was full of soldiers, mainly British and American. We shouted ribald comments at a tank regiment just moving in. We met a crowd round an American soldier standing in a jeep who was haranguing them. We removed three bottles of brandy from the back of the jeep and made our way back to our field, to the space, quiet and simplicity of our life.

The regiment had been in action since 1940, and had lost many officers and men killed in action.

CHAPTER NINE

From Limbo to Avalanche – the Italian Campaign

After the capture of Tunis 7th Armoured Division was hoping to be sent back to the UK, or to be granted extended leave in Cairo, or in and around Tunis. Not a bit of it. Within two days 1 RTR was sent into the heart of the desert to the wilderness of Bou Arada (where perhaps the fiery Tunisian brandy, available unofficially, would be beneficial). A few days there and back into Libya to Homs, 60 miles east of Tripoli. The tents were set on the seashore among palm trees between the sea and the road. Homs too had brandy – date brandy. Corporal Peter Roach recalled 'the training courses, sea to swim in, marvellous divisional theatre, amphitheatre of Leptis Magna, the rest camp in Tripoli, horse racing and the tote for bets, cricket, soccer, cinema (*Gone with the Wind*). Vivien Leigh and Laurence Olivier with an ENSA party played by moonlight to a packed house in the ancient Roman theatre, but also yellow mepacrin tablets against malaria.' Monty came, of course, as did Lieutenant-General Brian Horrocks, and King George VI was greeted with enthusiasm on 20 June.

Major Gus Holliman went back to the UK and was replaced by Barry O'Sullivan who had fought with 3 RTR at Calais in 1940. Captured in the action, O'Sullivan had been sent to a prisoner-of-war camp from which he subsequently escaped. The Crusader tanks were discarded and all three squadrons received diesel-engined Shermans. The Recce troop was re-equipped with Daimler scout-cars and Bren-carriers. All the AFVs had to be laboriously water-proofed (presumably for a possible 'wet' landing). Every item of equipment had to be checked, engines stripped down, all weapons cleaned, aligned, tested and cleaned again. Wireless sets were tested in the field. Landing-craft practice was carried out and live firing took place. The CO, Lieutenant-Colonel Carver, held frequent TEWTS in the hilly countryside between Homs and Tripoli. Carver wrote: 'We did not know where we should be going next – Sicily, Sardinia, Italy or the Balkans. We would have left the desert behind and would have to fight in totally different conditions.' On 10 July the invasion of Sicily took place (Operation Husky). The division was not involved but several 1 RTR officers were sent over to study the battle terrain conditions and tactics. Combined operations training took place and a Landing Ship Infantry

(LSI) arrived in Homs harbour for loading and unloading troops. The CO was not happy with the desert tactics of keeping armour and lorried infantry separate.

After the capture of Tunis Lieutenant-Colonel Carver, CO 1 RTR, wrote a report on the lessons learned, and made appropriate recommendations for an armoured regiment in desert conditions and Algerian/Tunisian battlefields. The full report is in the Public Record Office, Ref WO 169/9362 (1943). What follows is a brief summary.

Light Squadron The Sherman, Crusader Mk II and the Stuart tanks are compared. The latter with improved range (miles per fuel tank) and improved gun (equivalent to 6-pdr) would fit admirably requirements of light squadron.

Recce Troop Dingoes, Bren-carrier and small half-track compared. Ideal would be composition of ten Bren-carriers plus an intercom troop of 8 Dingoes with an officer in command.

Heavy Squadron The Sherman, with its effective high explosive and machine-gun fire, speed and accuracy, is the most effective weapon for dislodging anti-tank guns, mortars, machine-guns and OPs. A supporting RHA battery is essential to take on large calibre anti-tank guns such as 75mm or 88mm.

Tank *v.* Tank The new powerful Tiger Panzer Mk VI is heavily armoured and can only be tackled by a tank with a 17-pdr gun.

Liaison Importance of Recce troop providing information about progress of 'friendly' as well as enemy dispositions. The Intercom troop should have at least three wireless sets in addition to the CO's set in his HQ armoured car.

Mines Every man in an armoured regiment should be trained to remove mines. Every tank and scout-car in 1 RTR should be equipped with six nails and 50 yards of old signal cable for mine removal.

Bombing 1 RTR was bombed by 'our' light bombers on five occasions. Orange smoke not released *before* bombs were released. Bombing of dispersed armoured vehicles ineffective. Light metal fragments do little damage. 'Noise is terrific, if prolonged has considerable effect on morale.'

Wireless Communications difficult; most frequencies had at least three other groups on it, bad discipline, chat all day.

Observation The description of targets generally bad. Better training needed at troop and squadron level. A 50,000 map should produce an approximate map reference (but not in the desert where landmarks were rare).

Road Work Appropriate tactics in tackling opposition on a road in close country. Against enemy in strength, locate his first post by Recce troop, move up infantry, get tanks off the road. Against isolated anti-tank gun(s) lead with heavy Sherman squadron.

The key recommendation for a probable European campaign was the last paragraph.

★ ★ ★

On his return from Sicily the GOC Major-General 'Bobby' Erskine knew that Italy was the next divisional objective and planning revealed that Operation Avalanche would include the Desert Rats in General Mark Clark's 5th Army. The landing would be in the Gulf of Salerno, and X Corps under Lieutenant-General Dick McCreery would include 46 and 56 Infantry Divisions supported by the Desert Rats (22nd Armoured Brigade and 131st Queens Infantry Brigade).

The Italians surrendered on 8 September, five days after the Eighth Army had crossed the Straits of Messina. Nobody knew what the outcome of Mussolini's downfall would be. What was clear was the determined German resistance at the Salerno beach-head – indeed, at one stage it reached a crisis.

It was known that the German reception party would include 15 Panzer Division in the Battipaglia area and the battered Hermann Goering Division (recently driven out of Sicily) around Caserta. In Rome was the 3 Panzer Grenadier Division. The Eighth Army's landing on the toe of Italy was pushing 26 and 29 Panzer Grenadier Divisions northwards. D-day was 9 September and 1 RTR landed dryshod on Sugar beach on the 22nd, having embarked at Tripoli in four Landing Ships Tanks (LST). The two infantry divisions were to assault the northern sector of the landing area south of Salerno. 7th Armoured would then pass through them, heading north for Vesuvius and Naples.

Major Barry O'Sullivan commanded 'A' Squadron (with Barry Smethurst as second-in-command), Major 'Pedro' Pedraza was OC 'B' Squadron (Capt Withers) and Major Colin Sproull was OC 'C' Squadron. Major James Pink was second-in-command, Lieutenant Canham was OC the carrier patrol and the RMO was 'Doc' Wells. The RSM was C.V. Coke and the adjutant Captain D.L. Murison.

Sherman tanks of 22nd Armoured Brigade resting by the side of the main road to Naples, October 1943. (*Imperial War Museum NA-7427*)

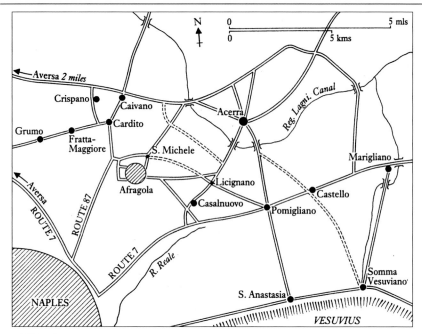

1 RTR advance around Vesuvius and Naples.

Corporal Peter Roach wrote:

We drove 70 miles to Tripoli, loaded on to LCTs for the journey to Salerno. The invasion had gone in but was meeting trouble although well established inland. Obvious 1 RTR was part of the follow-up. So it was goodbye to North Africa, to all the many races we had fought with and come to know with affection, to the desert which had been home for many of the men for some four years, no more open vista, weirdly changing shapes under the heat of the desert sun, no more sleeping under great ripe stars, no more the understanding, ribaldry and irreverence of this magnificent army.

On 28 September 7th Armoured Division passed through 46th Division to the pass between Vietri and Nocera beyond Salerno. 5 RTR and 1/6 Queens took Scafati and held the vital bridge over the River Sarno. 1 RTR found Somma Vesuviano a mass of rubble and demolitions but barged a way through. 1 RTR followed 5 RTR, grinding slowly along the only road in single file. It was very difficult to get the tanks off the road. It rained nearly every day and night and the mosquitoes were vicious and dangerous. By the end of 1 October 1 RTR was in the lead heading for Capua. Lieutenant-Colonel Michael Carver wrote a very detailed account entitled *Tanks in the Vineyards* about the skilful capture of Cardito in early October. The town is 5 miles north of Naples. The divisional axis was through Pomigliano, Afragola, Caivano and Aversa to Capua. Corporal Peter Roach described the terrain:

A toilsome dreary desolate advance through a tract of earth with tree-lined roads that stretched soullessly past squalid little towns of timeless dreariness. And all the time it rained.

The fields turned into mud and the water dropped into the turret of the tanks chilling the crews and leaving nowhere dry to fight, to cook or to rest. Beneath the leaden skies the bombed rubble of the town gave an impression of drab misery which the Italians themselves in their habitual black did nothing to alleviate.

The area was densely populated and intensively cultivated, with vines strung up on wires at the level of the tank turrets. 'We struggled forward, blown bridges and muddy vineyards causing more delay than opposition from the enemy. Towards the end of the day we had reached the large village of Afragola. The Germans had just left and had moved to the villages of Cardito and Caivano a few miles to the north,' wrote the CO.

Major Pedraza's 'B' Squadron led to Caserta and Lieutenant Canham of the Recce troop and Lieutenant Bobbie Gillespie destroyed a self-propelled 75mm anti-tank gun, but both Pedraza's and Captain Withers' Shermans went up on mines, shedding tracks. 1 RTR leaguered the night nose to tail on both sides of the road north of Afragola under enemy artillery and mortar fire. 'A' Squadron lost two Shermans knocked out and two more ditched, and the CO relieved the unlucky O'Sullivan of command over the regimental wireless net, ordering Brian Smethurst to take over. 'C' Squadron also lost two tanks, so 'B' Squadron supported the infantry. Cooperation from Lieutenant-Colonel Victor Paley's 1st Battalion Rifle Brigade and Lieutenant-Colonel Peter Gregson's 5 RHA was superb. Sergeant F.J. Williams of 'B' Squadron won the Military Medal at Cardito while supporting 1 RB against determined enemy counter-attacks. Lieutenant Smart led his troop south-east of Cardito and was fired on by a self-propelled 105mm gun in an orchard. The shell burst under his Sherman and blew a hole in the bottom. Smart's first shot with HE hit the top of the SP gun, penetrating the armour. His second shot with AP hit the gun mantle and knocked it out. Enemy snipers were dealt with by firing a round or two of 75mm HE with delay fuse into the building from which the firing was coming. Demolitions, mines and the rain-sodden tracks inevitably caused delays. Steady progress was made, however. Lieutenant Bob Stedman won the Military Cross for a recce on foot under fire to find a crossing over a damaged bridge at Grazzanise. Sergeant Robert Craig won the Military Medal in the advance from Vesuvius to the River Volturno, leading 'B' Squadron in an outflanking move round Aversa, and the crossing of the Regi Lagui canal. He was badly wounded at Carditello but survived. By the end of 5 October 1 RTR was on the outskirts of Capua. When the Queens Brigade arrived to take over, 1 RTR turned west to clear the open ground between the canal and the River Volturno defended by 15 Panzer Division. At the end of October the Desert Rats moved from the centre to the left of X Corps with orders to try to get across the canal beyond the Volturno. 'A' Squadron sent out a recce patrol and the CO crossed over the canal by a footbridge and swam about in the cold water checking the depth! 1 RTR crossed on the night of 29 October; its tanks encountered deep-laid mines and very soft ground intersected by ditches, and were engaged by enemy infantry. The whole area was overlooked by Monte Massico and 1 RTR's objective,

Mondragone, lay at the foot of it. No fewer than fifteen Shermans were bogged down; another four were disabled by mines, along with one knocked out and one broken down! The tank strength was reduced to twenty-four. The CO then flew to Algiers to attend a GHQ conference and Major James Pink took over. On the 30th Trooper B.C. Jones won the Military Medal when his tank was hit and set on fire. Under shell fire he rescued three severely wounded crew members, pulling them out and into cover until the ambulance party arrived.

Geoff Knights remembered: 'Rain, rain and more rain. I had two tank commanders killed – one by an airburst and the other by a sniper. We had Shermans but I was not a happy man. Action in close vineyard country was no fun after the open desert. We were all happy to be withdrawn to England as part of the "Imperial Strategic Reserve".'

Peter Roach wrote:

> We crossed the Volturno and fought our way slowly on. There seemed endless rivers, streams and dykes which frustrated our advances. Jerry was as thorough as ever and made us earn an advance, with here and there a tank and there a man. The fields were dense with crops blocking the views, dead bodies lay undiscovered among tall tobacco plants, arms and ammo among the tomatoes. All was lush and voluptuous, fat and greedy, soon to decay, to rot, to stink.

The 5th Canadian Armoured Division looked disdainfully at our ancient transport vehicles, and were horrified at the old wrecks of the 1 RTR Shermans.

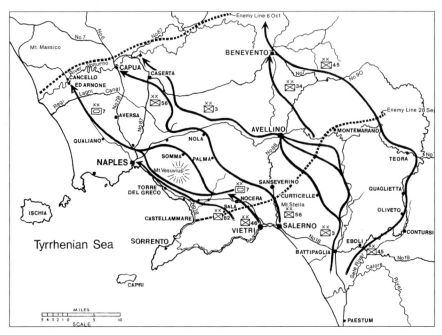

The advance to the Volturno.

A group of 1 RTR taken outside the church at Castelmare, Italy, late 1943. Second Warrant Officer Bob MacGregor, second on the left smoking a pipe, is wearing an MM ribbon. (*A.W. Green*)

The regiment moved into an empty macaroni factory at Castellamare near Pompeii. Cambrai Day – 20 November – was celebrated with many soldiers drinking mugfuls of Marsala wine since beer was in short supply. The regimental band appeared, hotels were commandeered in Amalfi and trips were made across the bay to Capri; hot baths were available in the Romanesque public baths, and there were visits to Pompeii to view the ruins and to Naples to try to buy some souvenirs. Parades and PT took place in the narrow streets and piazzi. Cinemas and dances were not 'successful' as the local ladies were well chaperoned! Early on 20 December the division including 1 RTR moved to Casoria to embark. The *Cameronia* carried 1 RTR, 5 RTR, 4th CLY, 11th Hussars and 1st Rifle Brigade. On Christmas Day the ship docked in Oran and moved slowly up the Clyde on 7 January 1944. Lieutenant-Colonel Michael Carver flew with the advance party via Algiers to Marrakesh and by USAAF Liberator to Prestwick in Scotland, returning six years after he had set sail for Egypt. He wrote:

I concluded that the right organisation for the regiment was to have three identical squadrons, each of three troops of four tanks, no longer regarding one of them as a reconnaissance squadron. Four tanks in a troop (instead of four troops of three tanks, as was laid down) meant that one did not have to change the organisation as soon as a few tanks fell out for whatever reason. Linked to this was the need for a vehicle of much better cross-country performance for the reconnaissance troop. There were many lessons to be learned about cooperation between all arms. In that close country the need for it had been even greater than in the desert. Whereas I found that my lack of previous direct personal experience of tank-versus-tank fighting in the desert was no handicap to me, it was clear that the greater knowledge I had of the characteristics of other arms, derived from my experience on divisional and corps staffs, stood me, my regiment and my supporting infantry, gunners and sappers in good stead. I now felt fully confident in my exercise of command.

CHAPTER TEN

Countdown to Overlord

The 22nd Armoured Brigade soon found itself in the Brandon area of Norfolk. Within three or four days 7th Armoured Division went on leave (2 years' service earned 2 weeks' leave, 2–4 years' service 3 weeks and over 4 years' service 4 weeks' leave) and sunburnt faces surprised barmen across the UK with their strident Arabic cries. The Desert Rats' uniform immortalised by 'Jon' startled the military establishment. The pubs and bars in Wisbech, March and King's Lynn did a thriving business. 1 RTR was in camp at Didlington, known as Sugar Hill, in Nissen huts, while HQ 22nd Armoured Brigade was at Cockley Hall, Swaffham. The Africa Star was awarded to all who had served under operational command in the Middle East, west of Suez, up to 12 May 1943.

The CO encountered several problems of morale. Quite a few NCOs with seniority and good records applied to transfer to units less likely to be in the front line. A few went but most stayed. Monty visited 1 RTR on 17 February, together with Major-General G.W.E.J. Erskine, the popular GOC. Kenneth Ward (born in Germany as K.R. Wurzburger) joined 'A' Squadron, and wrote: 'Before Monty arrived we daubed slogans in large letters on our tanks "No leave, no second front". Monty as usual jumped on to the bonnet of a jeep to address us and said, "There is one thing I am going to tell you right now – you are *not* getting any [embarkation] leave and you *are* getting a second front" and we all cheered.'

Monty's talk was brilliant for morale. The clipped, precise, confident voice, often using cricketing phrases, was very convincing – after all, he had not lost a battle since he arrived to command at Alam Halfa. The second morale problem concerned the new tanks. The CO wrote:

Morale was also raised as new tanks began to arrive. Most were the British Cromwell, with a British 75mm gun, which was new to us and which we liked, being less conspicuous and more lively than the Sherman; but we were glad to have one of the latter in each troop, armed with the powerful British 17-pdr anti-tank gun, which had an armour-piercing performance much superior to that of the 75 mm. There was much argument about whether we should put them all in one troop in each squadron or distribute them one to each troop. I was firmly in favour of the latter and was undoubtedly proved right when we went into action. The reconnaissance troop was equipped with a new model of the American Stuart light tank, from which it was decided to remove the turret. We trained on the Swaffham and Stanford training areas and fired our guns on the ranges there and, in the case of the 17-pdr, on the coast.

Buckingham Palace Investiture, summer 1944. Left to right: Sergeants Tom Harland DCM, H.A. Bennett MM, J. MacConnachie MM, F.J. Williams MM and Second Warrant Officer R. MacGregor MM. (*A.W. Green*)

The tank commanders had been driving and fighting their reliable Sherman tanks since late 1942. Now they had to get used to a brand-new tank and vital modifications had to be made, notably to the escape hatches, before they were fit for battle. There were changes among the senior officers. Major Gus Holliman came back as second-in-command only to leave in May to command 5 RTR. He was replaced by Major 'Stump' Gibbon, who had already won two Distinguished Service Orders, the first of them with 44 RTR in Operation Crusader, and the bar when he led a daring escape from a German prisoner-of-war train in 1943. Bob Crisp, who had won a Distinguished Service Order and a Military Cross with 3 RTR in Greece and the desert, took command of 'A' Squadron (and failed to get on with Carver!). There was an influx of quality young subalterns anxious to win their spurs in the coming battles. The CO then wrote:

During this period there was much discussion as to whether, as a result of the lessons we had learned in Italy, the organisation of the division should be changed to one which gave a more even balance of infantry and tanks than the official one of an armoured brigade of three tank regiments and one motor infantry battalion, and an infantry brigade of three infantry battalions, carried in 3-ton lorries, and no tanks. Under terms of great secrecy, within the confines of a Cambridge college, we were initiated into Montgomery's plan which forecast that, after a short period of battle in the close bocage country of Normandy, we should break out into the open country of northern France, ideal for tank action. It was therefore generally accepted that we should stick to the official organisation of the division, although it was clear that one of the tank regiments, initially at least, would have to be allotted to the lorried infantry brigade.

King George VI, last encountered by the tank crews near Tripoli in 1943, visited 1 RTR on 24 February and inspected the guard of honour at Brandon station. The CO travelled with him in his car to Divisional HQ at Didlington Hall. The route was lined by troopers and NCOs. The king met Sergeant Hall of 'B' Squadron, who had nineteen years of Army service under his belt. When the monarch was told this he remarked with his habitual stammer: 'G-g-g-good G-g-g-God, N-n-n-nineteen years in the army. How awful!'

Much of March was spent firing the new Cromwells at Kirkcudbright ranges in Scotland and also at Boyton. In April there was a gas respirator check for all the regiment, and outgoing mail was franked and censored. The GOC made another inspection. The strength of 1 RTR at this time was 41 officers and 746 ORs. The tank strength was 94, mainly Cromwells but also 3 ARVs, 4 Stuarts, 2 Sherman Fireflies and 2 Crusaders with anti-aircraft guns. Early in May the regiment moved to R-5 camp in Orwell Park between Ipswich and Felixstowe (the embarkation harbour). Waterproofing of all vehicles took place in case of a 'wet' landing. Exercises called Shudder, Shiver and Charpoy took place, as well as many TEWTS organised by the CO.

The divisional operation was revealed on 28 May by the GOC in the garrison cinema at Brentwood. The armoured brigade was to land on the Normandy beaches that had already been secured by the 50th Tyne Tees Division, and then concentrate around Ryes, 2½ miles inland, on the evening of D-day. The plan was for 50th Division to capture Bayeux and secure the road to Tilly-sur-Seulles. The armoured brigade (1 RTR, 5 RTR, 4 CLY) would push through Villers-Bocage and Aunay-sur-Oden towards Mont Pincon.

The armoured brigade embarked at Felixstowe on 4 June, with the rest of the division sailing from London and Tilbury Docks. Johnny Dingwall was 'B' Echelon commander; the adjutant was Captain J.W. Rogers. Major Bob Crisp was OC 'A' Squadron, Major R.W. Gillespie OC 'B' Squadron (his tank was called Miss Blandish II) and Major C.L. Sproull OC 'C' Squadron (his tank was The Old Firm). Captain B. Young was OC recce control and the RSM was C.V. Coke. As they sailed for France 1 RTR was composed of 12 17-pdr Fireflies, 49 Cromwells, 11 Stuarts, 6 Crusader anti-aircraft tanks, 3 Cromwell ARVs, 9 Humber scout-cars, 7 half-tracks and 10 Jeeps.

Trooper Kenneth Ward was in No. 7 Troop, 'A' Squadron. His tank commander was Sergeant Les Allen; Jimmy Hague was the Firefly gunner and Charley Adams the driver. Ward himself was the driver/operator looking after the 19 set and responsible for loading the 17-pdr gun and Browning machine-guns. The crew had waterproofed their tank, called 5C Ark Royal, to enable it to land in water up to just below the turret hatches. 'We were on an American LST, had excellent food and landed at Arromanches after lunch, blowing off the waterproofing as soon as we were on the beach and moving off the beach inland very quickly.' 'B' Echelon sailed in SS *Ignatius Donnelly* and were shelled by the German defence guns at Cap Gris Nez. The First of Track had set sail for their last great adventure which would – eventually – find them in Berlin.

CHAPTER ELEVEN

Normandy

Adverse weather conditions had postponed the landing operation by 24 hours. At dawn on 7 June (D+1) the invasion fleet was an astonishing sight, with hundreds of ships crowded in the Channel, some of them flying cable-balloons to deter low-flying Luftwaffe aircraft, and the Royal Navy busy bombarding targets inland. After de-waterproofing, the tanks went unscathed to Sommervieu where they leaguered. Corporal Peter Roach recalled:

I had my own Honey [Stuart] tank and two stripes and was the B tank in a troop of two. We landed early on D+1 and by D+2 Reconnaissance Troop was spread far and wide trying to establish what was ours and what was theirs. Working on our own we did our bit (collected 32 eggs from an abandoned farm). Two days later my officer was wounded and I took over the troop, with my operator taking over the B tank. At this point the division went into the line, moving south towards Tilly-sur-Seulles.

On D+3 the disembarkation of wheeled vehicles started. They were lifted out of the Liberty Ships' holds by derricks and slung into landing craft alongside. The tanks ashore moved to Rucqueville and took up battle positions. At 2000 hours the CO held a full conference. The armoured brigade would advance on the 10th with 1 RTR in reserve towards Condé-sur-Seulles. He noted that 'it was just like Italy all over again, except that the weather was better!' The bocage of Normandy consisted of small hills, valleys and small fields surrounded by high banks on which grew thick hedges. The apple orchards too gave the enemy excellent defensive cover. The long-range power of the German tanks and 88mm anti-tank guns was partly nullified in the close countryside, but the deadly German multiple-mortar minenwerfer (known as 'moaning minnies') were responsible for more casualties (particularly among the infantry) in Normandy than artillery, tanks, mines, sniping or the Luftwaffe. On the 10th the armoured brigade, with 5 RTR on the right and 4 CLY on the left, made slow progress towards Ellon and Jerusalem respectively, with 1 RTR guarding the bridges over the Seulles. The division was then switched to the right and aimed at Villers-Bocage. 'B' Squadron supported 1/5 Queens and 'C' Squadron 1/6 Queens. On the 13th disaster struck as 4 CLY and most of the 1st Rifle Brigade passed through Villers-Bocage and rather casually 'parked' beyond the village along the roadside towards Ellon. Here a Tiger tank squadron of 2 Panzer Division ambushed and destroyed the Desert Rat column.

1 RTR's task was to hold the village of Briquessard and the two crossroads north of it. Trooper Geoff Knights was plotting enemy troop movements on the map in Lieutenant D.A. Wickenden's 'B' Squadron 8 Troop 'Minerva' near Verrières on the 12th:

> The arrows I was plotting all pointed directly at us. The CO Mike Carver called for immediate artillery support. It was a mass of vehicles of Panzer Lehr division – lorries, tanks and half-tracks coming straight at us. B Squadron opened up with everything before they got too close. Our main armament kept the main front under fire. My troop bagged a tank destroyer at about 50 yards range.

The enemy counter-attacked on the 14th near Amaye, but was checked by 1 RTR. 'C' Squadron quickly knocked out two Panthers, a Tiger and several Mk IVs, and drove the enemy over the crest into thick apple orchards. Sergeant Alfred North won the Military Medal while commanding a Reconnaissance Troop patrol, which engaged enemy infantry with machine-gun fire and helped destroy an anti-tank gun. The CO wrote a report for the War Diary about the three-day action.

> 12 June 1 OR KIA, 5 wounded, 3 tanks temporarily damaged. Information about own and enemy troops before op. started was almost nil. Never knew 4 CLY were at St Bazire, nor did OC 1/6 Queens know the Essex bn were in wood 804692. No time spent on Recce. There seemed to be a lack of general inquisitiveness to discover what the opposition was and where it was. About 20 enemy tks in whole area, not more than 6 seen. Countryside exceptionally favourable to A/Tk defence. Rumour of presence of a few German tanks still puts a brake on any operations and causes excitement quite out of proportion to their potential material effect. No excuse for tying down our tks to the local A/Tk defence of infantry positions. Task should be to cover the gaps between infantry positions and not act as reserve to counter a tank attack from an unexpected position. Main task for 1 RTR was to hold Briquessard firmly in view of threat from south.
>   Casualties 13/14 June 2 officers killed, 2 wounded: ORs 7 KIA, 4 wounded, 1 missing. In 3 days operations 1 RTR gave close support to infantry, acted as additional A/Tk defence, covering screens carrying out Recces, seizing ground and holding it by day and night. Tanks should never be separated from their artillery OPs whatever task performed.

Lieutenant C.H. Gray 'Apres Vous' ('A' Squadron), Sergeant W. Tibbles 'Achilles' ('A' Squadron) and Captain J.A. Shambrook ('C' Squadron) all had their tanks knocked out in the three-day battle.

Lieutenant A.M. Walker was OC 5 Troop, 'B' Squadron. His tank was named 'Oor Wullie'; the others in the troop were 'Atalanta' (Sergeant W. White), 'Lili Marlene' (Sergeant E. Tait) and 'Wheresatiger' (Corporal N. Jenkins MM). What follows is Walker's report of the actions on 14 June at Amaye-sur-Seulles:

> The battle line south of A. To protect right flank. 5 Tp into orchards near Pt 198. Two sections 1/6 Queens were in orchard behind forming rear and flank protection, 8 Tp on my right. At 1600 my A Tk [Sergeant White] on left flank reported infantry moving at a junction, fired BESA at them. Then I saw the muzzle-brake of a gun moving along a hedge top and then part of a tall turret. I fired the 75mm at the hedge below the turret and at the same time Sergeant White engaged. The third shot scored a hit and the Tk drew out from the hedge into the middle of the field, but continued across our line of fire. I observed the broad track and 'Christy' suspension indicating either a Tiger or a Panther. My three

Cromwells were now scoring hits, but although the turret crew baled out and sought shelter in the hedge at the 3rd hit the Tk continued to move. I had no Firefly with me and asked for one to be sent up. 8C [Sergeant Richards] 'Juno' immediately moved up to my 'B' tank [Sergeant Tait] and engaged. By this time the Tiger was reversing towards the cover of the wood but at the third 17-pdr shot it stopped and did not move again. At the time the first Tiger began to reverse, a second Tiger moved from the shelter of the second line of hedge to the top of Pt 198. Sergeant White and I engaged it with 75mm and it pulled in behind a clump of bushes with its tail projecting. Then it moved back in reverse towards cover. A troop of C Squadron had been swung round and their tks then engaged, one shot causing the turret to brew.

Later Lieutenant Walker fired five 75mm and three 17-pdr, all direct hits on the first Tiger and it did not brew. When he was satisfied that it was U/S he ceased fire. The Tigers were painted light brown desert colour with green dazzle stripes on the turret. Long barrel and muzzle brake very conspicuous. In the open, broad track Christie suspension was very noticeable. At 1000 yards 40° angle at least 50 per cent of 75mm shot were deflected by side and front armour. Neither tank attempted to engage with their gun. Although 1 RTR had encountered the occasional Tiger in Tunisia this encounter confirmed the view that the 60-ton German Tiger was the queen of the battlefield, and the British Firefly was the only tank able to deal with them. But Walker was fortunate!

The 8th Hussars had previously shot at 1 RTR Cromwells, mistaking them for German Panthers. On the 15th 'B' and 'C' Squadrons were moved to hold the flank between Les Crailles and Parfourn L'Eclin. Shortly afterwards 22nd Armoured Brigade went into reserve and was out of action until the 23rd. Corporal Peter Roach again:

We came out of the line to reorganise; both our officers had been killed [Captain B.S. Young, Lieutenant E. Elgar] and we had a new squadron commander [Lieutenant J.M. Storey MC]. I was moved to a Honey tank without a turret which one of the officers used. [On a typical 'recce' day] it was difficult to stop tanks firing on barely seen tanks of a sister regiment on their flanks. The only way was to have someone listening on the radio to both regiments. The day was endless – my crew slumbered, brewed tea, read and slumbered while I fought to stay awake and listen. Eventually the day ended. Last light was around 1130 hours and first light 0330 hours, so in the four hours of darkness we had to return to the unit, leaguer, refuel and ration, do any necessary maintenance, do a guard duty and get some sleep before the 0315 hours start up.

On the 27th Lieutenant-Colonel Michael Carver DSO was promoted to command 4th Armoured Brigade at the age of twenty-nine. He had commanded 1 RTR brilliantly for fifteen months. He said his farewells with a talk to each squadron in turn. 'I hated the idea of leaving this splendid body of men, for whose lives and well-being I felt a keen responsibility,' he said. His adventures in command of 4th Armoured Brigade are related by this author in *Monty's Marauders*. Carver's talk was very interesting. The following are excerpts:

Aggressiveness There is marked difference between the aggressive spirit whose first reaction to enemy fire is to find out where it is and what it is, so that he can get at it and destroy it as

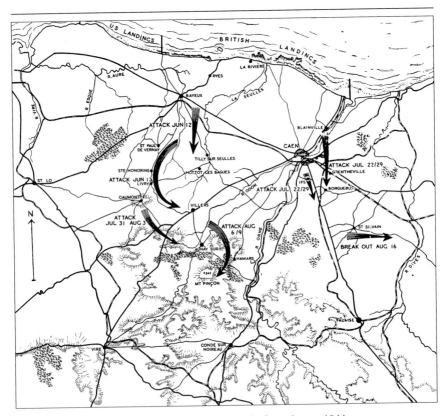

The battle centre lines of the Desert Rats in Normandy, June–August 1944.

quickly as possible, and the spirit who adopts a passive attitude, either merely reporting what he sees or hears and doing no more about it, because from where he is at the moment he cannot do anything about it being in no great danger himself, and doesn't very much care; or again two worse degrees of passivity, the man who restrains from taking aggressive action for fear of provoking reprisals, or the man whose reaction is best to avoid the danger. This is often only recognised as disgraceful if a man runs away. A great deal of unnecessary caution is due to an inability to gauge the effectiveness of enemy fire. British training with its emphasis on steel helmets and concealment on all and every occasion, its awful warnings about your fate if you don't do this or don't do that, is apt to make men worry far too much about their personal safety. A proper appreciation of the chances, the ability to realise whether the fire you hear and see is aimed at you or not, a general contempt for the enemy and above all a determined, aggressive and confident spirit are worth all the camouflaged steel helmets in the world. I have deliberately seen the good morale effect of the arrival of an officer of this division in corduroy trousers, a beret, and a pipe in his mouth among a collection of harassed-looking individuals looking like scarecrows herded together in a ditch.

This was powerful stuff from the Field Marshal in the making. Major E.H. Gibbon DSO was promoted to lieutenant-colonel and assumed command of 1 RTR, while Major C.L. Sproull MC was promoted to second-in-command and Major Johnny Dingwall was appointed OC 'C' Squadron. The 2nd US Armored Division took over from 7th Armoured.

The regiment leaguered around Ellon, spending two weeks preparing for Monty's mammoth Operation Goodwood with VIII Corps' three armoured divisions, 7th, 11th and Guards. The Corps Commander was Lieutenant-General O'Connor, the brilliant Western Desert hero of 1940, who had been a prisoner-of-war for several years and had little experience of the sophisticated armour/infantry/RAF battles of the Montgomery era. Ironically the War Diary of 2/3/4 July stated: 'Much thought was given to problem of infantry cooperation with tanks.' 1 RTR's battle operations in Italy had combined very well with Queens Infantry and Rifle Brigade motorised infantry. 'Officers of the unit discussed the matter with officers of Queens Brigade and much exercising was done with troops of the Queens. In essence Operation Goodwood was a massive armoured assault from north-east of Caen, led by 11th Armoured, followed up by the Guards and Desert Rats, to clear the area east of the River Orne and the Faubourg de Vaucelles. 1 RTR moved from Rucqueville, Bieville, across the River Orne via 'London Bridge' to Ste Honorine La Chardonette and Giberville.

The tanks and men of the 11th Armoured ('Black Bull') Division bore the brunt of Goodwood and 1 RTR saw no action on the first day (18 July), but on the next day Major Gillespie's 'B' Squadron had a difficult time taking the village of Four encountering heavy firing all afternoon from enemy anti-tank guns and mortars. Sergeant F. Wildegoose's 'Venus', Lieutenant D.A. Wickenden's 'Minerva', Sergeant J. Moat's 'Defiant' and Second Lieutenant

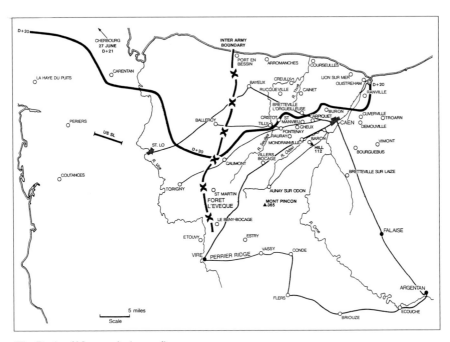

The Battle of Normandy (general).

Fletcher's 'The Saint' were all knocked out, incurring eight casualties including Major 'Bob' Crisp DSO.

Geoff Knights in 'B' Squadron's 'Minerva' recalled: 'Our 'B' Squadron was all but wiped out when attacking the Bourguébus ridge which was swarming with Panthers and/or Tigers. I lost my tank and four other members of my crew. That ended my career in the tanks.'

Corporal Peter Roach and his Honey crew were up in front, liaising with 5 RTR. They felt very vulnerable without a turret (Stuarts were built so tall that their turrets presented an easy target, hence the decision to scrap the turrets). On the second day of Goodwood, near the village of Ifs, Roach realised that 5 RTR and 1 RTR were firing at each other and 'between us we managed to quell the fight'.

Quite soon after D-Day Sergeant 'Chuck' Moat's Cromwell 'Defiant' was hit by an AP shell which damaged the front right-hand track. On the front of the tank was a painting by Corporal Tony Telford of a saucy young lady showing a leg. During Goodwood Moat's new Sherman Firefly was blown up on a Teller anti-tank mine which blew a hole in the petrol tanks. At base workshops a few days later Moat and his crew took over another Sherman Firefly – with the 'Defiant' saucy lady painted on it. The fitters had welded together the two good halves of the knocked-out tanks!

Operation Goodwood was a near-disaster for 11th Armoured Division but the Guards and 7th Armoured Divisions got off relatively unscathed. Rommel had fortified thirty small villages and hamlets, many of which had not been touched by that bomber armada. Bourguébus ridge in particular harboured many 88mm anti-tank guns and Panzers which took a terrible toll. Major C.L. Sproull left on the 20th to attend a Staff College course and his role was taken over by Major 'Pedro' Pedraza MC. Johnny Dingwall was promoted to OC 'C' Squadron. Captain B. Smethurst was promoted to OC 'A' Squadron, after Bob Crisp was severely wounded.

★ ★ ★

Operation Totalize was Monty's next plan. The 2nd Canadian Corps was to drive south towards Falaise, while the 7th Armoured Division supported the 3rd Canadian Division. In artificial moonlight created by searchlights, their objectives were Verrières and Rocquancourt in Operation Spring. On 23 July the Luftwaffe bombed heavily the forming-up points and anti-personnel bombs caused 1 RTR casualties. The next day 1 RTR moved to Pt 72 ridge but very strong opposition held up 'A' Squadron just beyond Tilly-la-Campaigne. They had a hot time and two troops of 'C' Squadron took over at 1000 hours. Very accurate AP fire and mortar/nebelwerfer fire caused heavy casualties. By 1400 hours 'C' Squadron's position at Verrières was untenable and it had to be withdrawn. Major Johnny Dingwall asked for RAF Typhoon support (called 'Limejuice'):

On a forward slope – not very clever – faced with three Panthers (one turned out to be a Tiger). Our firepower was not having much effect. I could not manoeuvre round their flank. The RAF flying at great speed spotted C Squadron on the forward slope, a pretty good target, although 2000 yards from the enemy – so they engaged us! A most frightening experience. After firing their rockets, they flew off without doing any damage. 1 RTR RHQ [received the] message: 'Target engaged and destroyed'.

One 'C' Squadron tank commander wrote:

25th, All No 5 Tp except its Firefly brewed up – Thomson and Smalley killed. Lieutenant G. Boak [in 'Slaphappy'] wounded in shoulder by HE, Fishes went slap-happy and Musdes is missing. Nothing known yet of 6 or 8 troops. 7 Troop's Firefly must have got it. 'B' Squadron hasn't suffered as bad but have lost some tanks. RBs and Queens knocked up.

Tilly was recaptured by the Germans. All the 1 RTR Fireflies were brought up to help 'C' Squadron which had eight tanks knocked out in the three-hour battle. During Operation Spring 'B' Squadron lost SSME Brown's 'Buonaparte', Lieutenant A.M. Walker's 'Oor Wullie', Sergeant F. Williams MM's 'Fairmaid of Perth', Sergeant A. Elvy's 'Betty Boop 1', Corporal F. Brown's 'Jeanne D'Arc' and Sergeant J. McConnachie MM's 'Diana'. 'C' Squadron lost Corporal Dutton and Sergeant G. McCarty's tanks, as well as Lieutenant G. Boak's 'Slaphappy' and Lieutenant R. Frost's 'Crippen 1'. 5 RTR relieved 1 RTR and then on the 29th was itself relieved by 4th Canadian Armoured Brigade.

CHAPTER TWELVE

Breakout – August 1944

On 27 July enemy counter-attacks inflicted more casualties, this time on the Recce troop's Corporal V.R. Luesley, Second Lieutenant Hanbury-Sparrow and Sergeant A. North. 4 CLY left 22nd Armoured Brigade and merged with 3 CLY in 4th Armoured Brigade. The 5th Royal Inniskilling Dragoon Guards ('The Skins') joined the Desert Rats and the 11th Hussars ('The Cherry Pickers') rejoined to lead the way.

Monty was determined to keep up the pressure on the western part of Operation Overlord while the US Army captured Cherbourg and threatened a break-out into Brittany. Operation Bluecoat was a massive three-corps operation – practically the whole of the British Army was involved. The Desert Rats were part of XXX Corps under Lieutenant-General Brian Horrocks, with the main objectives of Aunay-sur-Odon and the dominant Mont Pincon.

1 RTR moved back through Caen and St Leger and leaguered at Ellon. Operation Bluecoat started on 1 August and 1 RTR followed the Queens Brigade through Caumont and south-eastwards through Cahagnes on to Robin crossroads. The next day 'C' Squadron moved east to Sauques near Coulvain, despite thick mist, 88mm anti-tank guns and bazooka teams. The AP fire and mortaring was so intense that 'C' Squadron was obliged to withdraw. At 1700 hours a small set-piece attack with Queens and artillery support cleared the area. Sergeant E. Wainwright's 'Guts' was mined, and Trooper 'Hobby' Bullet was killed. Sergeant 'Ginger' Lincoln in 'Cumon Thith Way' suffered a head wound and Trooper Ted Daniels a stomach wound, while Trooper Durrant was wounded for the second time.

'C' Squadron counter-attacked when 'A' and 'B' Squadrons became isolated as the enemy closed round them, but nine out of the twelve remaining 'A' and 'B' tanks got out through the ring during the night. One tank commander wrote: 'Had to stop up in the wood until midnight when the [Norfolk Yeomanry] SPs came up to take over – glad too because Tigers were milling about somewhere in front.' 5 RTR then took over and the regiment remained in reserve at Robin crossroads. The advance continued on the 5th and 6th despite heavy mortaring from Campandre-Valcongrand east of Mont Pincon.

Condé-sur-Noireau was the next objective but heavy opposition was met around Cauville, and the brigade was pulled out of action on the night of the 7th, and 1 RTR moved to Roucamps for a week. Lieutenant-General Brian

'B' Squadron 1 RTR Baker Cromwell tank crew, Nordewick, Belgium, September 1944. Left to right: Trooper D. Wells (turret gunner), Trooper H. Barnett (co-driver), Corporal Spittles (commander), Trooper Billy Bagguley (wireless operator/gunner loader), Trooper Albert Garrett (driver). (*Reg Spittles*)

Horrocks, a tall, imposing commander, addressed officers and senior NCOs on the 11th, and the new brigade commander Mackeson talked to them the next day. The so-called 'night of the long knives' occurred on 3 August when Monty and Dempsey, furious at the apparent lack of drive, relieved General Bucknall, General Erskine and Brigadier Hinde of their commands.

Major General G.L. Verney was now GOC Desert Rats. Everyone was sorry to see Erskine and Hinde go. They were understandably cautious with the lives of the men they had led with such great distinction since El Alamein. Lieutenant-Colonel E.H. Gibbon was succeeded by Lieutenant-Colonel Pat Hobart, nephew of the great 'Hobo' and a successful leader since the 1940 Western Desert days. Two days later, on the 19th, 1 RTR moved from St Pierre-sur-Dives to Boissey, well to the north-east of the famous Falaise–Argentan gap where the bulk of the German Army had been trapped and demolished. Every forward unit in the British Army in this week was heavily bombed by the RAF and often by the Luftwaffe. Despite white star markings on all AFVs the RAF strafed and strafed. Some British formations turned their anti-aircraft guns on the Thunderbolts and Typhoons. The break-out was moving so fast that RAF pilots could not interpret their target areas – moving tanks *must* be Huns, but they weren't! Then it was on to Livarot and St Martin-de-la-Lieue, where 'B' Squadron took the high ground to secure crossings over the stream, which were subject to anti-tank fire.

On the 19th 'A2' Echelon had seven trucks blown up in an air-raid with several casualties, but 'A' Squadron led 'B' Squadron into Livarot to receive a splendid 'liberation' greeting: 'Post office girls – très jolis – in first-storey windows, throwing flowers down on us. Older women were weeping and throwing kisses,' wrote one tank commander. At St Martin-de-la-Lieue a bazooka team knocked out Sergeant Burnet's and Sergeant German's tanks, killing Corporal J. Maybury. No. 5 Troop put some HE shells through a German truck which produced a great deal of loot! East of Lisieux Sergeant John Caulfield commanding a Firefly won a bar to his Military Medal by tackling a Panther while supporting 1/5 Queens. Trooper J. Dinning joined 5 Troop in a 'B' Squadron tank called 'Little Audrey', crewed by Johnny Firth (driver), Trevor Gundry (co-driver) and Corporal Taffy Glenton (wireless operator): 'The last two had come through the entire North African campaign. There was I, very keen and naïve, amongst fighting soldiers of the finest quality who accepted me at face value and made me welcome. It was the experience of the crew with which I fought which saved my life on more than one occasion.' Trooper Dinning heard the church bells ringing in Lisieux and was 'very moved'. On the 22nd 'C' Squadron tried to push through Lisieux to get on to high ground to the east, but took casualties and returned to their start line having lost two tanks. At Beuvilliers, on the outskirts of Lisieux, Sergeant Harry Shelcott in 'Sidi Rezegh II' was killed by a sniper after the tank was hit by 88mm anti-tank guns and the crew evacuated. A combined attack by 51st Highland Division and 1 RTR found a way round the town centre by the Basilica of Ste Thérèse. Tigers and Panthers of 1 SS Division and infantry and guns of 272 Division put up a spirited defence. Snipers held out in the cathedral and 1 RTR and 1/7 Queens fended off a counter-attack around St Jacques. The 24th found 1 RTR in reserve moving east along minor roads towards St Georges du Vievre and Le Quesney. 'B' Squadron suffered casualties from SS troops on the 26th and 27th around Brestot Routot. Beyond the Forêt de Montfort the whole regiment was in action and casualties were fairly heavy.

The River Risle was crossed at Pont-Authou early on the 26th, as 1 RTR moved north along the river bank through Glos-sur-Risles and Montfort-sur-Risles. 'C' Squadron led up hairpin bends on the very steep salient. The Recce troop's Honey was brewed by an anti-tank gun. As 6 and 7 Troops went left of the road, 5 and 8 cut around to the right, supported by 1st Rifle Brigade. Lieutenant Ambridge, Sergeant Bennett and Sergeant Stennet's tanks were brewed up and Troopers Oakes and Williams suffered minor wounds. But the regiment had a liberation welcome in Routot, 2 miles west of the Seine. For three days 1 RTR was out of the line at Boslon. Plans were being made for a long move across the Rivers Seine and Somme. Each tank would carry 40 gallons of tinned petrol on the engine covers. It had been a tough eleven days of non-stop pursuit of a highly skilful and determined enemy. Bridges and culverts were blown and mined. Every day the armoured brigade lost men and tanks. The casualty list for 1 RTR in the break-out month of August 1944 was as follows:

2 August (in Operation Totalise): 24 casualties and 6 tanks
3 August: 1 tank
5 August: 2 tanks
7 August: 4 killed in action, 8 wounded, 1 tank
19 August: 2 killed in action, 11 wounded, 2 tanks
22 August: 9 wounded, 2 tanks
24 August: 2 wounded
25 August: 2 killed in action, 10 wounded, 1 tank
26 August: 2 wounded, 2 tanks (but captured 30 PoWs)
27 August: 4 killed in action, 12 wounded, 4 tanks
Total: 90 casualties and 21 tanks knocked out

CHAPTER THIRTEEN

The Great Swan

The astonishing armoured pursuit of the German Army from the River Seine through northern France and Belgium and back into Holland by the three famous British armoured divisions became known as the 'Great Swan'. It was a unique and exhilarating experience as the miles sped by, punctuated by sharp, bitter little rearguard actions and tumultuous, rapturous liberation welcomes.

The 43rd (Wessex Wyvern) Division under their brutal GOC Major-General Thomas had fought a five-day battle to secure crossings and a bridgehead over the Seine. Major-General Verney GOC 7th Armoured Division named the advance Operation Goodwood Meeting and was pleased to take under his command 4th Armoured Brigade under Brigadier Michael Carver. The plan was for XXX Corps (with Guards Armoured on the right and 11th Armoured on the left) to head for Brussels and Antwerp, while XII Corps would protect XXX Corps' flank and aim for Ghent. The 1st Canadian Army had the unpleasant tasks of surrounding and capturing all the Channel ports on the French and Belgian coast, and clearing the V-1 and V-2 flying bomb sites.

Major-General Verney's orders were for 4th Armoured Brigade with the Royals leading to take the right-hand centre line, with 22nd Armoured Brigade led by the Cherry Pickers on the left. The Queens Brigade was in reserve to follow up and 'mop up' if required. 1 RTR's move started at 0530 hours on 31 August. The tanks crossed the Seine at St Pierre de Vauvray and via Louviers and Lyon La Forêt reached the Gournay area, having covered 61 miles. The next day was tedious and was spent watching the 53rd Welsh Division passing through. On the 2nd they moved on to Hornoy, then Molliens-Vidame, across the River Somme at Picquigny, Vignacourt, Leger lès Domart and Bernaville, north-west of Amiens. At Cauchy and again at St Pol resistance was by-passed. The 1st Rifle Brigade was helpful but Lillers was more difficult. Most of the small towns set in wooded river valleys were held by an enemy force of about 200 with a couple of anti-tank guns. But the valley of the Lille coalfields was a maze of canals, dykes, factories and collieries. Two strong Grenadier regiments of 59 Infantry Division held the line of La Bassée Aire Canal. The regimental group 1 RTR/RB/RHA got through Lillers early on the 3rd and reached the Aire/Lys canals. The bridges were of course blown. Behind, parties of enemy soldiers with machine-guns, mortars and bazookas had broken the

The Great
Swan from
the Seine to
the capture of
Ghent.

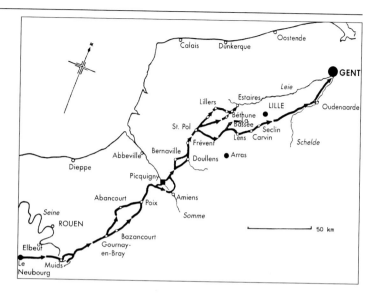

divisional centre line in Busnes and Lillers. The regimental group spent
most of 3 September mopping up, with considerable help from the FFI
(French Forces of the Interior or French Resistance).

When Major Freddy Pile joined 1 RTR to command 'A' Squadron at the
end of August, he already knew the CO Lieutenant-Colonel Pat Hobart,
Major Johnny Dingwall and Major Jack Greenwood. He wrote:

> My squadron was allotted the southern part of the town [Lillers] as our objective, and I was
> given a platoon of the Rifle Brigade to help with the clearing of houses; it was my first
> experience of clearing a town, albeit a small one, and I had the feeling that there were
> Germans popping up everywhere. We seemed much too 'thin on the ground' to deal with
> them all. However, bit by bit, we moved closer to the centre of the place and, by nightfall, the
> enemy seemed to have evacuated it; there was, however, a lot of movement in the buildings
> and hedgerows just outside and every tank (including my own) was needed to guard the
> approaches in case the enemy counter-attacked and came back. There was no sleep for
> anyone that night; all had to be fully alert or we would have been an easy target for enemy
> bazookas (called by the Germans *Panzerfaust*) – they were short-range, hand-held weapons
> which fired a shell of enormous power; a direct hit on tank almost invariably knocked it out
> or at least killed a member of the crew. By the time we were withdrawn, in the early hours of
> the morning, we had killed or captured some eighty Germans and had taken possession of a
> considerable number of guns, pistols, cars and much other enemy equipment. Two RTR
> tanks were lost and casualties were 2 KIA, 2 wounded.

When the town was cleared and garrisoned by the FFI, the regimental group
moved to Essars, Hinges and Locon, north of Bethune. Major Freddy Pile
with 'A' Squadron engaged enemy moving north-eastwards out of Bethune
and considerable damage was done early on the 4th on MET. Pile's
Cromwell was hit twice in the turret by a 75mm anti-tank gun 800 yards
away. 'Not for the first time was I grateful that the Cromwell tank, despite its
poor armour, had such speed and manoeuvrability,' Pile wrote. He went on:

The towns and villages through which we advanced were mostly inhabited and, in all these countries, the local people gave us the most enormous help. They helped us over intelligence, telling us how far we were likely to get without meeting enemy – and often fairly exactly where we were likely to meet trouble. If they felt reasonably secure they would come out of their houses and give us an unbelievable welcome. If we planned to remain overnight they often – most generously, because they had little enough themselves – gave us food and drink. Of course, they were intensely relieved to be 'liberated', but such help and kindness was also very encouraging for us – and made what we were doing seem even more worthwhile. The attitude of these people was not merely kind, however, it was frequently very courageous. It was by no means unknown for us to advance leaving a village we had captured temporarily unoccupied, due to the speed at which things were moving; in these circumstances Germans sometimes managed to return and they were invariably vicious to the inhabitants.

Trooper L.J. Dinning of 'B' Squadron put a single HE shot through the window of a house 1,200 yards away: 'We were holding a station [Lillers] on a level crossing. There were some houses across open ground to our right with German troops in them. There had been a battle royal to get the level crossing. There were bodies lying around all over the place. We were on the level crossing for two or three days and stayed in the tank most of the time because of mortaring from which the infantry copped it.'

By midnight on the 3rd 'C' Squadron had reached the bridge at Estaires, already blown of course, some 20 miles beyond Lillers. On the way they destroyed two 88mm anti-tank guns and caused considerable damage to 59 Infantry Division grenadiers. But the regiment had five tanks knocked out and 1 RTR had in fact been left behind! 5 RTR, the Skins, the Cherry Pickers and 1/5 Queens had liberated Ghent on 5 September, receiving a splendid welcome, and between them all the Desert Rats had captured 10,000 prisoners-of-war. On 11 September 1 RTR moved through Lens, Carvin, Oudenarde and Lede (halfway between Ghent and Brussels), before reporting to Brigade HQ and moving into billets at Wavre Ste Catherine. A dance was held in the village that night for the British troops. The next two days were spent guarding a stretch of the Albert Canal in preparation for Operation Market Garden, which started on 17 September.

Corporal Reg Spittles joined 'B' Squadron from the disbanded 2 Northants Yeomanry on 20 August, together with Sergeant George Ferguson. The squadron leader was Major 'Ginger' Gillespie. On 21 September, while guarding part of the Albert Canal opposite Herentals and other points around Veghel, the point tank was stalked by a German soldier who threw a grenade into the turret. The tank was disabled and the crew baled out. The wounded, including Spittles, made it back to the LAD and Spittles returned with a Firefly to tow back the knocked-out Cromwell.

★ ★ ★

It was definitely the end of the Great Swan! The great hopes in mid-September of an early, dramatic end to the war diminished, faded and ended.

CHAPTER FOURTEEN

Winter in the Peel Country

The Desert Rats played no major part in the gallant but ill-fated operation to capture Arnhem and force a bridgehead over the Rhine. On 24 September they moved south of Eindhoven to protect the long flank of the Guards Armoured and 43rd Wessex Divisions which had tried so bravely to link up with the 1st Airborne Division in Arnhem. Two German divisions had cut the XXX Corps centre line between Eindhoven and Veghel, a 20-mile-long single road. The division was tasked with its clearance.

Captain Tom Craig had been captured in the Western Desert. Escaping in September 1943 from a prisoner-of-war camp in Italy, he joined 1 RTR in Oss in Holland as second-in-command of 'B' Squadron. Captain Smart was due to be posted to the Gunnery School at Lulworth, while the OC Major Bobby Gillespie was earmarked to command the new Divisional Battle School being formed in Holland. 'Initially the squadron was taking part in defensive patrols near Geffen and Nuland in support of 1 RB. Towards the end of September the division was given the task of clearing the area of north-west Brabant [known as the Peel Country] bounded roughly by 's Hertogenbosch, Tilburg and the north of the Wilhelmina Canal, through Oosterhout to Gentruidenberg.'

Major Freddy Pile of 'A' Squadron 'drove in my Dingo [scout-car] behind the Guards Armoured as they advanced and saw at first hand what a hammering they had had. There were burnt-out tanks everywhere on both sides of the road. Desperately though they tried it had been impossible for them to manoeuvre off the road itself, flanked by canals and low-lying swampy country. The tanks were a sitting target for German, greatly superior, anti-tank guns pointing straight down the road.'

On the 26th 1 RTR moved up the divisional centre line, with 'B' Squadron probing the road towards Olland. The leading tank of each troop came under fire from bazookas and machine-guns. The next day 'A' Squadron moved towards Dinther on the Veghel road and on towards Nistelrode. Around Nulands-Vinkel two Honeys and a Cromwell were lost in a few minutes to bazookas, with four casualties. On the 28th and 29th messy skirmishes cost 'C' Squadron two tanks. Sergeant George McKee of 'A' Squadron won the Military Medal while in support of the 1/5 Queens around Dinther and Middelroode, destroying an anti-tank gun and several machine-guns and killing many infantry. SSM MacGregor gained a bar to the Military Medal he had won in the Western Desert while attacking enemy in Middelroode; he

1 RTR in Eindhoven,
18 September 1944.
(*Bert Dowler*)

knocked out several anti-tank guns and machine-guns and captured twenty prisoners. Sergeant 'Chuck' Moat also of 'B' Squadron acted as OP at Corso on the 30th until his tank 'Defiant' was knocked out by mortar fire, killing two of his crew. Climbing back into his tank, he engaged and destroyed a Spandau with his Browning. He then ordered the tank to be towed away and went forward on foot, locating the mortar crew and capturing twelve prisoners. He and the driver were both wounded and had to be flown back to England. In four days 1 RTR had had 3 men killed in action and 21 wounded, and lost seven tanks. One tank commander in 'A' Squadron wrote:

> Sept 28 and Jerry is fairly strong on this side of the corridor with Spandaus, mortars and 88s. One B Squadron tank knocked out by a bazooka, the commander killed. Sept 30. Had a nasty day, ran into all sorts of staff – small arms, sniping, bazookas, Spandaus, 88 and 105s. Lost 3 tanks brewed. Sergeant Smith's 'Johnny Wooder' was all right, operators Pete Eccles killed, Shep and Sergeant Smith moderately wounded with blast and shrapnel. 2nd tank had to get it, had three killed – turret people. Driver and George Travis brought it back to echelon. 3rd tank Captain Stephens hit with two 105mm, Micky Perrin killed. Jock Brady and the rest baled out and tank immediately brewed, Jock with burns and blast wounds.

Brigadier H.J.B. Cracroft took command of the armoured brigade but had to go to hospital and was replaced on 16 October by Brigadier A.D.R. Wingfield.

The regiment spent early October in Hess. The new adjutant, Captain A.H. Hills, took over from Captain J.W. Rogers. One of the oddest happenings in the midst of mortal combat in the long, bitter winter of 1944 was the sudden arrival of a piece of paper, via the adjutant, suddenly posting the recipient to a far-flung unit in a peaceful area (Salisbury Plain or Brussels) or to a course to improve their military knowledge!

On 22 October Operation Colin started. This involved 7th Armoured and three infantry divisions, tasked with clearing the area of Middelroede, Doornhoek and Berlicum against the enemy 712 Division. 'B' and 'C' Squadrons supported the Queens in very soft going in a successful three-day operation, hoping to capture the last two objectives, although two tanks were lost in a surprise attack on enemy anti-tank guns facing the wrong way. On the 26th the regiment moved from Boxtel across the Esch bridge to Udenhout, 10 miles on. By nightfall they had captured the town for the loss of two tanks hit by bazookas but had taken eighty prisoners and destroyed an anti-tank gun. The German CO of 1036 Grenadier Regiment was put in the bag. The regiment then passed through the next day Loon-op-Zand directed on Oosterhout. The next day they did rather well. They mopped up many infantry despite SP guns firing AP, reached Dongen at dusk, captured four guns, many MET and took a further eighty prisoners. GOC 7th Armoured sent them a signal of congratulations. But 'B' Squadron lost three tanks to AP fire on the 29th, before in turn destroying the enemy guns. 'At the capture of Oosterhout SSM McKees' troop excelled themselves by capturing in half an hour a group of anti-tank guns and enemy infantry,'

'B' Squadron, 1 RTR, 's Hertogenbosch, 1944. (*Reg Spittles*)

recalled Major F. Pile of 'A' Squadron. He also described the day-to-day life of a tank crew and the responsibilities of a squadron commander:

In the 1st Royal Tanks we were equipped with Cromwell tanks. These had a crew of four – driver, gunner, radio operator and tank commander. Each had a short 75mm gun, not to be confused with the German 75mm gun in the Panther tank which was long and vastly more powerful; but our tanks were, as we have seen, very fast and manoeuvrable. A troop had three such tanks; there were five troops and a squadron headquarters (of four tanks). These, together with some twenty-five 'soft' administrative vehicles, comprised the armoured squadron. At a later stage a few Sherman tanks, especially fitted with 17-pdr anti-tank guns, were issued in view of the disparity between the power of our guns and those of the enemy. These (known as Fireflies) added to the squadron strength and they were far more effective against the German tanks than the Cromwells – but there were very few of them.

As a tank crew our lives revolved entirely around our individual tanks. In these we kept everything we needed – food, water and our 'bedding rolls' containing perhaps a blanket, groundsheet and washing materials; there might also be an odd bottle of brandy if one happened to come across such a thing. The food was in the form of a box of 'composite' rations – some of it dehydrated to take up as little space as possible, together with bully beef, rice pudding, tea, milk and sugar; the milk, of course, being powdered. The tank's equipment included a small primus stove and we made cooking utensils out of old tins. Our 'plates' were mess tins – deep square aluminium tins with handles; each officer and man was issued with one of these.

During pauses in operations, if we had some indication that we might be twenty minutes or more in the same place, the crew would get out the primus, tea and a 'brew can' (old tin) and brew up a cup of tea for themselves; it was a welcome break, particularly on cold days. As dark fell we were nearly always ordered to discontinue the advance and to find a place as secure as possible – perhaps a wood, a field off the beaten track or even a small village. Directly we halted we posted guards round the squadron perimeter; all, including myself as squadron leader, would take their turn at guard duty throughout the night. Within our perimeter we made room for our 'soft' vehicles which came up each night that it was safe to do so with petrol, rations, ammunition and our mail, if any had arrived. As soon as they arrived the senior NCO fitter would go round and ascertain from each tank crew any mechanical defects. These would then be worked on – often all night – and in the morning I would be given a detailed account of the condition of every tank. I could then report to regimental headquarters what my fighting strength would be. While all the work of replenishment and tank maintenance was going on, the squadron leaders would normally be called to a meeting at RHQ where the colonel would give us orders for the following day; when we returned to our squadrons we, in our turn, gave orders to the five troop leaders. After this we bedded down by our tanks and got as much sleep as we could.

During November and December the regiment had a relatively peaceful time, based initially on Oosterhout for the first half of November before moving on to Neerhoven. Duties included patrolling and manning infantry posts, and life was enlivened by church services, regimental dances and some football. In mid-November various training courses started up, including wireless, driving, maintenance, gunnery, small arms and intelligence subjects, along with anti-gas lectures.

Cambrai Day, 20 November, was a regimental holiday, and special issues of rum and beer were made to all ranks. The day's highlight was a football match between officers and sergeants. On the 22nd the first 'Python' party left for Ostend, made up of desert veterans who had five years of war service. 'Lilop' was an alternative 'Leave in lieu of Python'. Major-General L.O. Lyne DSO came from the disbanded 50th Tyne Tees Division to command the Desert Rats. The Queens Brigade lost their 1/6 and 1/7

Monty inspects 1 RTR in Holland, winter 1944. (*Patrick Delaforce*)

battalions in exchange for the 2nd Devons and 9th Durham Light Infantry. On the 25th notification came that the CO had been awarded the Distinguished Service Order to add to his Order of the British Empire and Military Cross.

On 7 December 22nd Armoured Brigade moved over the River Maas and took over the area Roosteren–Nieuwstadt. Corporal Peter Roach recalled: 'It was now raw, wet November and we were out of the line apart from a short period before the Ardennes offensive when we were dismounted acting as infantry. Before Christmas we were in Limbourg on the German border, behind the infantry. Apart from patrolling it was a case of trying to keep warm and wishing it would all end.' Major Freddy Pile of 'A' Squadron wrote:

We spent two weeks in late December 1944 and early January 1945 in and around the Dutch town of Sittard. It was incredibly cold and there was deep snow on the ground throughout the period; since we were positioned in open fields and sometimes slept alongside our tanks, it was a major problem to keep warm. Luckily for us the authorities had just produced a 'tank suit' which was being issued to all crews; it was a sort of overall, but very warm, waterproof and comfortable. We slept well in these in the snow. Despite the extreme cold it was a pleasant break and a welcome one.

There was a good deal of leave available, either locally to Tilburg, Antwerp or Brussels, or, for the very fortunate, to the UK (usually restricted to

An 'A' Squadron Sherman 17pdr Firefly is cheered on by the Dutch in Eindhoven, September 1944. (*Bert Dowler*)

officers of the rank of lieutenant-colonel and above). A divisional concert party, ENSA and cinema shows boosted morale, as indeed did the warm reception from Dutch (and Belgian) villagers to those billeted there. Corporal Peter Roach recalled: 'It [Brussels] was gay and sleeping in a bed and having a bath were luxuries which I enjoyed to the full. Beer was plentiful and there were plenty of pretty girls to look at.'

On 20 December the regiment moved from Enighausen to Broek Sittard, just as rumours and stories began to circulate about the Battle of the Bulge in the Ardennes. For a time the units were widely scattered: 'C' Squadron was in Germany, 'B' was half in Holland and half in Germany, and 'A' and RHQ were in Holland. 'B' Echelon was in Belgium!

Christmas day was spent traditionally with an excellent Christmas dinner served by the officers in a large hall used as a cookhouse. Not many of the desert veterans who had landed in Normandy seven months earlier were present – casualties, postings and Python leave had all taken their toll. As they ate their Christmas meal, some of the Desert Rat units in the front line could hear the Germans singing 'Heilige Nacht' on the far side of the very cold, desolate, dangerous no-man's-land.

CHAPTER FIFTEEN

Operation Blackcock

The New Year opened with a bang. Early in the morning the Luftwaffe made a determined and widespread attack on British and American airfields in a last-ditch effort to prevent the RAF fighter-bombers from smashing up the German Army's progress in the Ardennes. On 15 January the CO issued final orders for Operation Blackcock.

Lieutenant-Colonel P.R.C. Hobart DSO OBE MC commanded, Major J.J. Dingwall DSO was second-in-command, the adjutant was Captain M. Jewell, the IO Lieutenant Brian Watkins, OC Recce Troop Captain Jack Storey MC, OC HQ Squadron Major J. Greenwood, second-in-command Captain G. Finden. 'A' Squadron was commanded by Major F.D. Pile MC, with Captain John Cordy-Simpson as his second-in-command; troop leaders were Lieutenant Keith Dyson, Lieutenant R.R. MacGregor, Lieutenant Stanton and SSM Paddy McKee MM. 'B' Squadron was under the command of Major T.S. Craig MC, with Captain D.W.A. Ambidge MC as his second-in-command; troop leaders were Lieutenant Vic Tilly, Lieutenant John Hockton, Lieutenant Chris Gain-Vickery, Lieutenant Tom Harland DCM, Lieutenant Stan Witheridge, Lieutenant Joe Newton and SSM Paddy Caulfield. 'C' Squadron was under the command of Major Bill Mather MC, with Captain D.S. Bowling-Smith MC as his second-in-command; troop leaders were Lieutenant Alan Parks, Lieutenant Peter Haderson and SSM Jim Dauncey MM. The Quartermaster was Captain Charlie Foot and the RTA (technical adjutant) was Captain Stan Canfield MM. The MQMS was of course 'Dodger' Green of Tobruk fame.

★ ★ ★

The three divisions that made up XII Corps (7th Armoured, 52nd Lowland and 43rd Wessex) had been tasked with the clearance of the area between the Maas and Roer Rivers in preparation for the northward drive to the Rhine by the US 9th Army, which in turn would coincide with 21st Army Group's Operation Veritable – the breaking-into and capture of the formidable Siegfried Line in the Reichswald.

The enemy were the 176 and 183 German Infantry Divisions, supported by SP guns, a few tanks and many bazookas. During Operation Blackcock 1 RTR was in action for two weeks supporting 1/5 Queens and 2nd Devons infantry. The reconnaissance squadron lost several Honey tanks. Corporal

Peter Roach wrote: 'Christmas itself was bitter cold until we took the offensive again to clear the country up the Roer river in mid-January. The ground was solid with frost and covered with several inches of snow when we set out. As the day wore on a thick fog developed so we parked along the road. While waiting we busied ourselves whitewashing the vehicles.' Roach liked the Honey tank. With its twin Cadillac engines and automatic gears, it was very reliable, very quiet and fast – excellent for its job. He went on: 'Sitting in a tank all night in that cold we dozed, passed a bottle of rum around on waking and dozed again. The centre line was moving very slowly because of blown roads, so in the afternoon we were re-routed on a left hook to rejoin the centre line beyond the trouble. The wretched Royal Engineers under constant mortar fire bridging a stream [actually two streams south of the Vloed Beek on the main Sittard–Roermond road].

Bakenhoven was taken by 1/5th Queens. On the 16th 9 DLI assaulted the Vloed Beek and the next morning 'C' Squadron moved across to support the Queens in Susteren. Trooper R.G. Knight, a Cromwell gunner in 'C' Squadron, wrote:

We now had about a week of intensive action around the towns of Susteren, Echt and Schilberg, confined to the turret of the tank firing at targets when required to do so. The ground was beginning to thaw and cause some problems for the tanks which no longer had a rock-hard surface to drive over. We crossed a stream over a scissors bridge carried on specialist [AVRE] tanks and unfolded to make a steel bridge.

Major Tom Craig, OC 'B' Squadron, wrote this report of Operation Blackcock:

15 January, the Regiment moved to the assembly area and formed up head to tail in the various Squadron/Infantry Groups. The weather was bitterly cold, damp and foggy. The initial bridgehead over the Vloed Beek, to include the village of Dieteren, was made on the night of 15 January by 9th DLI supported by 'flails' of the Lothian and Border Horse. In the original plan the Regiment, supporting 2nd Devons in 'Kangaroos', was to break out from this bridgehead when two class 40 bridges had been built over the Beek by the Sappers; to advance rapidly at first light on two centre lines, 'A' Squadron on the left, 'B' Squadron on the right; to seize Echt and Schilberg; and 'C' Squadron, in reserve, to support if necessary, 1st/5th Queens in the clearing of Susteren and open the main N–S road.

Owing to strong enemy opposition and intensive shelling of the Beek crossings, causing very heavy casualties to the Sappers, the bulldozing of the tanks and laying of the bridges was greatly hindered and delayed. This, combined with fog, postponed an early morning break-out, which was unfortunate as surprise was lost.

On the morning of 17 January, the 1st/5th Queens, who had entered and almost cleared Susteren, were counter-attacked at 0900 hours by a German force which included tanks and SPs. 'C' Squadron was called for and reached Susteren at 1130 hours to restore the situation. On the way they met inaccurate SP fire, knocked out one 88mm and helped 1st/5th Queens to take nearly 100 PoWs.

At 1100 hours the main column, 'A' and 'B' Squadrons with their infantry groups in 'Kangaroos' and carriers, moved off, RHQ and Recce following behind. It had started to thaw and the going was very bad, especially in the low-lying soft ground, already churned up, near the bridges. One of 'A' Squadron's leading tanks slipped and completely blocked the only scissors bridge. The sole alternative was a causeway bulldozed over metal pipes, and the remaining tanks of 'A' Squadron managed to get across it. This, however, made the going so bad that some of the carriers and scout-cars of the Infantry and RE sections became hopelessly bogged and their loss was regrettable as they were badly needed later on.

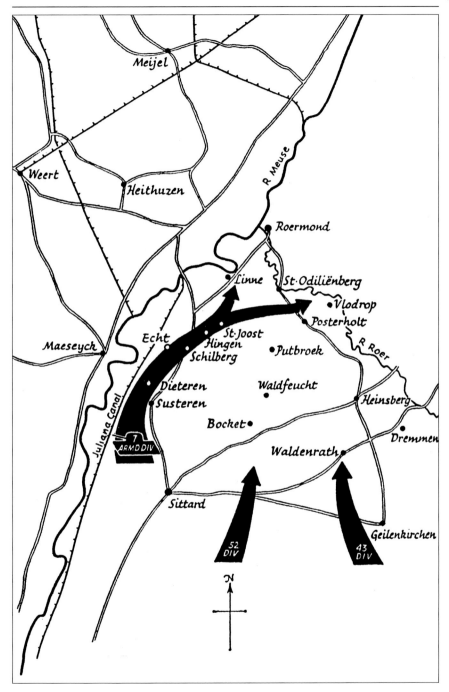

Operation Blackcock, January 1945.

The Advance

Just after 1500 hours both squadrons had assembled in Dieteren where they were subjected to heavy shelling, and at 1540 hours the break-out began. A Squadron on the left advanced rapidly with little opposition and an hour later reported leading tanks entering Echt, having knocked out one 88mm and disposed of several Germans on the way.

B Squadron, on the right, was not so lucky. Their centre line was along the main road to Schilberg, and on debouching from Dieteren they were engaged in open ground by three 75mm SPs and one 88mm. Two of their tanks were knocked out, the OP tank mined, and two tanks bogged in deep snow while going for cover. One enemy SP was damaged and the 88mm was later found abandoned. Invaluable help was given by C Squadron which laid smoke and helped to evacuate casualties while B Squadron was taking up fire positions.

At last light B Squadron reformed and, with infantry dismounted, attacked up the main road as far as the railway level crossing half-way to Schilberg, killing several Germans and taking prisoners. Leading tanks were then stopped by a strongly held road-block. After some fighting the enemy withdrew, but the road-block and the level crossing were subjected to very heavy DF artillery fire including Nebelwerfers. One tank and one 'Kangaroo' were knocked out and casualties caused to our infantry. Attempts were made to clear and by-pass the block, but owing to bad light, mines and enemy fire, it had to be abandoned.

'A' Squadron

'A' Squadron, with its infantry, had cleared Echt and on the morning of 18 January advanced east towards Schilberg, inflicting heavy casualties on the enemy and knocking out one anti-tank gun. The street fighting was particularly violent, especially around the main Schilberg crossroads. Through casualties, our infantry were becoming rather thin on the ground, and the tank crews had some very tricky moments with the enemy infantry infiltrating through houses. In the afternoon the squadron was forced to withdraw by enemy infantry supported by SPs and one Royal Tiger. Three of the 'A' Squadron tanks were knocked out, but they damaged one SP later found abandoned and killed at least 20 of the enemy. During the afternoon 'C' Squadron, with very strong artillery support which, incidentally, was a feature of the whole operation, attacked and cleared Heide with the 1/5th Queens. No tanks were lost and many of the enemy were killed or taken prisoner. The enemy attempting to escape north from Heide were heavily engaged by 'B' Squadron.

During the morning 'B' Squadron, with RE assistance, had cleared the road-block, which consisted of twelve large trees, and had engaged enemy infantry, an SP and an anti-tank gun in the area. At 1600 hours, reinforced by 'A' Company of 9th DLI, the squadron attacked again up the main road with strong artillery support. But the leading tank was mined and knocked out by an 88mm, so had to withdraw once again to the level crossing. The gunners later knocked out this 88mm, plus another one nearby, killing the German gun crews.

'B' Squadron

At last light 'B' Squadron supported a left-flanking infantry attack, which gained 1,000 yards, where another road-block was encountered. About 40 Germans were killed or taken prisoner. Following an hour's delay the advance was resumed, and after two more road-blocks had been cleared as well as mines, the final objectives in Schilberg and Peij were reached and the main road opened. Another tank was mined in Peij leaving only five operational.

In the meanwhile Recce Troop had been doing very valuable work keeping contact with the enemy and pushing out to the north. One patrol entered Hingen and reported it clear after taking 28 PoWs. During the next few days Recce continued to operate in this way, killing and taking prisoner many of the enemy and destroying transport.

Major Freddie Pile, OC 'A' Squadron, wrote:

In late January near the small town of Echt, near Maeseyck on the River Meuse, we were told to occupy the town, together with the neighbouring village of Schilberg, and to clear them of enemy. The advance to Echt presented no difficulty which was just as well as we were, as so often in Holland, flanked on each side by a large ditch (canal is probably a more apt description). In the middle of Schilberg, however, the leading troop came under heavy anti-tank gun fire, and the first two tanks went up in flames in a matter of twenty seconds. In an attempt to ascertain exactly where the enemy gun was, I got out of my tank and went up to the top floor of a house, and saw a Panther tank 800 yards straight down the road. I summoned up the No. 2 Troop of Cromwells, who got direct hits. There were red glows, but no penetration of the armour. The Panther knocked out one Cromwell, another bogged down in a deep ditch trying to outflank the enemy. I got No. 3 Troop up and tried from a different angle to attack the Panther's thinner side armour. By nightfall seven Cromwells were out of action, destroyed or bogged down. Most of the crews were saved. At nightfall the Panther withdrew. We took a considerable number of PoWs and instructed them to walk back up the road to Div HQ.

Corporal Peter Roach in his Honey tank 'chased a fleeing enemy out of the village where we saw and shot up a horse-drawn supply wagon'. In the nearby farm Roach's dismounted crew captured thirteen prisoners, putting them into an air-raid shelter until they could be collected. 'We spent a most uncomfortable day for there were Germans on three sides of us and a third Reconnaissance Troop tank was shot up and set on fire.' The next day a bazooka man hit the Honey tank, killing the lap-gunner and wounding the main gunner, the driver and Roach – 'So ended our war.'

One of the 1 RTR heroes was 'Conky' Harland, a strong, determined and brave NCO who had already been decorated with the Distinguished Conduct Medal, the Croix de Guerre and the Belgian Order of Leopold, and was later commissioned. Trooper Les Dinning was the gunner in Harland's 'B' Squadron tank during Operation Blackcock: 'We were harassing enemy troops withdrawing across the German border from Holland in great haste. I was using the MG on the road-side hedges to eliminate any bazooka teams attempting to ambush us.' Suddenly a cart with 20 enemy soldiers pulled by two horses was seen galloping furiously along a road, half a mile away. Dinning lined up the 75mm gun on the target determined to hit the rear of the cart and not the horses. He fired and the horses were saved, but not the occupants of the cart.

Lieutenant Alan Parks, a troop leader in 'C' Squadron, received orders to capture the small village of Heide, east of Susteren, across a railway line. Simultaneously on the 18th 'A' and 'B' moved north to Echt and Schilberg: 'By first light I was approaching the railway for a quick dash through a tunnel under the line which led straight into the village. We were on our own with no infantry . . . the point tank came to a grinding halt and the commander waved his arms. The whole of the subway was flooded and impassable.' Bravely Parks led his troop up and over the embankment, where they were very vulnerable to the enemy, before they roared into the village and took up their posts at the far end.

Major Tom Craig, OC 'B' Squadron, continued his report:

From 19 January to 22 January the regiment was responsible for the defence of the Schilberg–Echt area. 'B' Squadron being in reserve, 'A' and 'C' Squadrons watching north and east, Recce patrols maintaining contact and continuing to inflict casualties on the enemy for the loss of two of their own vehicles. During this period C Squadron had one tank knocked out. The enemy was active with his artillery and SPs, and the main crossroads near RHQ was heavily shelled. Occasionally enemy aircraft dropped flares and anti-personnel bombs by night. On 23 January 'C' Squadron successfully supported a Commando Brigade

1 RTR and Devons take Schilberg, 18 January 1945. (*Tank Museum*)

in the clearing of Maasbracht and Brachterbeek, inflicting heavy casualties on the Germans with no loss to themselves. 22 AB had, in the meanwhile, passed through to the north-east and the regiment, still under 131 Brigade, received orders for an advance eastwards towards the Roer.

Advance began at 1300 hours on 24 January, 'A' and 'B' Squadrons leading, supported by 9th DLI. The objectives – Putbroek and Aandenberg – were reached with little opposition but 'A' Squadron had one tank knocked out by an SP in the woods to the east, and Recce one tank mined.

Enemy resistance on the whole front was breaking up, and the main opposition now was the odd roving SP, small rearguards armed with bazookas, MGs and mines. Mines had inflicted many casualties on our infantry and tanks during the whole operation. They were laid in large quantities over a large area and were difficult to locate because of frost and snow. Those laid hastily, however, could be spotted on top of the ground, the enemy having had no time to break the hard surface.

On 25 January 'C' Squadron passed through between 'A' and 'B' and reached its objective of Aanendaal. 'A' and 'B' Squadrons, with 9th DLI, cleared the thick woods to the east. Mines were encountered in increasing quantities and caused 'C' Squadron one tank casualty. The leading infantry of 9th DLI, supported by a troop of tanks, attempted to enter Posterholt from the south, but withdrew in the face of opposition. Aanendaal was heavily shelled during the night.

On the morning of 26 January 'B' and 'C' Squadrons formed up with the 9th DLI for an attack on Posterholt from the north. The leading tanks of 'B' Squadron entered the village at 1100 hours, little opposition being met except for a road-block, mines and light shelling. A few prisoners were taken.

This attack was the last operation undertaken by the regiment in the Roer area with the exception of a very spirited action by 6 Troop of 'C' Squadron, when, supporting 1st/5th Queens during an enemy counter-attack on Paarlo, on 30 January, 40 Germans were killed by the troop alone and the remainder withdrew.

After two weeks' hard fighting under the most appalling conditions of cold, with snow, frost and thaws alternating, it was a pleasant change to become static and to get some rest in reasonable billets in Posterholt. All members of the regiment had put up a most excellent show, especially the tank crews, who in the initial stages had no sleep for 48 hours at a time. During the operation the regiment had played a major part, participating in the heaviest of fighting and inflicting very heavy casualties on the enemy. Official claims were over 300 enemy [killed, wounded] or PoW; at least 7 anti-tank guns knocked out and several SPs damaged. The regiment stayed at Posterholt for about a month supporting 131 Brigade. The enemy were active with their artillery and night patrols.

On the 23rd Lieutenant-Colonel 'Gus' Holliman, CO 5 RTR and a long-term valiant 1 RTR officer, was killed on the doorstep of RHQ 1 RTR as he came to attend a conference. The Western Desert heroes were sadly diminishing in numbers.

The battle still continued on the 24th. The CO went on leave and Major 'Pedro' Pedraza took command but five days later he was posted as brigade major to Brigadier Michael Carver's 4th Armoured Brigade. Thus Major Johnny Dingwall now assumed command. On the 24th Sergeant D.A. Johnstone of No. 1 Troop, 'A' Squadron, won the Military Medal. The woods around Putbroek were covered by enemy soldiers, SPs and mortars. Two of the troop's Cromwells were hit by AP. Johnstone dismounted and under fire helped two wounded troopers back to safety, before driving their disabled tank to safety.

Bryan Watkins, the Regimental Intelligence Officer, was now troop leader of 6 Troop, 'A' Squadron. His troop sergeant was Joe Pitt. Ted Skinner was the second-in-command to Major Freddy Pile. The No. 7 Troop leader was John King and his troop sergeant was David Johnson. In Watkins' tank was the careless Lance-Corporal Neachell and little 'Ginger' Coates, the gunner. On the 25th 'A' Squadron was ordered to occupy a group of farms called Posterholt. Major Freddy Pile took half the squadron round one side of the objective and Captain Cordy-Simpson and Lieutenant Watkins took the other side. An enemy SP destroyed 6 Troop's corporal's tank and killed his turret crew and 7 Troop lost a tank on a mine. Watkins wrote: 'My troop brought up the rear. We approached the farm in which Squadron HQ was sited. There were two blinding flashes and loud explosions. My tank and a Recce Tp Honey had been mined and their crews badly hurt.' When it later thawed, the Sappers discovered a huge minefield in the area, mainly double Tellers!

Les Allen, the sergeant troop commander of Seven Charlie Firefly 'A' Squadron, had as his driver Charlie Adams, with Jimmy Hague as his gunner. Both were Desert War and Italian Campaign veterans. Kenneth Ward was the radio operator/gun loader. On 19 January Major F. Pile, described by Ward as 'the major with his bristling moustache and carefully knotted desert scarf' sent his squadron down the road from Echt to the small village of Schilberg: 'Our troop advanced to a crossroads, turned right and moved up 300 yards. We were told [by the troop leader Lieutenant Kirby] to stop at a junction. [There were] infantry boys [Devons] on either side of the road. The radio crackled, telling us of fighting in close proximity. Suddenly the other three tanks of our troop appeared at great speed driving past us without stopping. The troop leader ordered us to stay and shoot up any enemy tanks which might be following. The shelling and small arms fire grew louder and nearer and German troops started firing on us.' A rifle grenade hit the tank and wounded the commander. On the radio Major Pile ordered: 'Sunray here. A7C watch out at the crossroad. SP gun on your right, over and out.' The German SP destroyed a nearby Churchill Crocodile (flame-thrower). A7C survived, but A6C did not, with two men killed in action before the SP was knocked out.

The final objectives of Operation Blackcock were Posterholt, St Joost (taken after a ferocious fight by Group Hubner against the 8th Hussars, 1st RB, the DLI and flame-throwing Crocodiles) and St Odilienberg. 1 RTR had been one of the spearheads of the Desert Rats during Blackcock and were still fighting hard on 29–30 January. The finale came on the 31st when the enemy blew up the last remaining bridge over the Roer at Vlodrop. Blackcock was a very creditable Battle Honour for the regiment.

'A' Squadron 1 RTR group includes Captain 'Freezer' Frost, Lieutenant Eric Smallwood and Corporal Neachel. (*Bert Dowler*)

Captain H.M. Stephens MC composed this cheerful ditty:

'Tanks in Line'
(to the tune of 'Tales for Vienna Woods' by Strauss)

Tanks, tanks, tanks, in line
Sweeping up towards the Rhine
The First, the Fifth, the Skins, the guns,
We're out to bugger up the Huns.
Cromwells, Honeys, Fireflies too,
A floating punch to see us through.
The Engineers with Scorpions
And troop of Bofors,
Half-a-dozen loafers
And the Navy, nice and wavy,
RAF umbrella, nothing could be sweller,
Deutschland, here we come – run, run.

The First are always at the front,
C Squadron picked to bear the brunt.
The 'iron ring' well at the back,
The Sergeant Major's thrown a track
The fitters then will do the trick,
But only with their usual tick.
The 88s are banging,
The 95s are wamming.
Major Dingwall's slanging
Tank Commanders hazy,
Operators lazy.
Office staffs are playing,
Tank crews are saying
'It's about time we had a brew – too true.'

1 RTR was indeed advancing on the Rhine!

CHAPTER SIXTEEN

Operation Plunder: on to Berlin

The division remained in its positions overlooking the Maas, with 1 RTR initially at Andenberg then at Bree, supporting 1 Queens, 9 DLI or 2 Devons with patrols and indirect shooting. On 21 February the division went into reserve, having been relieved by the 8th US Armored Division, and spent seven weeks training, re-equipping, being inspected by Brass Hats and playing football and boxing, around Weert and Bree. Firing ranges were sited at Lommel and Zomeren. On 26 February Monty visited 1 RTR and on 6 March the brigade commander inspected 'A' Squadron's cookhouse, 'B' Squadron personnel and 'C' Squadron tanks! Operation Veritable had been a long, dangerous attritional slog in mud and rain through the intricate pill-box defences of the Siegfried Line. Now Operation Plunder was planned for the crossing of the Rhine and the invasion of Germany. Part of General Neil Ritchie's XII Corps, the Desert Rats' centre line of advance was to be towards Bremen, via Borken, Stadtlohn, Ahaus and Rheine.

Trooper R.G. Knight of 5 Troop, 'C' Squadron, recalled:

> First we had to cross the Rhine but all the hard work had been done by the time we got there [by the airborne forces, commandos and 15th Scottish Division]. The assembly areas and roads leading to the river were very congested because we had just the one pontoon bridge to use [at Hamminkeln, 2 miles from Wesel]. The Rhine was far wider than any other river I had crossed before. On the other side I could see scores of gliders, some landed safely, some had crashed, others were burnt out.

The regiment arrived in Walbeck on the 25th, and sent an advance party over the Rhine the next day to organise a regimental harbour. On the 27th 1 RTR crossed the Rhine, with RHQ leading, followed by Recce, 'C', 'A' and 'B' Squadrons. They were following the Yellow route via Raesfeld, and soon captured Heiden against light opposition, seizing 18 guns and their crews, 10 lorries and 60 prisoners. Some 50 enemy soldiers were killed. The next day was more difficult. Directed north to Ramsdorf, and having passed a large ammunition dump in Heiden burning fiercely, 'B' Squadron lost a tank to a bazooka. As the rest attempted to cross over a stream by a flimsy wooden bridge, it collapsed under the weight. SSM Leonard Dauncey won the Military Medal when he organised a party of men to build a ford or causeway. For three hours, under mortars and sniper fire, which wounded three men, Dauncey and his helpers finally succeeded and 'C' Squadron got across the stream. Rain was falling and crews were reluctant to go off the roads on to the soft fields. On the main road the Reconnaissance Troop met bazooka teams in the centre of Ramsdorf, which knocked out two Honeys and held up the advance for four hours. The 1st RB helped to clear the town and then 'C' Squadron arrived, crossing another stream via a fascine built by German prisoners. 'A' Echelon lost a marked ambulance to an SP gun. Casualties during the day were 4 killed and 8 wounded. The regiment then returned to Sudlohn to clear the centre line for 11th Armoured Division to pass through. The enemy in front had been identified as two battalions of 857 Grenadier Regiment and 33 Panzer Grenadier Ersatz Battalion with infantry, SP guns, 88mm anti-tank guns and many Panzerfaust bazooka teams. On the right wing of the 22 Armoured Brigade front 1 RTR encountered some heavy fighting. The CO wrote:

On March 30 the regiment was ordered to move north through Sudlohn and Stadtlohn to Ahaus, Heek and Rheine. 5th Dragoon Guards with 4th DLI had the task of leading to Stadtlohn, which they found occupied at midday. The clearing operations took some time and it was not until 1600 that 1 RTR was able to pass through. 'B' Squadron led the right on a subsidiary road while 'A' Squadron was echeloned back moving down the main road.

Soon after moving out of Stadtlohn both squadrons found themselves faced by a thick wood which extended for five miles down the two axes about half-way to Ahaus, the main objective. Both squadrons were held up and the ground was too soft for movement off the road. Several tanks were knocked out by SP guns and, as it grew dark, the wood appeared to be alive with enemy who were now getting bolder and attempting to capture the crews of the burning tanks.

The advance was to be continued by night, for which task each squadron was supported by 'A' Company of the 1/5th Queens in armoured personnel carriers. The task appeared to be a formidable one; however, it was a moonlight night. Good leadership and a midnight charge, as so often before, did the trick and by 0230 the leading tanks of 'A' Squadrons were in Ahaus, having advanced ten miles.

During the advance, enemy rear installations and billets were shot up and many cars were burnt. To our certain knowledge the enemy lost ninety men killed, wounded or prisoners. The casualties to the unit were two officers and one other rank.

Ahaus was cleared by the 1/5 Queens during the morning of March 31, but about midday the 11th Hussars patrolling north of the town were held up, so 1 RTR was called upon to resume the advance with the object of capturing the villages of Heek and Nienburg ten miles to the north. After cross-country fighting by 'A' and 'C' Squadrons throughout the afternoon, the main road was opened before dark by 'B' Squadron. The villages of Heek and Nienburg were occupied by 1 RTR on the morning of April 1.

Major Tom Craig, OC 'B' Squadron, wrote of

the all-night thrust with 'A' Squadron on the main road, B on a minor road to the right with C initially close behind in reserve. We had infantry in APCs and CC Battery 5 RHA in close support, 'artificial moonlight' to light our way and covered some 10 miles before dawn. It wasn't plain sailing with opposition from an SP gun and the inevitable hand-held Panzerfaust anti-tank weapons. We sadly lost two tanks. Captain Martin Stephens my 2 i/c was badly wounded and died some weeks later. Captain 'Freezer' Frost 2 i/c of C Squadron on foot for a recce was shot dead by our own infantry. Chris Vickery and his crew were all wounded by a bazooka.

When Captain Frost was killed SSM Dauncey of 'C' Squadron took over command of the two CS tanks of HQ Squadron. When 'C' Squadron was ambushed Dauncey brought down quick and accurate fire. 'On the 30 March advance out of Stadtlohn, into a thick wood where the two leading tanks, Lieutenant Simmonds, Sergeant Johnstone, were bazooka'd and brewed. Trooper Justice was killed, Lieutenant Simmonds wounded and four men captured,' wrote Major Pile of 'A' Squadron. 'Ahaus captured in under an hour from the time we left Stadtlohn . . . 'A' Squadron reduced to 7 tanks as many were bogged in the soft ground.' Pile described Lieutenant Bob MacGregor DCM, MM, as 'a man of immense courage, skill and as far as fighting was concerned, cunning'.

Captain H.B.C. Watkins has written a detailed account of the capture of Ahaus, and Major F. Pile has described the 7-mile advance, attack and capture of Heek. Lieutenant R.R. MacGregor of 'A' Squadron led all the way, knocking out anti-tank guns, mortars and machine-gunners. Major William Mather, OC 'C' Squadron, won the Military Cross in the Heek engagement. After the leading tanks were knocked out and his scout-car had been ditched, he regrouped his squadron and pressed on, taking forty prisoners and preventing the Heek bridge from being blown.

On the 31 March 1 RTR suffered fourteen casualties. Major Pile estimated that at least 25 Panzerfausts had been fired at his squadron and ordered his troop leaders to go flat out to defeat the bazooka parties lying in ambush. Usually the combined armour/infantry tactics were successful – often with 1/5th Queens and frequently with the motorised 1st Rifle Brigade.

Metelen was the concentration area for the first three days of April. Major Tom Craig, OC 'B' Squadron, reflected on the battles for Stadtlohn, Ahaus and Meek:

It was really worth it all, in spite of losses, because we realised that we had broken through the main enemy opposition. As the ground and going improved, so we were able to move off roads, bypass bottlenecks, towns and villages. With our well-known RHA FOOs up with us any kind of opposition located was quickly 'stonked' by the guns of 3rd or 5th RHA – on occasion the whole of the divisional artillery.

The advance between the main river and canal barriers was almost reminiscent of the September 'Great Swan', as Major Freddy Pile relates:

As the advance started we normally moved down roads or tracks for speed; one troop (a different one each day as it was a demanding and frequently dangerous role) would be ordered to lead the squadron. Squadron HQ would come next and the four other (reserve) troops behind. Nearly always, after a short time, we made some degree of contact with the enemy. Sometimes it might be a small detachment – perhaps some infantry in personnel carriers with a few motor cycles; on other occasions it would be something more solid – possibly two or three tanks or self-propelled guns which could, with their superior guns, inflict enormous damage on our Cromwell tanks if these were caught in the open. If the enemy resistance was quite minor the leading troop would deal with it with its own fire power, then continue the advance as soon as possible. If, on the other hand, the opposition was clearly substantial the troop would 'fan' out off the road under cover, keeping the enemy under observation. At that stage I would go forward in my Dingo to speak to the troop leader and to see the situation at first hand; if I did not consider he could deal quickly with the enemy position I would make a plan to outflank it by using my reserve troops (or some of them) to move across country. Often I would accompany the outflanking troops to ensure that they got to the right place to engage the enemy effectively. By this means the enemy position could often be dislodged and the advance continued. If all our efforts failed, and we started sustaining heavy losses, the commanding officer would almost certainly come forward and would bring in another squadron, or possibly supporting infantry or guns to assist. We were required to keep going at all costs, and enemy resistance had to be overcome without much delay or there would be sharp criticism on the radio from our Brigade HQ. Despite any plea that one was incurring heavy losses and was therefore being a bit more cautious, the instruction from above was always the same – 'Sorry, but you must press on regardless.' The phrase 'pocket of resistance' is rather a misnomer; it was usually a small but very well-armed mixed group of tanks, guns and infantry. They were normally sited on a main approach road, or in a wood or village which it was difficult for us to circumvent. Because we often ran into them without much warning we had casualties quite out of proportion to the size and importance of many of these actions. Perhaps it is understandable therefore that, as we approached towns or villages, we often used incendiary machine-gun ammunition and set fire to the houses in the path of our intended advance. This, of course, did cause much damage.

On 4 April the regiment advanced through Bourgsteinfurt and Techlenburg (bypassing the fanatical resistance on the Teutoburger Wald) towards Halen with the task of protecting the centre line from Halen to Hinter. On the same day another hero of Tobruk, Lieutenant-Colonel Rea Leakey, became CO 5 RTR. On the next day 'A' Squadron pushed patrols forward to the bridges over the River Weser and the Ems Canal to Branen – both had been blown – but the Recce Troop found two bridges over the river prepared for demolition but still intact. During the 5th forty prisoners were taken and ten assorted 88mm, 40mm and 20mm guns were captured.

During the night of 5th/6th the regiment with 1 RB advanced east to capture Nienburg. 'C' and 'A' led, with 'B' in reserve, via Stemsholm and Liebenau. But at Kirchdorf new orders were received to move north-eastwards via Barenberg and Siedenberg to Hoya (due south of Bremen) and Suligen was bypassed. Lieutenant-Colonel Pat Hobart decided to try a night attack to seize the Hoya bridge. At midnight 'A' Squadron swept down the centre line flat out with all guns blazing and, despite two roads being blocked, covered 40 miles in the night, finding just before dawn that two bridges had been blown. During the next day seven more bridges were reccied; some had been blown and the rest were very well covered. 1 RTR took 270 prisoners during the day and caused heavy casualties despite snipers. On the 8th Major Pile's tank was brewed up by one of three SPs. Lieutenant MacGregor in turn knocked out two of them and the third made off. 'B' Squadron moved towards Beppen while 'C' cleared Inshede and then moved south-east to Rehr and Ritzenbergen; between them they disposed of two SPs and 6 guns and caught 30 prisoners. In Twistringen two tanks collided and the unfortunate Lieutenant MacGregor died later of wounds. Corporal Leslie Clarke, a tank gunner, won the Military Medal on the 10th in the wooded Langeloh Forest. His tank was hit by a bazooka, killing its commander outright and badly wounding the operator and leaving the turret ablaze. Clarke calmly directed fire from the BESA and after an hour managed to put out the fire.

'B' Squadron in action north of Harpstedt. (*Tom Craig*)

The River Weser, running south from Bremen, was being strongly defended. With 2 Devons the regiment captured Harpstedt despite resistance from panzer grenadiers and this opened up three roads for an advance. Finally on the 13th 1 RTR crossed the River Weser at Drakenberg and the CO discussed plans, not for an attack on Bremen, which in the event needed four British infantry divisions for its capture, but for an advance to the River Elbe.

Major Tom Craig, OC 'B' Squadron, had been deeply upset when SS cadet troops escaping from Ibbenburen had retreated to the north-east ahead of 7th Armoured Division. They specialised in ambushing HQs and B vehicles, letting the Cromwells pass through. In this way they killed Captain John Cordy-Simpson in the forest of Langeloh:

> We had a lucky stroke of revenge shortly after John was killed. North of Soltau, the usual stand-to at dawn, we moved on 16th towards the village of Jarlingen. After checking an abandoned SP gun, I was right behind my leading troop, was astonished to see marching across a T-junction about 300 yards ahead, a group of about forty SS cadets marching towards the village towing eight carts, laden we discovered later, with Panzerfausts and ammunition. I quickly ordered the troop behind me to go off round to the left to stop the cadets getting into the village, brought the Squadron HQ and remaining troop up into line and all opened fire at once with every weapon we had and firing HE into the trees above the cadets. It was quickly over. There were no SS survivors.

Trooper Peterson won the Military Medal as a gunner in the leading troop. His tank was hit by a bazooka near Jarlingen village. His commander was badly wounded and Petersen took over; grabbing a Sten gun from the top of

Benny Branson's Cromwell, 'C' Squadron 1 RTR. (*Reg Spittles*)

the turret he shot dead the SS officer who had fired the bazooka. He then withdrew the Cromwell, firing both the hull BESA and Sten, until he reached cover so that his commander could receive treatment.

Now across the River Aller, the Desert Rats liberated Fallingbostel prisoner-of-war camp, which contained some 10,000 British/US PoWs. Many small villages were occupied or captured, including Freilingen, Fulde, Hunzingen, Widingen, Schneverdingen, Welle, Sprengel and Wesseloh. Each day prisoners were taken and bazooka parties and snipers encountered, but there was nothing to match the scale of the defence of Rethem. This town, south-west of Walsrode, was guarded by a determined Marine Brigade which had given the 53rd Welsh Division a hard time. 'We were on the road to Hamburg, via Ramsdorf, Stadtlohn and Soltau. Sometimes we would be speeding down roads, sometimes feeling our way through towns and villages. Too often we were clearing pockets of resistance. These were the worst, usually in woods and with no idea of what the Germans had lined up against us. We were glad to have infantry with us to guide us through and happy to give them support when needed,' wrote Trooper R.G. Knight, a 'C' Squadron Cromwell tank gunner.

Sergeant Donnelly was an expert in bazookas, having survived eight attacks by the 18th. In the thick wood near Tostedt the ninth attack put out of action his tank's 75mm gun and BESA. Despite heavy small arms fire, he used a Sten gun and grenades most effectively, personally killing five of the enemy. Later on he returned with infantry flame-throwing carriers (WASPS) to clear the wood.

Captain H.M. Stevens joined 1 RTR in Normandy and was twice recommended for the Military Cross and was later awarded it. Later on he commanded both 'B' and 'C' Squadrons in action. He wrote this little lyric:

> I'm a rambler, I'm a rambler, I'm a long way from home
> If you don't like me just leave me alone
> Johnnie Dingwall's our Fuehrer
> Pat Hobart's Sieg Heil
> And if I'm not bazooka'd, I'll live till I die.

Sadly, on 30 March west of Ahaus, as 'Steve' was firing a Bren gun from his tank turret, he was severely wounded and was paralysed from the waist down.

If the resistance was difficult, an RHA 'stonk' was usually sufficient to subdue the defenders; against really tough defences RAF Typhoons – occasionally a cab rank of them – would be requested. They frightened friend and foe alike!

North of Schnevendingen on the way to Welle, Major Craig of 'B' Squadron encountered a Cherry Picker armoured car by a lone farmhouse observing a well-hidden 88mm anti-tank gun in scrub by the side of the road 'just waiting for us'. He was indeed lying in wait, and his fourth shot hit SSM Paddy Caulfield's Cromwell.

It damaged the storage bins on the side. We all made a rapid 'high reverse shunt' into cover. My mad Irish SSM said, 'It's all right, Sir all the Squadron rum is in the other containers.' He'd been saving it up for the end of the war. We then brought artillery fire down on the gun which was firing at every movement. I then launched an attack with two troops of tanks supported by all of us and some smoke shells, but two tanks were hit and commanders killed so we pulled back. Finally it took a flight of four RAF Typhoons to fix the anti-tank gun for good with their rockets.

Many German houses hung out white sheets to indicate surrender, but the Germans – now mainly Volksturm (Home Guard), very young Hitler youths, Wehrmacht with disabilities (stomach or other problems) and occasionally, as in Rethem, marines or grounded Flak or Luftwaffe ground troops – often fought with desperation as the Third Reich crumbled about them. On the 18th the defences in the wooded country around Todtglusingen, with SP guns and 88mm anti-tank guns, were so strong that both artillery concentrations and Typhoons were needed.

Dibbersen, Emsen and Dangersen were cleared on the 20th and 21st. 'C' Squadron was lent to the 53rd Welsh Division and the next day an Allied prisoner-of-war camp was liberated. 'A' Squadron was in Soltau, 'B' in Bispingen and 'C' at Hozingen supporting Welsh infantry battalions. Sergeant E.J. Stennett of C Squadron won the Military Medal in two consecutive actions at Onegan on the 21st, when he silenced several Spandau positions, reccied an important bridge on foot and returned – despite sniping – with a full report. The next day in action at Harber he knocked out an 80mm hollow-charge anti-tank gun, engaged and destroyed a second, captured at the far end of the village a 75mm anti-tank gun and its crew and finally advanced with his troop 2,000 yards to high ground and destroyed an armoured car and a lorry!

The 23rd was a 'field' day. The War Diary stated: 'Opposition had virtually collapsed and final PoW bag was at least 1,200, and MET destroyed or captured 33, and 19 Panzerfaust written off.' 1 RTR moved back to the Dibbensen area in reserve. Lieutenant-Colonel Pat Hobart, the CO, wrote a report on the lessons to be learned from the 'Great Swan' advance from the Rhine, on 25 March to 20 April, including topics such as clearing villages, road-blocks, bridges, stream crossings, bazookas, static positions, night advances and rapid advances.

Major-General L.O. Lyne, the Desert Rats GOC, and Brigadier Wingfield of the 22nd Armoured Brigade visited the regiment on the 24th. 'Finally we arrived at the outskirts of Harburg, just south of Hamburg. For a couple of days all the tanks were lined up and we fired as if we were artillery by setting the guns on bearings,' recalled Trooper R.G. Knight.

Offensive patrolling and minor skirmishes continued during the last week of April. The last tank in 1 RTR, probably in 7th Armoured Division, was knocked out on the 27th. It was from 'C' Squadron. In April the Regiment had suffered 22 casualties and lost only 5 tanks (many hit were subsequently repaired). The Recce Troop south of Glusingen engaged in an official psychological war by broadcasting an amplified message in German from a Chaffee tank, suggesting, even recommending, that the marine defenders in the south Hamburg defences should surrender. The remnants of the German First Parachute Army were still trying to escape northwards to the Elbe crossings and ferries. Prisoners were swept into the divisional cages every day – SS troops, parachutists, submarine crews, stevedores from Hamburg docks, policemen and firemen, Volksturm, cadets, Hitler Youth, Flak and Luftwaffe units – but they had contested every yard of the marshy areas and the forests and Luneburg Heath.

1 RTR remained in reserve around the autobahn north of Buchholz. On 2 May staff cars with negotiators for the surrender of Hamburg came through the regimental lines to Divisional HQ and thence to Commander 21st Army Group. The next day 1 RTR moved into Hamburg with 9 DLI to seize and hold the eight road and rail bridges into the city from the south and to occupy the dock area. Admiral Doenitz had told General Keitel to order General Alwin Wolz to surrender the city. Lieutenant-Colonel Wainman with the Cherry Pickers was first into Hamburg. They had conducted with panache their own desert war in 1940 and, like 1 RTR, had been fighting ever since. Now they had led the Desert Rats to the final victory.

The CO went on leave on the 4th and Major Johnny Dingwall assumed command. That night at 2000 hours news of the cessation of hostilities in north-west Europe was announced to the regiment at Rellingen.

Major Tom Craig, OC 'B' Squadron, recalled:

> We started to move into Hamburg on 3 May over the great Elbe bridges. My squadron was ordered to occupy Blohm and Voss's shipyards. We were astonished to find in large covered sheds, several new ocean-going U-boats on the slipways virtually completed and ready for launching. We also took the surrender of a fully manned huge Flak tower quite undamaged, [which] soared above all the wrecked buildings in the area. A day or two later we moved off north towards the Kiel Canal in Schleswig-Holstein with maps marked all the way to the Danish frontier. We were in the neighbourhood of Pinneburg and Elmshorn when the CO suddenly came on the air and said 'The war is over – I say again the war is over!' He added: 'You all can say or do anything you want to, but after that, calm down and get back on "net"'. We all came to a speedy halt, guns and Very lights were fired in the air. We all cheered and shook hands and were so happy that unbelievably the war was really over. But at the same time we thought of all of our friends who had not survived or who had been disabled and most of all, of our loved ones at home. It was an unforgettable moment.

Craig then celebrated the official VE-Day and the end of the war by flying under all the bridges of the Kiel Canal in an Auster aircraft of the divisional Air OP Flight!

'The advance to Hamburg did not unfortunately leave us unscathed,' recalled Major Freddy Pile. 'We lost 3 officers and 17 ORs (either killed or wounded), a quarter of our tank crew strength, in under three weeks, including Captain G.E. Cordy-Simpson, the 2 i/c killed in the Forest of Langeloh and Lieutenant J. Noble badly wounded by a sniper on the autobahn.'

The 5th was spent according to the War Diary as 'Consciousness with many hangovers' but with a possible move to Denmark on the cards. But no, it was to the Kiel Canal area at Thaden. Winston Churchill spoke on the radio on the 8th and announced there would be two VE-Days. King George VI spoke at 2100 hours and afterwards a giant bonfire was lit by firing into it a mass of Very lights. The SSMs had by now 'released' their hoarded rum to the thirsty participants. The War Diary recorded: 'The fireworks display put Crystal Palace to shame.' Operation Eclipse was then mounted to collect and confine German troops into three peninsulas on the west coast of Schleswig-Holstein. The next day Major Dingwall addressed all ranks on their role in Eclipse but also explained the necessity for an immediate and severe improvement in the standard of turn-out and discipline. Captain M. Jewell was the adjutant, and he and RSM E.C. Foote soon transformed the war-battered tinkers into respectability. On the 20th Lieutenant-Colonel Pat Hobart returned and resumed command.

1 RTR officers at Gluckstadt, Germany, VJ-Day, 1945. Back row, left to right: Captain Stan Camfield MM, Lieutenant Alan Parks, Derek ?, Lieutenant Keith Dyson, Lieutenant Peter Henderson, George ? (REME), Captain Freddy Simmonds, Captain Brian Watkins, Lieutenant Chris Vickery, ? Wycke, -?-, Second Lieutenant Stan Witherridge, Captain (QM) Charles Foot. Second row: Captain 'Pip' Williams, Eric ?, Captain George Finden, -?-, Captain M. Jewell (Adjutant), Captain Derek Bowling-Smith MC, Lieutenant Vic Tilly, Johnnie ?, -?-, Captain Jack Clemson. Front Row: Lieutenant Tom Stanton MM, Lieutenant Tom Harland DCM, Major Johnie Dingwall DSO (2 i/c), Lieutenant-Colonel Pat Hobart DSO, OBE, MC (CO), Major Jack Greenwood OBE (HQ Sqn), Major Tom Craig MC ('B' Sqn), Captain Frank Gutteridge, Lieutenant Alan ?, Second Lieutenant Joe Newton. Absent Major Freddy Pile MC ('A' Sqn), Major Bill Mather MC ('C' Sqn), Captain Jack Storey (recce troop). (*Tom Craig*)

From Gluckstadt 1 RTR moved back to Lommel in Belgium to collect new Comet tanks (11th Armoured was the only division to have Comets for Operation Plunder) before returning to Itzehoe. The move to Berlin came in late July to Gatow barracks, and was followed by participation in the large international Victory Parade with the Russian Marshal Zhukov taking the salute. Another parade was put on to mark Field Marshal Montgomery's appointment as Colonel Commandant of the Royal Tank Regiment.

★ ★ ★

The regiment had come a long way from the Western Desert. Among the many heroes were the names of Carver, Leakey, Holliman, Hynes, Hobart, Harland, MacGregor, Moat and many, many others. But even more were left behind, buried in well-kept cemeteries in North Africa and north-west Europe.

Salute to the 1st Royal Tank Regiment

We've travelled far since '39
From Alamein across the Rhine;
The road was paved with sweat and blood,
Our pals that fell asleep in its mud.

Side by side we fought together
In scorching sun and filthy weather,
Through sand and wadis across the blue
We stopped just only for a brew.

We cursed this thing they called a tank,
Inside of which the air was rank;
Cordite fumes and stinks untold,
Hellish nights that were freezing cold.

Italy, with its cypress groves:
Huns fought hard, they fell in droves;
Italian skies that shed the sun,
Bloody battles fought and won.

Thoughts of Dover's cliffs so grand:
Homeward bound for our native land;
Leave with loved ones missed so much,
Fireside radio, Bing and Hutch.

Months of liberty, love and cheer,
Until that historic day drew near:
Working hard night and day,
Preparing for another fray.

Came the night the fourth of June:
We sailed without the Channel moon;
Here it is the shore at last,
Countless memories of beach-heads past.

Into the water, up the beach,
Caen objective, soon to reach,
Not without its toll of life:
Toil and sweat, blood and strife.

Battling on through countless miles,
Each one brought its tears and smiles:
Holland, Belgium, now the Rhine,
Bringing war home to the swine.

'V-Day' is here and soon 'VJ',
Time now for a holiday;
No more war but lasting peace,
End of black-out, lend-and-lease.

Now are the days of spit and shine,
The ENSAs good, the Winston fine;
Tanks are gleaming like a pin,
For the march-past in Berlin.

Roll on swiftly now demob.
Put us back in our civvy job;
The work is easy, sport is fine,
But how I miss that home of mine.

Danny Bourne, Tony Patterson and Reg Knott,
'C' Squadron, Berlin
November 1945

Part Two

Second to None
(2 RTC/RTR)

CHAPTER SEVENTEEN

2 RTC/RTR in the First World War

The author acknowledges an immense debt to Kenneth Chadwick's *Seconds Out* and is grateful to his family for permission to quote from it.

'B' Company, Heavy Section, Machine-Gun Corps, was formed at Bullhouse camp, Surrey, in May 1916 from 'D' and 'K' companies, Armoured Car Services. Most of the 250 officers and men came from Cambridgeshire, Bedfordshire, Norfolk, Suffolk, East Kent or London. The company commander was Major T.R. McLellan from the Cameronians regiment.

In July the company moved to Elvedon camp, Thetford, and trained with Vickers and Hotchkiss machine-guns and 6-pdr guns. In 'John O'Groats camp' tanks were shown for the first time – they were still a highly secret species, but driving instructions and demonstrations took place. What the men saw, the Mk I tank, was still in very short supply and 'B' Company eventually only received its *own* tanks for training in January 1917 – *after* they had arrived in France. Captain Vandervell sailed for France on 30 September 1916 with 2 and 3 Sections, each with five crews, followed two weeks later by 1 and 4 Sections under Captain Bennewith and Captain Lord Rodney. The total strength of the tankless company was 255 all ranks. The troopship *Caesarea* berthed at Le Havre, and troop trains took the company on to Acheux. On 18 November the company was renamed 'B' Battalion, but it was not until 2 January 1917 that three Mk I tanks for each of the six companies were collected. The battalion workshops were erected at Pierremont.

Courses were arranged in map reading and sketching the battle terrain, reconnaissance (often to be done on foot in front of the tank or tanks), signalling (using flags, discs and wireless), gunnery (for both Lewis guns and 6-pdrs), visual training (VT), use of compass and revolver, and the basics of foot drill and PT – and of course handling pigeons!

The battle practice range was sited in a valley 1,500 yards north-west of Fleury and the Lewis gun range was near Sautricourt. 'C' and 'D' Companies had been the first to land in France and had seen action – with thirty-six of the original Mk I tanks – in September 1916. The male (gun) tanks were equipped with 57mm guns, the female (machine-gun) tanks with Vickers water-cooled machine-guns. Powered by a 105hp Daimler engine, the Mk Is were unreliable and slow (up to 4mph). It took four of the eight-man crew to operate the three separate gear-boxes. Accurate and precise teamwork was needed in the noisy, cramped and stifling conditions. The special tail wheels that acted as a steering aid and counter-balance were quickly discarded. However, the practical tank expert Lieutenant-Colonel E.D. Swinton had followed the adventures of 'C', 'D' and 'A' Companies in November 1916 and subsequently wrote his *Notes on the Employment of Tanks*:

It emphasised that the simplest and surest way of destroying entrenched machine-guns was 'by rolling over the emplacements and crushing them. Hostile machine-guns which it is impossible or inconvenient to crush will be attacked by gunfire'. This would usually be done by moving close to 'pour in shell at point-blank range'. If progress was quick, however, the tanks might soon approach the German artillery position, and then in that case should open fire at long range. 'The 6-pdr guns firing at reduced charges will give accurate shooting up to a range of 2,000 yards, and they can be fitted with telescopic sights so that full advantage may be taken of a chance of this nature should it occur.'

For communication with the rear the tanks should not be entirely dependent on the accompanying infantry. Alternative means were under experiment; they were that, first, about one tank in ten should be equipped 'with small wireless telegraphy sets'; second, equipping a similar proportion 'with apparatus for laying a field telephone cable'; third, a system for visual signalling to the tanks from the starting-line by means of miniature kite balloons; fourth, a system of signalling *from* the tanks by smoke rocket.

The tanks would probably be put out of action by any kind of high-explosive shell, and also by land-mines. 'Special stress is laid on the vulnerability of the tanks to artillery of different natures as it represents their chief weakness . . .' The risk might be reduced by indirect measures, such as counter-battery fire.

Since the chance of success of an attack by tanks lies almost entirely in its novelty and in the element of surprise, it is obvious that no repetition of it will have the same opportunity of succeeding the first unexpected effort. It follows, therefore, that these machines *should not be used in driblets* (for instance, as they may be produced), but that the fact of their existence should be kept as secret as possible until the whole are ready to be launched, together with the infantry assault, in one great combined operation.

The sector of attack 'should be carefully chosen to comply with the limitations, i.e. their inability to cross canals, rivers, deep railway cuttings with steep sides, or woods and orchards'.

At the end of 1916 'B' Company became 'B' Battalion with 4, 5 and 6 Companies.

The winter of 1916/17 was long and hard. For a three-week period tankodromes previously knee-deep in mud were now knee-deep in frozen mud, and every tank was of course firmly grounded! Fuel was scarce and billets were wretched. The officers in their Armstrong huts fared as badly. March 1917 saw the introduction of dummy tanks (nicknamed LLs after a certain lady entertainer). Made of canvas and wooden struts, they were crewed by seven troopers and in movement resembled a startled centipede. The result was an 'attack' on Galampin and Libessart. But tanks sent to practise on the German trenches at Wailly near Arras found them deep and wide and difficult to cross. On 18 May 1917 the first Mk IV tanks were drawn. They had the same engine and transmission as the Mk Is but had thicker armour, an external fuel tank and improved reliability and safety, and eventually 1,200 were built. Three sections were equipped with four Mk IVs and the remaining section had six supply tanks.

The battle of Messines started on 7 June 1917. The battalion started from Zwartemolenhoek, and preparations for the attack were thorough. Observation posts on Kemmel Hill and Hill 63 had excellent views ahead. Practice artillery barrages were carried out daily and of course cratered and churned-up the attack ground! Out of 36 fighting and 6 supply tanks employed, 19 and 4 respectively were back at the rallying points and ready for action again the next morning.

Of the 72 tanks of the brigade ('A' and 'B' Battalions) supporting X, XI and II Anzac Corps, 40 launched from the start line and 27 reached the first Blue line where tank/infantry cooperation was to start. Most rendered valuable help in the reduction of Fannys Farm, Lumms Farm, Staenyzer and Wytschaete.

Major E.D. Bryce's 6 Company had one section working with the 25th Division in the attack on the Black Line north of the New Zealand Division's sector, another section with the 36th Division for the attack on Wytschaete and the third in reserve for the Anzac II Corps. Second Lieutenant B.R. Clarke reached and dealt with Wytschaete and Second Lieutenant M.A. Tuite engaged a hostile battery successfully. Second Lieutenant N.H. Hallam won the Military Cross for unditching his tank under fire, while Lance-Corporal L.C. Hill won the Military Medal, as did Pte L. Donaldson.

Major J.D. Bingham's 4 Company supported the New Zealand Division attacking Messines. Many tanks were bogged in the Steenbeck stream and five ditched in the German first line of trenches, but two tanks, those of Second Lieutenant C.E. Rice and Second Lieutenant W.G.A. Whittle, cooperated in the capture of the Black Line defences and Pte W. Green was awarded the Military Medal.

Major F. Tucker's 5 Company took part in the attack on the Osttaverne line. Captain B.E. Dudgeon took his section south of Messines ahead of the infantry and achieved his objectives. Lieutenant F. Vans Agnew and Corporal R.A. Tait won the Military Cross and Military Medal respectively by putting out a fire caused by enemy shelling, moving about in the open under machine-gun fire and shelling. The other two sections went north of Messines, in support of the infantry. The Blauwepoertbeck stream bogged four tanks, but three (those of Lieutenant W.L. Hoyland, Lieutenant G.E. Porte and Second Lieutenant G.E.V. Thompson) reached the Osttaverne line successfully. Captain R.C. Knight won the Military Cross for early reconnaissance of no-man's-land before the attack. On 11 June 'B' Battalion returned to Giles camp. Casualties in the battle of Messines were 3 officers and 5 ORs killed in action and 12 officers and 43 ORs wounded. Congratulations were sent to the 2nd Brigade Heavy Branch ('A' and 'B' Battalions under Lieutenant-Colonel A. Courage) from the GOC Second Army, from the Corps Commander and from the GOC 3rd Australian Division.

Lieutenant-Colonel R.C. Hill DSO commanded 'B' Battalion and endured many inspections by Brass Hats, including those by Major-General J.E. Capper (Director-General of the Heavy Brigade, Machine-Gun Corps), Brigadier-General H.J. Elles DSO (the senior tank officer in France), General Plumer and, on the 26th, the King and Queen of the Belgians. On 4 July King George V and the Prince of Wales visited 'B' Battalion. On this occasion, 'B' Battalion, as well as taking the King for a ride, staged a demonstration of tank action over a steeplechase course. The war correspondents wrote vivid accounts of the terrifying agility of these 'Leviathans' and 'Behemoths', but a more illuminating inside story of the spectacular final turn is provided by Lieutenant-Colonel Alan Scrutton, who was then a senior subaltern in 'B' Battalion:

July 1917. There was a very solid concrete cover to an ammunition dump in a hedge, and my recollection of it is that the approach at the back was probably some 15ft high, and the descent in front to much lower ground was probably about 25/30ft. It was decided to ramp the approach at the back with earth and sods, to give the tank a grip, and let it come down the front and see what happened. To avoid spoiling the surprise or leaving marks, a descent was not tried before the event. The battalion therefore waited in the field below, opposite the descent, and the King was placed just in front and everyone waited with bated breath. The tank, under the command of a very cheery little subaltern called Haseler – who was afterwards killed – came up with a great deal of noise, appeared on the flat top, balanced for a second on the crown of the descent and as it dropped, inch by inch, it suddenly lost all grip and shot to the bottom, burying its nose several feet in the mud of the field below, in front of His Majesty. We all stood holding our breath, wondering whether anyone inside was still alive when, to our amazement, after a short pause, the tank went slowly on its way and came to a level keel alongside the King. Out hopped Haseler and two other men, looking very shaken, but Haseler, with a grin all over his face, made light of it and was congratulated by the king, who, of course, had no idea that the remainder of the crew were still inside the tank unconscious!

Alan Scrutton also tells the story of a visit from the King and Queen of the Belgians, who came to express their thanks for the liberation of Messines and Wytschaete:

Again we planned a steeplechase course, and this was to finish with a race between a male and female tank. The female tank had been specially cleaned inside, had a strip of carpet down and a chair for the Queen to sit in, and this tank was to win the race – the male tank merely being a stooge. I – because of my ADC experience – was detailed to act in the same capacity, and happened to be standing near the King when the preparations were made for this race. When King Albert saw the Queen hopping into the female tank helped by General Gough, he turned to me and indicated that he wished to get into the male tank. I was completely at a loss what to do because I knew it was filthy and he would have a very uncomfortable journey, but he insisted, handed me his cane (which had a beautiful Belgian lion carved out of the top) and got in. All went according to plan, the Queen's tank won the race and she emerged, helped out by General Gough. The King did not seem nearly so pleased at his very rough journey in a filthy tank in which everything he touched had been red hot!

Field Marshal Haig now planned a new offensive east of Ypres. It was a very wet summer so the water table was high, artillery had smashed up the terrain, wrecking any drainage systems, and reconnaissance was impossible

The cap badge of the Tank Corps from 28 July 1917 until it became the Royal Tank Corps on 18 October 1923. (*Tank Museum*)

apart from balloons which were of course promptly shot down. In short, it was the worst possible scenario – 28-ton tanks would have to progress through a quagmire. Aerial photographs of water-filled shell-holes and the pockmarked battlefield showed that a successful attack was unlikely. Still Field Marshals always know best.

The battle of Ypres was destined to last from 30 June to 5 September 1917. 'B' Battalion was supporting 2nd Corps to try to establish a new line to include Broodseinde through Noordeurhoek, through the centre of Polygon de Zonnebeke, south-east of Veldhoek, with the right of II Corps' sector being midway between Zillebeke and Zanduoorde. The approach march started on 28 June and almost immediately 6 Company was subjected to heavy shelling (gas, HE and shrapnel) and there were 7 officers and 33 OR casualties before the fourteen tanks reached Valley Cottages. The CO sent an officer of 4 Company to check that the camouflage at the rendezvous was effective. There was a heavy thunderstorm during which lightning struck the crew down, possibly because of their tin hats. Major B.M. Jager's 4 Company was in reserve and waited at Elton Point. The other two companies supported 18th, 24th and 30th Divisions in the attack on the 2nd, 3rd and 4th defence line objectives.

It was not a success. No. 5 Company got eight out of twelve tanks into action around Bodmin Copse and Dumbarton Woods. Four of these were disabled by direct artillery hits, two became ditched and two returned to the rallying point. Major E.D. Bryce's 6 Company got five of its ten tanks into action. Lieutenant A.C. Harcourt's 9 Section was in action west of Inverness Copse and Glencorse Wood, but three ditched and one was knocked out. One of these losses was that of Second Lieutenant C.M. Evans. When his first tank broke down he transferred to another and went back into action, subsequently winning the Military Cross. Major Bryce and Corporal N. McGuire won the Distinguished Service Order and Distinguished Conduct Medal respectively. Captain H.V. Diamond also won the Military Cross and five ORs were awarded the Military Medal. No. 4 Section did not go into action. The battalion lost 2 officers and 6 ORs killed, and 9 officers and 45 ORs wounded or gassed.

On 22 August 4 Company supported 14th Division in an attack on Inverness Copse and Herenthage Château. Two tanks saw action and caused many casualties, and in 3 Section Captain J. Reardon won the Military Cross and Private W.H. Howard the Military Medal. The next day Captain H.B.M. Groves led 1 Section to capture Fitzclarence and L-Shaped Farms. Three tanks led in front of the 14th Division infantry and had a heated action. Groves won the Military Cross trying to get the inexperienced infantry into action and for rescuing a badly wounded officer of his section who was lying in the open. Lance-Corporal A. Daglish received the Military Medal. Three days later Captain Partington led a section of 4 Company forwards but all failed to get into action. In these actions 4 Company suffered 5 officers and 39 OR casualties.

'B' Battalion tanks were usually christened with names starting with the letter B, such as 'Badger', 'Ballybogan', 'Bayardo', 'Beelzebub', 'Bellerophon', 'Bison' and 'Black Night'. ('Barrhead' appears later on!) On 27 October Lieutenant-Colonel Hill left to rejoin the Indian Army, and command passed to Major E.D. Bryce DSO. Captain F.S. Laskey from 'F' Battalion took over command of 6 Company.

A wounded London Territorial described the infantry view of the tanks:

Old Mother Hubbard they called her and lots of funny names as well. She looked like a pantomime animal or a walking ship with iron sides moving along, very slowly, apparently all on her own and with none of her crew visible. There she was groanin' and gruntin' along, pokin' her nose here and there, stopping now and then as if she was not sure of the road and then going on very slow but over everything. It was her slowness that scared us and the way she shook her wicked old head and stopped to cough. It was a circus – my word! She came bumpin' out of the fog at one end of the line and bumped into it again at the other like a great big hippopotamus and with a crowd of Tommies cheering behind.

A great deal of thought had gone into alleviating the problem of ditching. Captain Liddell Hart wrote:

The biggest trouble of all had been due to 'ditching', which happened in many ways. One of the most common was that the tank got its tail down in a trench and so wedged that it had not the grip nor the engine-power to pull the tail out. Another was when one or both tracks sank into soft ground while the belly became fixed on harder ground with the tracks revolving uselessly. Again, the tank might get 'bellied' on a tree-stump or mound. From this experience two devices were evolved. One was the attachment of 'spuds', or iron shoes, clamped at intervals along the tracks when the tanks were used on soft ground. Another was an unditching gear. In the first improvised form this consisted of a pair of wooden spars, strengthened with steel, that could be fastened to each track by chains, and were drawn round under the machine as the tracks turned, so providing a firm purchase by which the tank could extricate itself, climbing out over them. This improvisation was helpful, but not good enough, as the spars were too short and weak. The following summer a superior gear was developed – a single squared beam, weighing nearly half a ton and long enough to stretch slightly beyond the tank's width. Carried on top of the tank, clipped to a pair of rails, it could be lifted down and fastened to the tracks by a couple of men sheltered behind the tank, and then by the revolution of the tracks be pulled forward along the rails, over the nose, and down under the belly. It enabled the tank to climb out of most 'holes'.

Although all the tank operations in the battles of 1916 and 1917 had been in 'penny packets' and widely dispersed, the next great battle planned would involve nine battalions totalling 378 fighting Mk IV tanks plus 54 in reserve. Reports suggested that the German infantry were by now distinctly apprehensive of the approach of the British tanks, although the German artillery were quite happy to take them on.

CHAPTER EIGHTEEN

Cambrai

At the end of October 1917 Sir Douglas Haig and his senior generals were in a very difficult position. Their attack on Passchendaele had failed and a morale-raising victory was urgently needed before winter arrived. A few months earlier Major J.F.C. Fuller had produced a complete plan for a massive tank incursion in the area south of Cambrai. The German General Ludendorff was confident in the strong defences there, known as the Hindenburg Line. A 40ft-deep trench was thought impassable, and a wide zone of wire entanglements protected the area in front of the three great German trench systems. Defensive works protected the places where three canals crossed the main fortifications. On 20 October the attack on the Hindenburg Line was agreed, deploying nine battalions of the Tank Corps – 378 Mk IV tanks plus 54 in reserve. Some 400 fascines made of 75 bundles of brushwood bound together by chains would be dropped into the deep trenches to allow the tanks to pass over. Each fascine was 10ft long, weighed 1¾ tons and was 4½ft in diameter. A thousand workshop members of the 51st Chinese Labour Company made up the 400 fascines. In addition, 110 tank sledges for hauling up supplies were made and 127 broken-down tanks were repaired, most of them salvaged from the Ypres swamps. On 4 November a demonstration with infantry involving three sections of 'B' Battalion was staged for General Sir Julian Byng, GOC 3rd Army. This took place north of Boiry Becquerelle. Extra tanks were equipped as wire cutters to deal with barbed wire, while others served as mobile wireless stations. The supply arrangements were magnificent, and mostly carried out at night. Some 165,000 gallons of petrol, 40,500 gallons of oil, 5 million rounds of machine-gun ammunition, 54,000 6-pdr shells and 166,000 rounds of pistol ammunition were required and allocated. It was calculated that the huge surprise tank attack would achieve considerable success and gain 48 hours before German reinforcements in strength would arrive.

'B' Battalion (and 'H') would support the 6th Division in their attack, specifically the 16th Infantry Brigade. Major B.M. Jager, OC 4 Company, deployed two sections to lead the 1st KSLI (Kings Shropshire Light Infantry) and two more to lead the 1st Buffs. Major L.S. Henshall's 5 Company and Major F.S. Laskey's 6 Company would support the 2nd Yorks and Lancs, the 8th Bedfordshires and 'A' Company of 1st KSLI.

The 2,000-yard frontage for the attack was along the Gouzeaucourt–Cambrai railway. Zero hour was 0320 hours on 20 November and final

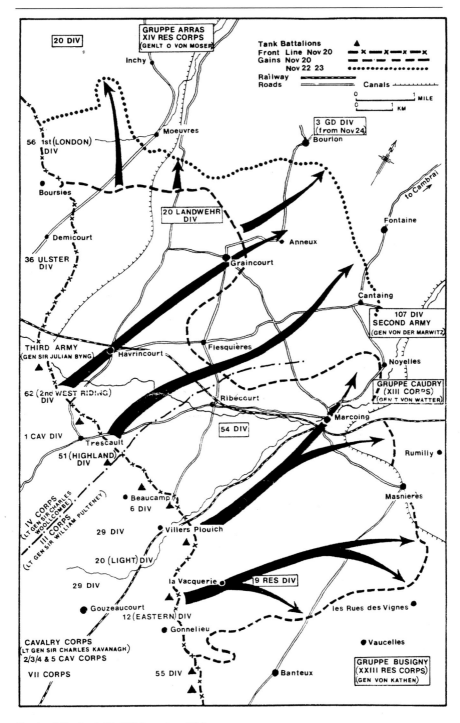

Battle of Cambrai, 20–22 November 1917.

orders had been given to the adjutant, Captain H. Dewhurst by Captain H.B.M. Groves MC. Twenty-four tanks of 5 and 6 Companies set off. The barrage had evidently subdued the defenders as the outpost line and first system of the Hindenburg Line itself were captured with very few casualties. Two tanks were ditched in the German front line system and another had autovac trouble. Lieutenant Alan Scrutton commanded a section of 6 Company, and had a chessboard painted on horns on the back of each tank! In the second phase 4 Company passed through and attacked (and helped to capture) the support trenches of the second Hindenburg Line and then rallied less 3 tanks (2 hit, 1 ditched) in a valley called the Grand Ravine south-west of Marcoing. Meanwhile 5 Company plus two tanks from 6 Company had begun the great race (at 4mph) to capture the bridges over the Canal de L'Escaut, east of Marcoing, as well as the railway bridge and canal locks. Major Huntback of 'H' Battalion wrote:

> I had a grandstand view of all 'B' Battalion tanks with some of 'C' and 'F' almost racing down Welsh Ridge, a broad spur. It was magnificent and it was war all right. They were doing what always paid with First World War tanks, maintaining fire against all local targets. Case-shot from the guns was a certain inducement to the enemy to go to earth or cock their hands up. The whole fleet took the wire in their stride and the cunning little manoeuvre of each section of 3 tanks at the two main trenches was perfectly executed.

Every tank battalion had practised a chess plan of attack. The advanced guard tank would go through the wire up to the enemy line, turn left and fire its starboard (right-hand) guns into the trench. The next, a female tank, moved up to the first trench, dropped its fascine, crossed it and turned left on the far side of the enemy trench. The third tank in the section crossed over the fascine already dropped, advanced to the support line trench, dropped its fascine, moved over and turned left. If all went well the first tank would then cross over both fascines, with one fascine in hand!

So 5 Company raced ahead and entered Marcoing at 1030 hours by the bridge and level crossing. Half the tanks cleared to the south, half to the north. Major L.S. Henshall had previously drawn up a traffic map to prevent chaos in the narrow streets. At Crucifix Corner north-west of the village armour-piercing machine-gun fire caused some casualties. In the southern sector Second Lieutenant A.A. Dalby prevented the enemy from blowing up the bridge south-west of the station. At 1230 hours the infantry arrived and mopped up. 'B' Battalion then concentrated in the Grand Ravine and refuelled from the supply tanks. 'B' Battalion was under the command of the 1st Cavalry Division, and after their breakthrough to Marcoing had succeeded the cavalry should have appeared immediately and advanced to Fontaine, Noyelle and Cantaing. Unfortunately they did not appear. On the first day of the battle of Cambrai casualties in 'B' Battalion were 2 officers and 3 ORs killed, and 1 officer and 35 ORs wounded.

On the second day 'B' Battalion was unfortunately ordered to support attacks by Lieutenant-General G.M. Harper's 51st Highland Division, rather unfairly nicknamed 'Harper's Duds' after their failure in a previous battle. Harper was a die-hard who did not believe in these 'new-fangled' machines.

However, the first operation on the 21st was successful. The attack was on Cantaing, 2 miles north of the Grand Ravine, with a composite company of twelve tanks from 4 and 6 Companies. From the crest of the hill at Premy Chapel another stirring race developed (still at 4mph!). Each section took its own line across country. The ground was firm and slightly downhill, and despite heavy machine-gun fire from sunken roads and shallow trenches in front of Cantaing the village was captured. Many enemy casualties were inflicted, indeed one tank captured sixty prisoners by itself. The village was a long street, about a thousand yards long, with houses on each side. All the tanks had advanced a long way ahead of the Scottish infantry. During lunch the CO Lieutenant-Colonel E.D. Bryce had a yellow flag raised (saffron is the 'B' Battalion colour). The enemy then commenced a very heavy bombardment of the village. The surviving nine tanks rallied at the Grand Ravine at 1730 hours.

The second attack on the 21st was against Noyelles, to help the 1st Buffs of 86th Infantry Brigade. The Germans had counter-attacked and regained half of Noyelles, so Captain A.C. Harcourt set off with two tanks and joined up with two tanks of 'C' Battalion before counter-attacking the German defenders in Noyelles. It was a splendid action. One tank went straight up the main street blasting the enemy with fire and securing a bridge-head. The second tank turned down a street to the right setting on fire a house containing a machine-gun nest and SAA dump. The Buffs sent up a fresh infantry company to consolidate the ground regained.

The third operation on 21 November was a disaster! On the night of the 21st/22nd 'B' Battalion received orders to support the Gordon Highlanders of 51st Highland Division in an attack on Fontaine-Notre-Dame. The front line then ran east of Noyelles, east of Castaing and east of Anneux. Major L.S. Henshall led a composite company of 7 tanks from 5 Company and 3 each from 4 and 6 Companies. From the Grand Ravine the thirteen tanks moved to a sunken road near La Justice Farm where they parked for the night. Zero hour was at 1030 hours and all tanks had started and reached Fontaine by 1100 hours. The Scottish infantry was already a considerable distance behind, and then halted *before* the village allowing the 'B' Battalion tanks to do all the dirty work of clearing the heavily defended village. The German infantry adopted anti-tank tactics for the first time, most successfully. Taking refuge in cellars or in the upper storeys of buildings, they waited for each tank to pass close by and lobbed hand-grenades at it, and fired machine-guns at close quarters. An anti-tank gun posted on the Bapaume–Cambrai road to the north-east of the village knocked out several tanks. It was a shambles. Although the composite company gave a good account of itself, without close infantry support they were sitting ducks. Five tanks eventually rallied, three from 4 Company, one each from 5 and 6.

'B' Battalion B57 Blarney Castle Mk IV female tank with dead crew, Fontaine-Notre Dame, 23 November 1917. (*Tank Museum 566/C3*)

There were 91 casualties, including many taken prisoner. There is a long, detailed and exciting account of the Fontaine battle by a young section commander. These are extracts:

> My section was allotted the right flank to the south from the last house in La Folie Wood to the centre of the village. Our tanks were to go with all speed into the village followed by the infantry, the village being screened by a smoke barrage . . . A tot of rum and we were off. In front of us perfect going and occasional shells bursting. Then I opened fire with the 6-pdr gun and our five Lewis guns opened up on a battery which was well screened by smoke. We were doing a good 4mph when, on nearing the village, German infantry ran out of a shallow fire trench. First a few and then about two companies legged it for the village. There was great excitement in the tank. Those who were handy to the Lewis guns took turns in firing at the fleeing infantry . . . I hopped about between the tank commander and driver in front and the 6-pdr gun giving orders.
>
> There were three field guns quite alone in the open. Our tank ran over the first gun, crumpled it up and fired shells into the breech of the second. The third tank of the section ran over the third gun. . . . so far it was all our luck – all smiles, laughter, excitement and thrills, but at this moment hell was let loose as we turned into the street. We were being fired at from the roofs, front, back and sides. A combination of splash and armour flaking made it most difficult to see anything when handling a gun. The gun ports were all lit up with sparks. Under immense fire every Lewis gun in the section of 3 tanks was put out of action. Two of the crew were wounded. All the crew's faces were covered in blood. The Hotchkiss LG gun was also out of action. The tank was on fire but using three Pyrenes it was eventually put out. Two tanks of another section were on fire in the centre of Fontaine, hit by a field gun firing up the street. None of the Gordons infantry were in sight, some 400 yards short of the village. My two female tanks were firing their revolvers out of loop-holes on their way out as they had not got a single gun left in action.

The young section commander, possibly Captain A.C. Harcourt or Captain H.B.M. Groves, who both won the Distinguished Service Order at Cambrai, then led his three crippled tanks out of the village. Meeting Major Hotblack, he told him about the action and then returned to the fight. Then the tank engine seized, the radiator tank riddled with bullets. The crew walked back to Marcoing pushing the wounded in a wheelbarrow, and then got another tank to tow theirs back. The action took altogether five hours.

Several awards were made for this action. There were Distinguished Service Orders for Lieutenant-Colonel E.D. Bryce, Major Henshall, Captain Harcourt and Captain Crouch, Military Crosses for Captains Groves and Dalby and Lieutenants Law, Dingley, Clarke and Symmons. The Distinguished Conduct Medal went to Private Irving, and Military Medals to Sergeants Hadlon and Morgan, Corporals Eidmans, Stilliwell, Strachan, Owers, Jupp, Bennett and Gilder, and Privates Hawgood, Moon, Stephens and Kinnis. Some time later Trooper R.G. Knight composed these verses:

Cambrai Day: The Reason for it All

When did this start, you might like to say,
Why do you celebrate? What is Cambrai Day?
What's it that happened on the Twentieth November,
For the Royal Tank Regiment, this day to remember?

In Nineteen-fifteen, the Tank was so named,
Its exploits in those days were not really famed,
As a new thing in warfare, the Generals weren't sure,
It was really worthwhile to ask for some more.

After nearly two years, they were still in some doubt
And in Nineteen-seventeen, it so came about,
A battle was planned around about Cambrai
And November the Twentieth arranged for the day.

Up to this time, no victory was won,
To show that the day of the tank had begun,
They were used in support but not on their own,
So this battle was based on their powers alone.

With General Hugh Elles leading the tanks,
Confusion was wrought in the enemy ranks,
He was flying the colours of the Royal Tank Corps,
The brown, red and green was well to the fore.

When the afternoon came, the battle was won
But the fame of the tank had scarcely begun

Crews at work on their tanks at Bermicourt Tankodrome. (*Tank Museum 887/C2*)

After that day, many battles were fought,
And many more honours to the Tank Corps were brought.

Through mud and through blood, to the green fields beyond,
That is our motto and to none we second,
The Royal Tank Regiment remembers this day,
November the Twentieth, the day of Cambrai!

Two unexpected actions took place on 30 November and 1 December. Under cover of a gas attack the Germans counter-attacked and captured Gouzeaucourt and Villers Guislans. Very quickly Major F.S. Laskey led two sections from the Tankodrome to retake Gouzeaucourt from the south-east and south. This was part of a joint operation with 'A' Battalion. Eventually 22 'B' Battalion and 14 'A' Battalion tanks under very heavy fire reached Gouzeaucourt, only to find that a superb counter-attack by 1st Guards Brigade had already recaptured the town. The following morning another composite force under Major A.G. Pearson of 'H' Battalion with seven 'B' Squadron tanks was formed to support a dismounted cavalry brigade in the capture of Gauche Wood and Villers Guislans. It was a disorganised, hurried little battle in which Gauche Wood and Quentin Ridge were captured after stiff fighting. Very heavy German artillery fire from Villers Guislans knocked out many tanks or forced them to seek the shelter of Gauche Wood. Four 'B' Battalion tanks were knocked out with four casualties. Second Lieutenant P.A. Symons won the Military Cross and Corporal Morgan the Military Medal.

From a camp at Fins the battalion left for their winter camp at Bray-sur-Somme, to a new Tankodrome near the Bray–Maricourt road. For four months there was regular training but sports of all kinds, concerts, cinema shows and generous leave periods made for good morale. Gunnery courses were held at Merlimont. Major Diamond organised the building of a theatre. Shortly after Christmas 1917 all the tank battalions were given numbers, so 'B' became the 2nd Battalion, Tank Corps.

CHAPTER NINETEEN

Amiens

In February 1918 Major H.V. Diamond became OC 'A' Company, taking over from Major B.M. Jager, and Major A.E. Scrutton became OC 'B' Company, taking over from Major L.S. Henshall DSO.

The great German Spring Offensive of 1918 soon put General Byng's 3rd Army of fourteen divisions under severe pressure. The 2nd Tank Brigade which included 2nd Battalion was placed in the Bapaume area. At about 1500 hours on 22 March reports came in that the enemy had broken through near Vaulx-Vraucourt and Morchies and was threatening Beugny and Beaumetz. Lieutenant-Colonel Bryce ordered 'C' Company to move to the west of Beugny to engage the enemy east of Vaulx and then push on towards Maricourt Wood. 'A' Company was also to move west of Beugny, and drive forwards to Morchies, while 'B' Company moved east of Beugny to fight west of Morchies. By 1630 hours the battalion had covered 3 miles and was in action again. It was a desperate business. There was no infantry support and little artillery cooperation. Crossing the main Cambrai–Bapaume road the tanks were greeted by very heavy machine-gun and heavy artillery fire and several tanks were quickly knocked out. But the German infantry were surprised and disorganised; they retreated some distance and delayed further enemy attacks in that area for about a day. Of the 25 tanks that got into action, 16 received direct hits and failed to return. Another 3 received direct hits but were able to return and 6 returned undamaged. As for the crews, 19 officers out of 25 became casualties and 108 out of 175 ORs. In all, 3 officers and 2 ORs were killed and 51 ORs were wounded, while 8 officers and 55 ORs were missing. It was a complete disaster. The survivors moved back to Bray and rallied at Aveluy with just 14 fighting tanks and 6 tenders. On the 24th a composite force was cobbled together under Major Diamond with 6 fighting tanks and 2 tenders hijacked from the 2nd Brigade Training School, plus two borrowed with crews from the 13th Battalion. A force of forty Lewis gunners was also assembled. Orders came on the 25th for the composite force to leave Corbie for the 3rd Brigade camp on the Albert–Bray road under Majors Laskey and Scrutton. The camp at Bray was set on fire deliberately to keep it out of enemy hands. The composite force with gun teams and twenty Lewis guns moved to Bois des Tailles. Captains Hooper and Hoyland led dismounted Lewis gun teams under infantry command. Major Laskey was wounded and Major Scrutton took his detachment to Bonnay, then to Querrieu on the 27th.

2nd Battalion Mk IVs at Aveluy, 25 March 1918. (*Tank Museum 66/B1*)

The 2nd Battalion RTC was now scattered throughout the area around Albert: Major Diamond had 7 tanks and a tender at Henencourt (to the west); Major Scrutton had Lewis gunners on Corbie Road (south-west); Captains Porter and Black had about 7 tanks near Acheux (north-west); Captain Hooper had Lewis gun teams with 17th Division infantry near Meaulté (south-east); Captain Hoyland also had 17th Division infantry and Lewis gunners; Captain Hamlet was with the 3rd Tank Brigade; Captain Cockell was with Echelon at Corbie (south-west) and Captain Appleton had kits and details at Humières. The 2nd Battalion rallied at Acheux and then moved to Blangy, south-east of Amiens, to take over brand-new Mk V tanks as part of 5th Tank Brigade.

The German Army had taken 80,000 British prisoners and made a salient some 40 miles deep south of the River Somme close to Villers-Bretonneux, only 10 miles from Amiens. The 2nd Tank Brigade started the battle with 98 tanks but this figure was reduced to 27 at the end. It had been a bitter experience for the men of 2nd RTC (and 1st RTC), who were mainly fighting as dismounted infantry with Lewis gun teams. Lieutenant A.H. Goodall received the Military Cross, while Military Medals were awarded to Corporals Kinnis and Sotting and Privates Kilminster, Evans and Dowdall. At Blangy Colonel A. Courage DSO, MC, OC 5th Tank Brigade, briefed all the officers in each battalion about the seriousness of the British Army's position. Only three weeks were allotted for reorganisation and training with the new Mk V tanks. Reinforcements poured in to replace the near-150 casualties. Hotchkiss guns replaced the Lewis machine-guns and practice was carried out at Fleury range, with driving and mechanical courses at Sautricourt and gunnery courses at Merliment.

If the reader looks at the map of the battlegrounds around Albert he will see that there are more than thirty well-kept British cemeteries. They include many brave tank men who lost their lives in the battle for Amiens.

Early in May training was completed and the battalion went by train east to Querrieu Wood, 10 miles north-east of Amiens, because 4th Army needed tank support around the Amiens area. The weeks passed. The mornings were devoted to training and the afternoons to sport – football, cricket, boxing, even quoits, bathing and fishing in the River Ancre. A considerable amount of time was spent on cooperation with the 2nd Australian Division at Vaux-sur-Somme. On the night of 4 August the battalion left for Fouilloy, a few miles to the south-east, through Daours.

The battle of Amiens was to be the final blow from which the German Army never recovered. It was unique in that a major assault was begun *without* the usual tell-tale bombardment. No fewer than 450 British tanks were launched against the German lines east and south-east of Amiens with almost total secrecy and surprise. The new cavalry-type Whippet tanks, armoured cars and gun-carrier tanks plus the new Mk V tanks were deployed with conspicuous success.

The 5th Tank Brigade under Colonel Courage consisted of 2nd, 8th, 13th and 15th Battalions, Tank Corps, supporting the Australian Corps under General Sir John Monash. Covering a 13-mile frontage, some 10 miles south of the River Somme, the objectives were marked out as Green, Red and Blue Lines. The opposition in front consisted of General von der Marwitz's seven depleted divisions of the German 2nd Army.

On 8 August 2nd Battalion supported 2nd Australian Division. Major Scrutton's 'B' Company led 5th Australian Brigade towards the village of Lamotte-Warfusée and the valley north of it, which was full of field gun batteries. Major Crouch's 'C' Company led the 7th Australian Brigade towards the south of Lamotte-Warfusée, with the railway as the southern boundary. And Major Diamond's 'A' Company was to pass through 'C' and lead the 15th Australian Brigade towards Harbonnières. In a thick mist which hindered accurate progress 'B' Company almost immediately lost three tanks, two on land mines, the third hit by a shell. The eight survivors then cleared Lamotte-Warfusée. Lieutenant Craig's tank was hit while towing an enemy field gun back to our lines. When it was hit a second time and set on fire, Craig and Sergeant Jessop rescued the wounded under fire. Second Lieutenant Coe captured two machine-guns and many prisoners but was killed shortly afterwards.

The first objectives were reached at 0630 hours and 19 out of the 24 2nd Battalion tanks got there. 'C' Company's twelve tanks reached their first objective. Lieutenant Percy-Eade helped the Australian infantry into the village of Marcelcave and obtained a written receipt from the infantry to that effect. He had knocked out six enemy machine-guns single-handedly and in the next

2nd Battalion Mk V male tank, Battle of Amiens, 8 August 1918. (*Tank Museum 1557/C1*)

phase tackled a field gun battery and put their gunners to flight. The second phase of the attack, shared by 12 tanks of 'A' Company and 11 of 'A' Company, 12th Battalion, was followed by all the tanks of 'C' Company and the surviving six of 'B' Company assaulting the heavily defended village of Bayonvillers.

An anti-tank battery in Bayonvillers now proceeded to knock out no fewer than seventeen tanks – four each from 'A' and 'B' Companies and the rest from 13th Battalion. Luckily 'C' Company's tanks were able to dominate and finish off the German battery. Second Lieutenants Rothery and Botterill of 'B' Company distinguished themselves on the left flank. Eventually only 5 out of the 48 tanks of 2nd Battalion and 13th Battalion reached Harbonnières, which was found to have been deserted by the enemy.

The commander of tank no. 9003 'Barrhead' wrote a full account of his part in the battle of Amiens, of which what follows is a summary:

The approach march is always a most important and trying part of the tank's work. It must be done at night and every precaution has to be taken to prevent the enemy hearing our approach, as much of the success of the tank action depends on taking the enemy by surprise . . . Guiding tapes were laid down under the supervision of officers detailed for the work. The attack was to commence at 4.20am. Watches were synchronised and a final inspection was made of the tank to ensure that everything was ready for the attack . . . We arrived at the jumping-off point just when the barrage commenced and each tank at once got into its own sector in front of the infantry . . . a very thick mist made observation most difficult, used my tank compass and followed the barrage. Very little opposition met in the first phase . . . they put up a poor fight. Whenever a tank was sighted they ran forward with their hands up. We passed them and allowed the infantry to deal with them. A few enemy machine-guns kept on firing but they were soon silenced by running over them with the tank. Any of the gun teams who remained were dealt with effectively.

The village of Bayonvillers was entered by 'Barrhead' steering a zig-zag course and travelling behind houses and swinging round.

> We then set off for Harbonnières. Other tanks of 'B' Battalion were cleaning up the village and had captured an enemy train full of reinforcements . . . it was a good day's work. The crews were in excellent spirits, somewhat exhausted having been in the tanks for nearly 16 hours. 'Barrhead' was in splendid condition, gave no trouble during this its first action.

The next day, 9 August, the advance continued at 1330 hours south of Harbonnières, where 'Strong opposition was met from machine-guns, anti-tank guns were soon silenced. 'Barrhead's 6-pdr guns opened fire on some splendid targets and her machine-guns poured forth a leaden hail of bullets. Pushing ahead the artillery fire became very heavy.' Eventually 'Barrhead' was hit. Two crewmen were killed and four wounded, and although the tank was hit again and burst into flames, the intrepid commander escaped to fight another day. He had captured 10 machine-guns and 200 prisoners.

On the 9th the battalion strength was down to seventeen tanks, formed into a composite company under Major T.A. Crouch DSO supporting the 2nd Australian Infantry Brigade. The attack was now concentrated on Rosières and Lihons a few miles south-east of Harbonnières. Near Rosières station and a factory, enemy field guns knocked out eight tanks and casualties among tank crews and the Australian infantry were heavy. An abandoned German field hospital provided medical attention for the wounded. Major H.V. Diamond was then asked to provide two sections for a difficult night attack. Out of nine tanks that started only three actually took part in the action. Six tanks had troubles and were forced to drop out: two were ditched, one had oil trouble, one had auto-vac trouble and one caught fire while the sixth got lost and was captured. It was a very disappointing end for the 2nd Battalion. However, the Australian Corps captured 8,000 prisoners and 173 guns for the loss of only 650 casualties. When the battle of Amiens ended on 12 August, some 688 British tanks had been deployed, 480 of which were either damaged in action or had suffered mechanical problems and were handed over to the workshops for repair.

On 21 August Captain A.C. Harcourt DSO took the remaining battleworthy tanks into action supporting 1st Australian Infantry Brigade in its attack on the high ground running from Froissy Beacon to south-east of Proyart, north-east of Harbonnières. The battalion had been resting at Etampes near Corbie and the tanks were driven east to Amy Wood. Eleven tanks helped the Australians reach their objectives but later several tanks were hit by anti-tank guns. In all, 2nd Battalion suffered eleven casualties in this action.

In all, 13 Military Crosses, 5 Distinguished Conduct Medals and 16 Military Medals were awarded to 2nd Battalion for the August offensive. At the end of August Lieutenant-Colonel Bryce, Majors Scrutton and Diamond, and many other officers and ORs left for Wool in the UK to form a new battalion.

CHAPTER TWENTY

The Last Offensive

By late August 1918 there were no fewer than twenty-six battalions of the Tank Corps (including some armoured car battalions), with eight in England and eighteen in France. On 14 September King George V became Colonel-in-Chief of the Tank Corps. The shattered 2nd Battalion with most of its veterans back at Wool was now commanded by Major H.R. Pape from 13th Tank Battalion, with Captain H.J. Symons OC 'A' Company. Captain A.C. Harcourt DSO was OC 'B' Company.

By the end of September 230 British tanks were in position for another major assault on the Hindenburg Line south of Cambrai. From Villers-Bretonneux and Boisleux-au-Mont (a few miles south of Arras), 2nd Battalion moved by train south to Briost and Ytres. 5th Tank Brigade was to support three corps (IX, Australian and III Corps) in an attack on a 14-mile front half-way between Cambrai and St Quentin. The objective was to push the enemy back to the line of the Canal du Nord. Rather optimistically the battalion's twenty-one tanks were spread widely. Major H.J. Symons, OC 'A' Company, with eight tanks supported three divisions of III Corps; Major A.C. Harcourt, OC 'B' Company, with nine tanks supported the Australian Corps (with two divisions); and Captain D.V. Black, OC 'C' Company, was to support with its four tanks the 6th Division of IXth Corps. The three start points were, from north to south, 'A' Company from Lieramont, 'B' from Bois de Buire and 'C' from Monchy-Lagache. 'A' Company's objectives were Peizièrs, Epehy, Ronssoy and Lempire.

It had rained heavily and the 18th was a dull cloudy day. Visibility was bad as 'A' Company's six tanks took all their objectives, although Ronssoy was strongly held. Second Lieutenants A.E. Stammers, H.D. Harrison and R.W. Jameson handled their tanks with gallantry and the first two gained Military Crosses. 'B' Company's seven tanks headed for Hargicourt, Villeret and Cologne Farm, three being diverted to Le Verguier and Parker Post. All the objectives were taken by the Australians and the four tanks were soon in action (one broke down, one went up on land mine and a third got tangled in wire). 'C' Company's four tanks headed for Badger Copse, Fresnoy-le-Petit, Douai Trench and the Quadrilateral near Holnon. Only two got into action and both Second Lieutenant W.R. Hedges and G.F. Smallwood distinguished themselves. Once Fresnoy was taken heavy artillery fire, gas shells and machine-gun fire came from the Quadrilateral. Smallwood's tank got stuck crossing a sunken ditch. To his rescue came Hedges, personally driving his tank as both his drivers were dead or dying. Inside it was Captain Hamlet, the section commander. Hedges' tank was hit, burst into flames and both officers jumped out and were captured. Smallwood then took his machine-guns out of the ditched tank and successfully held out until the infantry came up. Smallwood was awarded the Military Cross, while Lance-Corporal G. Rivers MM won the Distinguished Conduct Medal for gallantry at Ephey. Lance-Corporal E. Sneath and Private W. Phipps both won Military Medals for brave actions in the attack on the Quadrilateral. On 18 September 2nd Battalion suffered twenty-seven casualties. The operations were all very successful except that on the southern flank, where the French troops failed to link up with the IXth Corps attack!

Still, the Australians and the Tank Corps HQ sent letters of congratulation and thanks to the CO, Lieutenant-Colonel H.R. Pape. But three days later the surviving eleven tanks were summoned to fight their last little battle in the First World War. Major H.J. Symons, OC 'A' Company, with seven tanks supported 53rd Infantry Brigade (18th Division) in an attack on high ground north-east of Ronssoy, known as the Knoll. Three tanks were hit and knocked out but Lieutenant R.W. Kerr in tank no. N9031 reached the Knoll; shortly afterwards he was badly wounded and his tank sergeant was killed by anti-tank fire. Two Mk V tanks laden with infantry machine-gunners also reached the Knoll but intense fire drove them back.

Major A.C. Harcourt, OC 'B' Company, with four tanks supported 231st Infantry Brigade (74th Division) on their attack on Guillemont Farm south of the Knoll. Only two tanks got into the action and both struck land mines before getting half-way to Guillemont Farm.

On 24 September 2nd Battalion went back to Guillemont and then to Suzanne, near Bray-sur-Somme, west of Peronne and stayed there until after the Armistice.

Kenneth Chadwick, author of *Seconds Out*, calculated that in *each* year of the war the turnover of personnel – for whatever reasons – was equal to the battalion's total strength. They had fought seventeen separate actions, eleven of which were on a large scale, and had been awarded 116 decorations including 5 Distinguished Service Orders and 9 Distinguished Conduct Medals – a truly impressive performance.

CHAPTER TWENTY-ONE

Between the Wars

The overwhelming impression of peacetime soldiering in the twenty-year period 1919–1939 is of army sport interspersed by tiresome parades, bullshit, occasional manoeuvres, vehicle maintenance, training on many subjects and generous leave! Kenneth Chadwick in *Seconds Out* lists 2nd Battalion team victories in all these sports – cross-country running, army athletics, boxing, swimming, water polo, football league, pole vault, officers' tennis, hockey championship, swimming relay, throwing the hammer, throwing the discus, hurdles, long jump, rugby, motor-cycling and cycling. There were also successes in the machine-gun cup and revolver competition, and even the Command cookery competition!

In 1919 Lieutenant-Colonel Courage DSO still commanded the 2nd Tank Battalion. The new yellow (saffron) whistle cord round the left shoulder of the Service dress jacket and the yellow shoulder patches were their official 'colours'. The 1st Battalion had Red, the 3rd Green, the 4th Blue and the 5th Light Blue and Red.

However, the war-time generals were still working out the lessons learned from two years of hard tank fighting in the First World War. Brigadier-General H.J. Elles DSO, commanding the Tank Corps, and his staff wrote the following report after Cambrai:

(a) weight makes for heavy going on heavily shelled wet ground; (b) speed over heavily shelled ground is only 10 yards a minute, and over unshelled ground from 1 to 5mph; (c) difficulty of maintaining direction because of limited visibility; (d) exhaustion of crews due to heat and difficulties of driving. This led to the following conclusions: (i) if the ground has been heavily shelled, tanks will cross slowly, but if soaked with rain as well, the majority will not cross at all. To employ tanks in such conditions is to throw them away (e.g. the tanks with the First Army operating against Vimy Ridge); (ii) tanks cannot keep up with infantry until the zone of heavy bombardment is crossed. This zone is about 3,000 yards deep. It is impossible for tanks to cooperate in initial attacks in this zone; (iii) tanks cannot proceed certainly during dark or twilight over ground which is intersected with trenches or shelled unless this has been reconnoitred; (iv) mist and smoke will bring tanks almost to a standstill; so will dust, not only that thrown up by shells but that picked up by the tracks and blown in the face of the driver. [Here it was suggested that goggles should be provided for driver and officer]; (v) on a hot day the temperature inside the tanks rises to 120° in the shade. This excessive heat causes vomiting and exhaustion. Eight hours' continual work is the limit of the crew's endurance, after which the men require 48 hours' rest; (vi) a tank's circuit of action is about 8 miles; (vii) tanks cannot operate through thickly wooded country or over ground covered with tree stumps. Tank unit commanders are the best judges of the ground they can cover; infantry commanders should be brought to realise this; (vii) tanks cannot pass through barrages with safety. High explosive barrages are the most dangerous. In a creeping barrage HE should not be mixed with shrapnel. The progress of tanks would be facilitated if heavy

King George V and Queen Mary inspect a medium C Cruiser, 2nd Battalion Tank Corps, *c.* 1919. (*Tank Museum 5581/B3*)

artillery and trench mortars were not used on the enemy's trench system; (ix) infantry should be warned not to bunch behind the tanks, and not be led off their objectives if the tanks are moving diagonally across their front; (x) the greatest assistance in the location of tanks during a battle is that provided by the Royal Flying Corps.

In March 1921 the 2nd Battalion moved to Pinehurst Barracks, Farnborough, in Aldershot Command and remained there until 1939. A total of 36 tanks (24 Medium Cs and 12 Mk Vs) were drawn from RAOC at Wool; 100 new recruits joined; trade tests for upgraded pay were held on the Medium C tank and on .303 Hotchkiss guns fired on Ash ranges. Captain Hotblack gave tank tactics lectures and practical demonstrations to other tank regiments. The 2nd Battalion tanks took part in the Ascot week grand military tattoo and Lieutenant-Colonel B.E. Hankey DSO became the CO. The next year (1922) the so-called Geddes Axe, the national economy crisis, forced the discharge of many able soldiers.

King George V and Queen Mary visited the Tankodrome and witnessed the effectiveness of the Medium C tank, and searchlight tattoos took place with 2nd Battalion tanks deployed. The American Mission visited Aldershot Command and the tanks 'Blair Athol' and 'Bayardo' showed off their skills. The Royal Review on 19 May 1923 was held at Aldershot and a composite section participated to favourable press reviews. The Tank Corps then became the Royal Tank Corps.

The next year the 2nd Battalion was equipped with the new Vickers tanks and spirited manoeuvres took place in the New Forest and with the Guards

Brigade in Sussex. The thirty-one Vickers tanks were all named, with seven As from the old 1917 'A' Company, nine Cs from the old 'C' Company and fifteen beginning with B: 'Badger', 'Ballyboggan', 'Bayardo', 'Beelzebub', 'Bellerophon', 'Bison', 'Blackcock', 'Black Knight', 'Blacklook', 'Blair Atholl', 'Blue Dun', 'Bow On', 'Buckwheat', 'Bugler' and 'Bulwark'. In 1925 the 2nd Battalion wore the Tank Corps black beret for the first time and these doggerel verses appeared in 1926:

A Superimposition on 'Sally in Our Alley'

Of all the caps that are so smart
There's none like our black Beret.
It captivates the fem'nine heart
From Lydd to Londonderry.
Bearskin – SD – the Forage Cap –
Shako – Busby – Glengarry –
Straw – Topper – Bowler – sleek Valour –
Can't beat the younger Beret.

'Tis fashioned in a coal-black cloth
And bound with leather binding,
Behind, a tape to tighten this;
In front, a badge quite blinding,
Which gleams above the left eyebrow
When worn per regulation,
The right side pulled to lobe of ear . . .
Voila! A chic creation!

The wearer's state of mind, I wis,
By wrongful mode of wearing
Can be made plain as though by his
Serenest smile – or swearing.
Yet all awry, badge not o'er eye,
The whole effect so alters,
The Sergeant-Major wants to cry –
The wearer gets 'Defaulters!'

One sees the man who has been swilled
With wild and wasteful lotion
With cap like fireman's, or of he
Who rides upon the ocean.
There is no head-dress on the earth
Of large or small dimension
Which causes such unseemly mirth
As this artistic French 'un.

Cartoonists, Punch and papers have
Made game of my old Beret.
That this is just green envy is
Not only plain, but very.
Of this I am not only sure
But furthermore I swear it,
They'd give a lot to try one on –
And if the cap fits – wear it!

I brush my Beret every morn,
My badge I clean and cherish.
My brasses brush is now quite worn,
Soon must entirely perish.
But when my seven long years are out,
I'll have to doff my Beret
From off my head. But then in bed
I'll wear my blinkin' Beret

Spooner

Each year the Royal Tournament took place at Olympia with two 2nd Battalion tanks showing off their obstacle-climbing techniques. A defensive operation manoeuvre in September was highly praised by the famous

Colonel 'Blood' Caunter briefing 2 RTC near the Surrey/Sussex border, 1928. (*Tank Museum 2714/C5*)

Medium Mk 1 (right) and Mk 1A of 2nd Battalion RTC on the Surrey/Sussex borders, *c.* 1928. (*Tank Museum 2714/B4*)

Captain Liddell Hart, military tactician, in the *Daily Telegraph* under the title 'Tanks in Defence'. During the General Strike the 2nd Battalion sent a Medium Tank Company to Chelsea Barracks 'just in case'!

In 1927, after four years as CO, Lieutenant-Colonel Cary-Barnard left and was replaced by Lieutenant-Colonel J.M. Hulton CBE, DSO. The next year King Amanhullah inspected the battalion at Tidworth and members of the Mechanical Warfare Experimental Establishment closely inspected 'A' Company tanks – a very 'hush-hush' affair. Probably unconnected with this, in 1928 'A' Company was issued with Carden Lloyd light recce tanks, known as 'Harold Lloyds'! Brass Hats have always liked inspections and General Sir John Capper, Colonel Commandant Tank Corps, arrived on Empire Day 1929, while in November the commander of the 2nd Division, Major-General Sir Astley Cubitt, paid a visit. The next year wireless was fitted to the tanks, a draft of soldiers left for India, and brigade and divisional training schemes took place over Laffen Plain, Long Valley and Chobham Ridges. In 1931 Lieutenant-Colonel 'Jumbo' Hulton left and one of the most controversial figures in the British Army became the new CO. Lieutenant-Colonel P.C.S. Hobart had transferred from the Royal Engineers in 1923. Kenneth Chadwick wrote of him: 'He was at the height of his powers. He brought with him originality of thought, determination, resourcefulness, enthusiasm and vitality. He had a strong personality with a

2nd Battalion RTC light and medium tanks on Salisbury Plain, *c.* 1930. (*Tank Museum 4328/E2*)

blunt outspokenness which made dangerous adversaries in high places.'
Certainly all the old-fashioned cavalry generals hated him! 'He was
impatient of delay and inefficiency. He knew what he wanted and
consistently reached the high standards he set. Slightly built, immaculately
uniformed in barracks, he sported a shortened polo stick for a walking stick.'
Nobody of course in 1931 knew that in the next world war (not even
looming then) 'Hobo' would create and form three separate formidable
fighting armoured divisions from scratch – a record impossible to beat. On 1
April 1931 the 1st Tank Brigade was formed at Tilshead by Brigadier
C.F.N. Broad DSO. Captain Basil Liddell Hart had recommended the use
of systematic tank attacks, with light tanks used to recce in front of the main
force, and forming a defensive screen if required, followed by the heavy
battle tanks which would then engage the enemy closely.

Kenneth Chadwick wrote: 'During early summer it was a common sight
to see the battalion's tanks careering over Long Valley or Hartford Bridge
Flats in changing formations with gay bunting hanging out of the tanks.' On
19 April 1933 King George V visited Aldershot and the 2nd Battalion
formed up in line in Long Valley and faultlessly carried out complicated
manoeuvres in front of the monarch, Sir John Capper and Brigadier Broad.
'Hobo' had predictably been promoted and Lieutenant-Colonel H.L. Evans
MC took command. Brigadier Hobart now commanded the 1st Tank
Brigade and was also the Inspector. He devised really professional exercises,
usually in mid-August. The old medium tanks could 'march' at 8mph and
cover 60 or 70 miles in a normal day of ten hours. Only 5 per cent of

mechanical problems caused tanks to break down, but they still required very careful maintenance work.

Hobart had seven concepts that the brigade manoeuvres had to take into account:

- (1) The medium battalions in close order drill; changes of formation from 'Trident' to 'line ahead', 'double line ahead' and new variations.
- (2) Practise the brigade as a whole in manoeuvring over open country.
- (3) A cadre exercise by radio-telephone, also a brigade change of direction when advancing along roads.
- (4) Complex tactical manoeuvre. The brigade crossed [the River Avon] in three columns and attacked the artillery positions behind the front of the hostile force in conjunction with the direct attack of their own infantry.
- (5) A demonstration by the tank brigade of circling round the opposing army's flank to disorganise communications and back areas.
- (6) Using Savernake Forest as a large 'city', the exercise showed how tank units could penetrate and disable essential services before withdrawing.
- (7) A test to force crossings of two rivers and a canal in face of anti-tank guns [of the 7th Infantry Brigade].

The arrival of the practical all-black tank overalls was now welcomed by the majority.

The year 1935 saw an inspection by a Chinese military mission, but only two of the fifteen visitors could be persuaded to take a ride in a medium tank! The royal review took place on 13 July. On joint infantry/tank exercises, the 2nd Battalion was impressed by the infantry's belief in the almost magical power of tanks to remove opposition. More Egyptian and

Lieutenant Colonel (later Major-General) Sir Percy Hobart leads his 2nd Battalion RTC from Tilshead camp during 1932 manoeuvres with adjutant Captain (later Brigadier) Lee standing in front hatch. (*Tank Museum 4318/E4*)

Indian drafts were dispatched. The practice was adopted of referring to the individual company and its commander by the name of his tank, e.g. 'Ajax', 'Badger' and 'Cyclops'. Early in 1936 the 2nd Battalion represented the Royal Tank Corps at King George V's funeral. The usual summer camp was held at Tilshead in August and a new brigade exercise area was chosen, at Cranborne Chase. In November a medium and a light tank took part in the Lord Mayor's Show, but found it difficult to leaguer in the Tower of London. The medieval gateways were too narrow and the bridges not strong enough! The BBC broadcast the procession from a Mk VII R/T set installed in a 2nd Battalion medium tank.

Lieutenant-Colonel D.H. Pratt commanded from 1936 to 1938. 'B' Company's medium tanks, resplendent in new paint, staged a demonstration for the visiting premiers of the British Empire and a selection of colonial troops in the summer of 1937. In September a certain Lieutenant Carver went on a hair-raising shopping expedition to Frome in a Mk IV tank driven by Lance-Corporal Madden. Also a new cavalry training directive was received at HQ. The tank brigade was to be part of the mobile division, together with two cavalry brigades. Not very usefully, the 'yellow book' told the tankmen how 'to sling lance', 'prepare to dismount' and 'what to do with the horse on outpost'.

Under their new Führer the German Army had followed closely Liddell Hart's tactical genius and Hobart's practical training brilliance. By 1934 they had their first panzer battalion; by October 1935 there were three complete panzer divisions, and by 1939 there were six.

Early in 1938 the *Sunday Pictorial* claimed that the British Army tanks were 'junk'. The *Daily Express* retorted that the British had big tanks which could do 50mph and turned corners at the flick of the wheel, and that RTC personnel were all tough men! In March Lieutenant-Colonel R.G.W. Rimmington took command. Major-General Hobart had left for Egypt in September 1938 to form and train the Mobile Division in Egypt. Life in 1939 continued undisturbed by threats of war, apart from the involvement in an ARP (Air Raid Precautions) exercise on 6/7 May covering the whole of Hampshire and much of Surrey. Early that year the Cavalry of the Line and the Royal Tank Corps merged to form the Royal Armoured Corps, and the Royal Tank Corps became the Royal Tank Regiment.

CHAPTER TWENTY-TWO

With the BEF, 1940

After the declaration of war in September 1939 the so-called 'Phoney War' existed for about six months. Poland was bombed and blasted by Hitler's Wehrmacht and Luftwaffe while London and Paris made placatory noises. However, the British Expeditionary Force was rapidly mobilised and some light Vickers Mk VI tanks swung ashore at St Nazaire on 11 September. By the winter of 1939 there were six divisions with the BEF and by the end of March 1940 no fewer than nine. On 9 April Hitler invaded Denmark and Norway. On 10 May the headquarters of the GOC, General Lord Gort VC, at Arras was bombed early in the morning, so advance parties of the BEF moved into neutral Belgium.

The 3rd Armoured Brigade under Brigadier John Crocker consisted of 2 RTR and 5 RTR and on 14 May they paraded for and were inspected by King George VI. Lieutenant-Colonel A.C. Harcourt DSO commanded 2 RTR while Major W.A.S. Rumsey, Major J.R.D. Carlton and Major J.P. Brown commanded 'A', 'B' and 'C' Squadrons respectively. The tank strength was 18 A-13s (armed with a 2-pdr gun and a co-axial machine-gun, with a crew of four, Christie suspension and a top speed of 30mph), 1 A-10, 8 A-9s (armed with a 2-pdr and three machine-guns, with a crew of 6), and finally 21 Light Mk VI Bs (armed with three machine-guns, with a crew of 3 and a top speed of 35mph). Second Lieutenant C.D. Williamson with two cruiser tanks sailed first with the 9th Lancers and rejoined the regiment in France. From Southampton 2 RTR sailed peacefully to Cherbourg, arriving on 23 May. By this time the Luftwaffe had destroyed Rotterdam and the Dutch surrendered on 15 May. Little Luxembourg was overrun and two panzer divisions crashed through the Ardennes. The advancing German armour poured across France in the direction of Abbeville, isolating the main BEF in the north from the French army in the south. General Martel commanded the 50th Motorised Division which included 4 RTR and 7 RTR, and the tank battle at Arras on the 21st gave the German panzers a nasty shock and bought a little time for the defenders. 3 RTR landed their tanks at Calais on the 22nd and were destined to fight a heroic week-long battle against desperate odds. 2 RTR arrived by train at Neufchatel, 15 miles south-east of Blagny. They were ordered to support elements of the French 5th Army 'around Abbeville'. On 27 May 3rd Armoured Brigade was on the west side of the Blangy–Abbeville road. Blangy town was on the River Bresle and the advance towards the River

2 RTR A-13 tanks on the Cherbourg quayside on 23 May 1940, when 2 and 5 RTR landed to join 1st Armoured Division. (*Tank Museum 2447/A2*)

Somme was to be made in three 'bounds', the first covering 3 miles, the second and third 5 miles each. The enemy had assembled a force of 1,500 infantry, 10 medium and 50 light tanks in the Blangy region. Their armoured cars and motor-cycle patrols dominated the area between the two rivers, the Bresle and the Somme. After a wet and chilly night the advance began at 0430 hours. 'C' Squadron cleared the first bound by 0525 and two hours later reached Miannay, a few miles south-west of Abbeville.

The countryside was rolling and open country, sprinkled with small woods, hamlets and steep-sided valleys. Soon mortaring was reported beyond and behind the regiment's left flank. 'A' Squadron on the right flank reached the Miannay–Toeuffles road, with Moyenneville as their next objective; this small town lay on a minor road to Abbeville. The tanks were crossing a very wide open plain and Second Lieutenant Ewart was sent forwards to liaise with two French armoured cars on the road about 900 yards ahead. Both these cars were discovered to be knocked out and German anti-tank guns then hit and destroyed Ewart's light Mk VI and also four 'A' Squadron cruisers following up. Within a short space of time 2 RTR had suffered their first casualties of the war. Second Lieutenant Ewart and 8 ORs were killed, while Major Rumsey, his second-in-command Captain Daniell, Second Lieutenant Powell and 8 ORs were either killed, wounded or taken prisoner. The CO then ordered 'A' Squadron back to Toeuffles, and later to Aigneville. 'C' Squadron reached Miannay (north of

Moyenneville) but encountered heavy artillery fire covering several road-blocks and they too rallied back to Aigneville. Brigadier J.T. Crocker came up to see the situation for himself, but without artillery and infantry progress was not possible. The French motorised cavalry failed to appear. The next day, the 28th, a composite squadron moved north to Chepy and Franleu to cover the right flank of a combined attack by the 51st Highland Division and the French; this attack resulted in tragedy at St Valery-en-Caux, where the brave Scottish division was surrounded and overrun. Many disabled 2 RTR tanks were retrieved from the battlefield by Scammells, taken to Blangy and then sent by train back to the workshops. Lieutenant G.T.A. Strong's light tank of B Squadron tried to tow away a fallen tree trunk being used as a road-block, but it was booby-trapped and he was wounded. From Franleu he saw the Highland Division troops marching towards the coast. Belgium had surrendered and it was clear that the BEF was in great danger. The regiment entrained variously at Gameches and Bouttencourt, and headed south to Catenay, a small town on the River Crevon, 12 miles south-west of Forges-les-Eaux. The French General Weygand, the Allied Commander-in-Chief, ordered his British allies, specifically including 3rd Armoured Brigade, to withdraw south to hold a 12-mile stretch of the River Andelle north-west of Gournay-en-Bray. On their way 2 RTR also defended the River Epte line north of Gournay and roughly parallel to the River Andelle.

On 7 June the brigade, augmented to a strength of 92 tanks from other sources in 1st Armoured Division, had reached the area of Beauvoir-en-

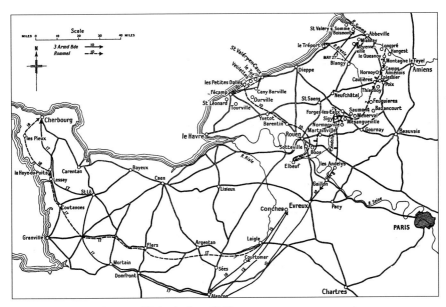

Movements of 3rd Armoured Brigade, June 1940.

Lyons a few miles west of Gournay. Brigadier Crocker ordered 2 RTR to advance across the River Andelle and establish standing patrols on the line of the railway running south-east from Forges-les-Eaux to Gournay. So 2 RTR sent five patrols on to the line of the River Epte between Cuy-St-Fiacre and Saumont, commanded by Captain P.R.C. Hobart (nephew of 'Hobo'), previously the battalion technical adjutant. Major H.O. Stibbard MC, OC 'A' Squadron, escorted the 'B' Echelon south to the Forêt du Bord. At Haussez, a crossing of the River Epte, Second Lieutenant D. Barker with 7 Troop encountered six panzer cruiser tanks. His tank, along with that of Sergeant Blades, was knocked out. Troopers Murwell and Maggs helped the withdrawal to Bremont.

Captain Hobart, commanding the recce squadron of light tanks, recounted:

> On rounding a corner I saw a German tank head-on about 300 yards down the road . . . I opened fire with the .5 machine-gun, which of course refused to fire more than the shortest of bursts without a stoppage. Hastily deciding that contact had been made, I withdrew. By this time I had lost touch not only with my other tanks but with Battalion HQ as well, and so ignominiously started to find my way back in the dusk towards Catenay, calling repeatedly on the wireless but getting no reply. I shortly encountered another German tank which appeared huge to my scared eye, but which could not have been anything bigger than a Mk III, I suppose.

2 RTR then withdrew to Bosc Edeline with patrols on the River Andelle from Sigy-en-Bray northwards. A certain rather brilliant German panzer commander called Erwin Rommel had been hounding elements of the BEF, and had sent armoured patrols to seize the bridges over the River Seine at Elbeuf. On the way they crossed the River Andelle at Sigy through a 3ft-deep ford. So back went 2 RTR south to Seraville and crossed the River Seine at Les Andelys with a composite squadron of 5 RTR, heading towards Gaillon. French requests for tank support at the bridges meant that Captain Carey-Thomas, Second Lieutenant H.W. Turner and two cruiser tanks arrived to help. Between 2000 and 0200 hours intermittent enemy shelling meant that the tank support had to keep moving south.

The brigade reached Les Andelys about midnight, simultaneously with Rommel's arrival on the banks of the Seine near Elbeuf! The town of Les Andelys was on fire from bombing and the bridge was closed. But Brigade HQ managed to cross the river at the Gaillon bridge after an hour's delay in clearing a passage. The units had crossed a little earlier. Captain Pat Hobart provides a vivid picture of that retreat:

> I can't recall much of these days except endless driving and a great tiredness, streams of pitiful refugees by day and straining tired eyes through the dark to see the vehicle ahead by night, and all the time a feeling of uncomprehended disaster and a lack of knowledge of what was going on, feet aching from hour upon hour of standing in the turret and bruised shoulders, back and chest from the jolting of the cupola ring. The only place I can remember in those three days is the Seine crossing at Pont de l'Arche. It was dusk as we wound down from the high ground on the north bank and the town was being bombed; by the time we

were clattering down the cobbled streets it was dark, some houses were on fire and by the light of a burning building just at the end of the bridge I saw the body of a young woman sprawled against the wall clutching her dead child.

Rommel's motor-cycle battalion actually entered Elbeuf while traffic was still pouring over the bridge. But the German troops wasted an hour in the dark and congested streets before Rommel himself came up and immediately organised them into two storming parties. The bridges were blown just as the assault was launched. The neighbouring bridges were destroyed at about the same time. If Rommel had gone further south he would have found the going easier. For at Les Andelys and Gaillon the only defence, apart from the demolition parties, was provided by a few cruiser tanks – two troops of the 2nd RTR. Crocker remarked: 'During that day thousands of French troops had streamed back across the river, yet no active steps seem to have been taken to organise resistance on this, France's last main line of defence.'

Early on the 10th the remnants of 3rd Armoured Brigade continued their fighting retreat south-westwards on a 90-mile march to the Forêt de Perseigne east of Alencon, arriving in dribs and drabs by the evening. A composite squadron was then formed from 2 RTR and 5 RTR, commanded by Major J.P. Brown with Captain Pat Hobart as second-in-command. The four troops were under Second Lieutenant M.F.S. Rudkin (light tanks), Second Lieutenant W.H.B. Bell (light tanks), Second Lieutenant J.K.W. Bingham (cruisers) and Second Lieutenant P.W. Stratton (cruisers). Squadron HQ had five assorted tanks. The remaining light tanks were formed into three troops under Second Lieutenants G.T.A. Strong, C.D. Williamson and T.S.M.C. Board. On 12 June the composite column of thirty-two tanks set off and reached Conches that evening. Patrols were sent out frequently. Second Lieutenant Bell's patrol, aided by a French 'agent' in a scout-car and chaperoned by Captain Hobart, had a nasty fracas near Combon. This involved Sergeant Cross, Corporal Jasper, Corporal Draper and of course Captain Hobart fighting off several anti-tank guns. The running battle ended with two surviving 2 RTR tanks and several enemy guns 'kaput'. On the 16th Brigadier Crocker's force of 29 tanks, 60 other vehicles and 409 officers and men was ordered to proceed to Cherbourg via Domfront, Mortain. 'We moved at wide distance at a steady pace, observing maintenance halts. Fitters' lorries brought up the rear of each squadron and tanks which broke down were repaired and came on,' wrote Crocker. The tanks covered 175 miles in 24 hours and 400 miles in the last six days. Only two tanks failed to reach the port of Cherbourg.

It was no minor achievement. The tanks had already been in a poor state before the last long journey began. Hobart wrote: 'I was bringing up the rear of one little column and was continually having to halt at some stopped tank to see whether it could be patched up or would have to be abandoned. One looked back down the road from time to time and was not anxious to hang about.' His uneasiness was well justified.

The regiment's various segments sailed from Brest on the 16th and from Cherbourg on the *Delius*. The Brest garrison and a party of twenty-four ORs under Captain Carey-Thomas destroyed the many Echelon vehicles left on the quayside. The composite squadron returned to the UK with its tanks disembarking at Plymouth.

★ ★ ★

Two young officers, Norman Plough and Eric Duncan, were posted to a holding camp in France as reserves for 2 RTR. On their arrival at Army HQ, the urgent need for reliable information about the French defence lines near the River Seine meant that the two reserve officers were sent out on motor-cycles to scout the area and report back. Plough's trio arrived on a high ridge overlooking the valley of the Seine and was astonished to see hundreds of French Army *poilus* running away in chaotic retreat. They had abandoned their weapons and each man carried only a cardboard box containing his gas mask! On their return to Army HQ with this news, they were told to get to Cherbourg and on the way to destroy any British Army reserve dumps they came across. At Le Mans racetrack they set on fire a petrol dump and eventually returned to the UK via St Malo. At Thursley near Warminster Plough and Duncan reported to the CO, who gave them command of a troop in 'A' and 'B' Squadron respectively. Rommel's panzers had finally helped push 2 RTR (and much of the BEF) out of France.

CHAPTER TWENTY-THREE

The Western Desert, 1940–1

The regiment reassembled near the Staff College, Camberley, and leave was granted, followed by training, visits (notably by the Prime Minister on 2 July), South Coast Protection (Sussex) and the arrival of new Mk IV A cruisers. When re-equipped, 'A' Squadron had A-13s, 'B' and 'C' Squadrons had A-10s and the Squadron HQs had A-9s. On 10 August orders were received to 'proceed overseas to a tropical climate forthwith'. Vaccinations took place, tropical kit was issued and the tanks moved to Birkenhead. Lieutenant-Colonel A.C. Harcourt still commanded, with Major R.F.E. Chute as his second-in-command; the adjutant was Captain J.A.C. Richardson.

On 20 August a large troop convoy set sail, guarded by fourteen warships including a battleship and an aircraft carrier. The vital reinforcements for the African campaign against Mussolini's vast army included the 3rd Hussars, 7 RTR and 2 RTR. Their personnel sailed in the liner *Duchess of Bedford* and their tanks, respectively light tanks, Matildas and mixed cruisers were carried in three fast merchant ships which travelled independently. After reaching Gibraltar the *Duchess of Bedford* and two cargo ships escorted only by the cruiser *York* sailed for Cape Town and finally reached Suez five weeks after sailing from Liverpool. Soon after arrival in the Delta, 'B' Squadron and its cruisers swapped places with 'B' Squadron of the 3rd Hussars and their light tanks – this was a divisional tactical decision. From October until early December 1940 all the units practised desert movement by day and night, 2 RTR being part of the 4th Armoured Brigade in the 7th Armoured Division. Lieutenant-General R.N. O'Connor had decided to make an aggressive move westwards from Matruh to capture Sidi Barrani and to drive through the line of fortified Italian camps. The enemy strength was 80,000, with 275 tanks. O'Connor's two divisional and support troops of 4th Indian and 7th Armoured Divisions totalled 30,000 men with 275 tanks (including 7 RTR's 45 powerful Matildas). The 7th Armoured Division's role was to cover the main strike force in the north, mask Rabia and the Sofafi group of camps and take on the Italians' mobile reserves. Colonel Horace Birks, General O'Moore Creagh's GSO-1 and also a former 2 RTR boxing officer, took over command of 4th Armoured Brigade. The first objectives were the Italian tank forces clustered round Azzaziya 10 miles west of Sidi Barrani.

The desert approach march which began that night was a great adventure and a complex undertaking, with thousands of vehicles moving forward. An account by P.R.C. Hobart, then second-in-command of 'C' Squadron 2nd RTR, gives an impression of the opening stage:

> Just before dusk on 7 December we started the move forward. I can vividly remember watching the tanks ahead with their hulls hidden in drifting clouds of dust, but with each turret standing out clear and black against the fading western sky, each with two muffled heads emerging and two pennants fluttering above from the wireless aerial. Late at night we halted for refuelling and a few hours of sleep . . . Daylight revealed a wonderful sight, the whole desert to the north was covered with a mass of dispersed vehicles – tanks, tracks and guns all moving westwards with long plumes of dust rolling out behind each of them. One wondered how the attack could possibly achieve surprise – however, no Italian aircraft appeared . . .

The 7th Hussars led the way, followed by 6 RTR and then 2 RTR. They moved at a speed of 8 miles in the hour, on a frontage of 2,000 yards, with a depth of 1,300 yards and a gap of 1,000 yards between armoured regiments. Each squadron moved in a box formation. By 8 December the Desert Rats (so-called after 7th Armoured Division's jerboa emblem) had moved astride of the enemy's line of retreat. 2 RTR was made responsible for the Sidi Barrani area to the coast. The Italian infantry put up little resistance but their gunners caused 'C' Squadron casualties and two A-10s were knocked

2 RTR A-13 Cruiser, December 1940. (*Norman Plough*)

2 RTR group, Alexandria, 1940. (*Norman Plough*)

out. The OC Major J.P. Brown, Corporal Draper and Trooper Lugg were all killed, while Second Lieutenant J.K.W. Bingham, Sergeant Horne and Trooper Lister were wounded.

Many Italian guns were destroyed by the 15-ton A-13 cruiser tanks running them over! By 10 December 1940 2 RTR's 'collection' of Italian prisoners of war totalled 30 officers and 1,000 ORs. Despite run-down tank batteries owing to leaks or wireless watch, the regiment was ready for the next phase after three days of continuous movement. O'Connor's first onslaught had been spectacular – 40,000 prisoners, 240 guns and 70 tanks had been captured at the cost of 600 casualties. 4th Armoured Brigade deployed mixed arms columns, called 'Birks', 'Combes' and 'Harcourt'. 'C' Squadron was now commanded by Captain P.R.C. Hobart with seven A-10s and two A-9 cruisers.

The brigade was now ordered to move into Libya to cover the road between Bardia and Tobruk, and on the afternoon of the 14th 'A' Squadron destroyed three Italian tanks despite being heavily bombed by the Regia Aeronautica. During the night two ambulances were captured containing twenty-five Italians and Libyans. General O'Connor was furious because he had expected a night attack to tackle the enemy who had rallied in the Capuzzo–Sollum area, withdrawing into the Bardia defences. On the 16th 2 RTR moved south and concentrated on the capture of an Italian-held fort at Sidi Omar, garrisoned by the 119th Black Shirt Fascisti Battalion.

Fort Capuzzo, December 1940. (*Norman Plough*)

The defenders were about a thousand strong and armed with 15 guns and 14 Breda machine-guns. The heavy guns of 4 RHA shelled the fort for quarter of an hour, after which 'C' Squadron was to make a direct attack and B Squadron (3rd Hussars) would block the exits to the west of the 'small white fort surrounded by field works and wire and with known mines on the east side', as Brigadier Caunter described it. The RHA barrage ceased at 1645 hours and Captain Pat Hobart's C Squadron launched its attack. He wrote:

We drove around to avoid the enemy shelling while the 25-pdrs did their bombardment, then formed up in line and advanced at full speed on the fort in what I imagined to be the best traditions of the *arme blanche*. The enemy must have suffered pretty severely from the attentions of the RHA, for in we went unscathed, with every gun and machine-gun firing. My orders to the squadron were to drive straight through the perimeter, doing as much destruction as possible, out the other side, and then to return again and rally back on the nearside. I was in the centre of the squadron line, and in an excess of zeal and enthusiasm charged the fort itself. The outer wall was built of solid blocks of stone, and in breaking it I knocked off my nearside idler, so that I found myself inside the courtyard of the two-storey fort with an immobilised tank . . . There were some hectic minutes, particularly as my second-in-command, David Wilkie, was shelling the fort from outside with his close-support tank. During this time I had inadvertently left my no. 9 set switched to 'send', so that all my frenzied orders and exhortations to my crew were going out over the regimental net – which caused considerable pleasure to my brother officers, later embarrassment to me.

Captain D. Wilkie's tank was driven by Sergeant 'Paddy' Bermingham:

Our tank was an A-9 cruiser which although poorly armoured had quite an assortment of weapons. Main armament was a 3.7mm smoke mortar, three Vickers MG1s and mounted for Ack-Ack we had a Bren. Our crew was quite a mixed bag of nationalities. Capt Wilkie, our Operator 'Tumbleweed' Crean, and nearside 'dustbin' gunner, Bill Lawe, were English. Corporal Sid Watkins, our main gunner, was a South African. In the offside 'dustbin' was Tom Carleton (my pal since squaddies); [he] and I, the driver, were Irishmen.

Wilkie's tank had arrived too early on the start line and was heavily shelled:

This kept us on the move and some lovely figures of eight were cut in the sand. Our party arrived and were soon putting concentrations down on the fort . . . After circling the fort once, my commander gave the urgent order 'sharp left'. This turn placed the tank facing a large breach in the fort. I sailed across it, with all machine-guns blazing, and came to rest beside the squadron commander's tank . . . Looking through the visor, I could see Captain Hobart, with steel helmet on, shooting away over the top of his cupola with a pistol. The sight of a second tank inside the fort must have been too much for the Italians and very soon they were appearing from nooks and crannies everywhere to give themselves up.

The battle was over within ten minutes from the moment that the tanks raced in upon the fort. Some 50 enemy soldiers were killed and over 900 taken prisoner. Nevertheless the Italian gunners here, who were Fascisti, had gone on firing resolutely until they were overrun. Fortunately for the attackers, most of the guns were sited on the east, or frontal side. Thus the value of the indirect approach, and of combining attacks from different directions, was clearly demonstrated – as Caunter emphasised in his report. Two 'C' Squadron tanks were mechanically disabled but there were no casualties. All the fort's guns, motor-cycles, mortars, machine-guns and transport vehicles were captured.

Derna Pass, February 1941. (*Norman Plough*)

★ ★ ★

The 6th Australian Division then replaced the Indian Division. 2 RTR passed a peaceful Christmas and the first week in 1941 found them patrolling the outer defences of Tobruk. On the 18th 6 RTR handed over 10 cruisers and 5 light tanks as well as 3 officers and 72 ORs as reinforcements. The main attack on Tobruk started on 21 January and immediately it fell 2 RTR was on the move across 100 miles of desert to Mechili.

Lieutenant R.A. Farran and Lieutenant J.B. Taylor were troop commanders in 'B' Squadron (actually 3rd Hussars' light tanks). On the 24th near Mechili they were attacked by fourteen enemy M-13 tanks which initially chased them. Fortunately 'C' and 'A' Squadrons came to their rescue and in turn attacked the M-13s from the east and south. Five were quickly destroyed and one was captured and driven in by its Italian driver, but the rest escaped. The cruisers' 2-pdr gun could usually deal with the Italian M-13s and Captain Jim Richardson of 'C' Squadron had a field day. Corporal Peter Watson of 'A' Squadron wrote:

> We got a message that the Italian Army was retreating from Benghazi and we had to cut across the desert to cut them off. We had to go through the Djebel which is mountains, rock and desert, sand, very rough territory . . . We travelled day and night for two days. We were so tired we were almost hallucinating. The rocks over which we travelled caused a lot of trouble to the tank tracks and suspensions and proved too much for a number of lorries. We were chasing a desert fox. We had our heads out of the turret and saw miles and miles of lorries as far as the eye could see in both directions. So we battened down and charged. There were eight of our tanks, all that was left out of our squadron's 16 tanks. The long column was seen on 28th January, estimated at 21 tanks, 6 guns and 40 MET. 'B' Echelon had not arrived the previous night so there were many 2 RTR tanks short of petrol, so the action was inconclusive.

The 4th Armoured Brigade remained a few miles west of Mechili on tank maintenance until at mid-day on 5 February the advance continued 90 miles south-west to Msus, a large village in the middle of the desert. The 3rd Hussars, 7th Hussars, 2 RTR, 2nd Rifle Brigade, 4 RHA and a battery of 106 RHA with anti-tank guns composed the brigade which was about to change the face of history – for a short time, anyway!

CHAPTER TWENTY-FOUR

The Battle for Beda Fomm

There are two excellent accounts of this famous battle, one in Captain B.H. Liddell-Hart's *The Tanks* and the other in Lieutenant-Colonel George Forty's *The First Victory*. They tell the story of 2 RTR's participation in the extraordinary battle. It assumed the main role but much honour is also due to the 11th Hussars (the Cherry Pickers), who first reached the coast road 70 miles south of Benghazi; to the 2nd Battalion Rifle Brigade, who first met the Italian forces head on; to the nine 37mm Bofors guns which 106 RHA carried 'portee' on the backs of 15-cwt trucks and which engaged Italian 75mm Italian field guns at 1,000 metres and knocked them out; to the 25-pdr guns of 'F' and 'D' Batteries 4 RHA which fired almost non-stop; to the brave, nippy little light tanks of the 3rd and 7th Hussars which harried, bit and helped destroy the long flanks of Graziani's retreating army; and to 1 RTR's ten cruiser tanks which arrived in the nick of time. But it was the nineteen cruisers of Major Gerald Strong's 'A' Squadron and Major James Richardson's 'C' Squadron that did the brutal business of destroying the Italian M-13 tanks of the 1st Ariete Armoured Division leading the huge column fleeing south from Benghazi. But first of all a look at the battleground is needed. From Benghazi to Ghemines the coastal road ran due south, parallel to the Gulf of Sirte, towards Agedabia. As the Italian 10th Army straggled south, just over half-way were the two modest landmarks of Beda Fomm and Sidi Saleh, both on the east side of the road. The three most noticeable points were a tall windpump, the Pimple (a small hillock) and the white Mosque ridge, clustered together between Beda Fomm and the main road. The steel-framed wind-powered waterhole at Beda Fomm was surrounded by Arab graves and mounds and could be seen from some distance away.

First on the scene – of course – were 'A' and 'C' Squadrons of the Cherry Pickers (who had so dominated the early war against the Italians). Next came the flying column of wheeled units from 2nd RB, 'C' Battery 4 RHA and 106 RHA's anti-tank guns which had left Msus and Antelat on 4 February and arrived at Sidi Saleh at noon on the 5th. Known as Combe Force, it was soon in action as the enemy column arrived at 1430 hours – about 20,000 Italians with guns and tanks against Lieutenant-Colonel John Combe's 2,000 men and 20 guns. The riflemen and the anti-tank gunners battled away until at 1815 hours the 7th Hussars leading 4th Armoured Brigade appeared and tore into the action; devastating the long line of MET,

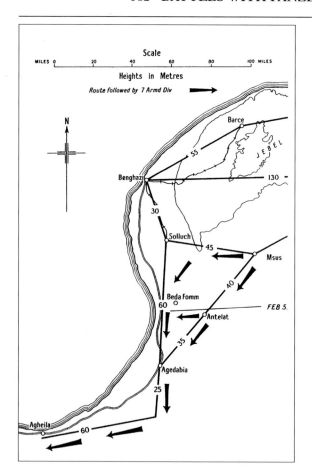

The advance through
Cyrenaica, 1941.

they took 800 prisoners and 'immobilised' well over 100 trucks and lorries.
The 3rd Hussars, 'A' Squadron (Major Gerald Strong) and 'C' Squadron
(Major James Richardson) 2 RTR arrived an hour before dusk. At 1700
hours Lieutenant-Colonel Harcourt, CO 2 RTR, had ordered Strong, then 10
miles away from Beda Fomm, to go forward at his top speed of 30mph to stop
the Italian column at all costs with his A-13 cruisers ('C' Squadron had A-9s).
They immediately attacked an Italian artillery column. Lieutenant Norman
Plough was a troop leader in 'A' Squadron and he later wrote a detailed report
of the battle with maps and photographs: 'We had identified Beda Fomm on
the map and with knowledge of the area, located on the main
Benghazi–Tripoli road, as a wind-generated watering hole and Arab
graveyard. On the last section [of the advance] from Msus our nine remaining
first A-13s were sent ahead . . . we dropped 3 or 4 on this last run, mostly loss
of tracks.' Major Strong radioed back to the CO: 'Have cut the road near a
white mosque.' From there he could see the main enemy column of the Babini
Armoured Brigade under Major-General Cona. There were tanks, supply

lorries, cars, buses, water-carts and petrol tankers stretching for miles. Strong
selected as his vantage point the little ridge named the Pimple. A short time
after their arrival two odd events occurred. Norman Plough recalled: 'Two
single-decker buses appeared on the road. A burst of machine-gun fire
stopped them near the cutting through the mound [Pimple]. They were full of
Italian civilians and women who were unloaded and sent to safety in the sand
dunes. We moved the coaches to form a road-block about 50 yards from the
cutting. Light faded and it was soon pitch dark.' About two hours later
Lieutenant Plough heard tanks and transport approaching the road-block. He
moved his A-13 closer. At the head of the convoy were two closed-down
M-13 tanks about 20 yards away. He told his radio operator Trooper Elfred
'Taffy' Hughes to go forward and tap on the lid of the first tank with his
revolver to see if there was a crew inside. Hughes did so, covered by fire from
two cruiser tanks. 'I marched the Eyties back towards our tanks past a big
naval gun on wheels.' Hughes 'persuaded' an Italian officer in beautiful

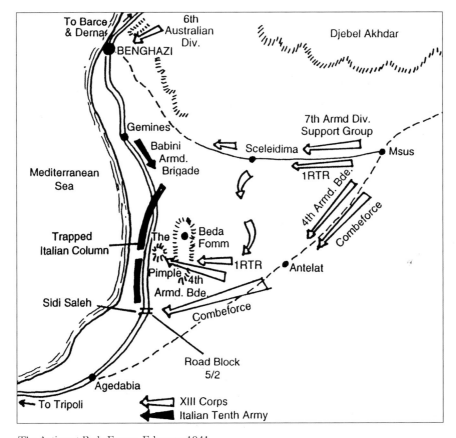

The Action at Beda Fomm, February 1941.

powder-blue uniform with gold braid to 'join' his prisoners of war. Hughes was later awarded the Distinguished Conduct Medal. During the night there was heavy rain and a howling gale. Sergeant Kenneth Chadwick wrote:

> First light showed what the battlefield was like – completely flat, sandy with a little loose scrub, empty 4-gallon petrol cans blowing about, muddy in places because of the rain. The road was a track with telephone poles marking the edge, and the 'Pimple', a small hill, a ridge with a tomb on it. A mile to the east was another ridge with a tomb, called the Mosque. Here stayed 'A' Squadron. Nothing could be seen [normally] up or down the road for some eight miles. Beda Fomm, two road houses, a road, some windmills, two ridges and a 'Pimple'.

Next morning, the 6th, the enemy's main columns began to appear escorted by over a hundred M-13 medium tanks, whereas Brigadier 'Blood' Caunter could only muster a total of 20 cruiser tanks (1 RTR had 10 and 8 lights, but they were some distance away, and 2 RTR had 19). The defences of 4th Armoured Brigade were clustered round the 'Pimple': Brigade HQ with 2 cruisers and 3 light tanks; 3rd Hussars with the borrowed cruisers from 'B' Squadron 2 RTR and 6 light tanks; 7th Hussars with 1 cruiser and 29 light tanks; 2 RTR with 19 cruisers and 8 lights; plus of course the determined and experienced 2nd RB, a battery of 3 RHA/4 RHA and 106 RHA.

Soon after sunrise Major Strong had reported to his CO 'a colossal column packed on the road, stretching as far as we can see'. Brigadier Caunter then ordered the 7th Hussars to locate the rear of the column and the 3rd Hussars to threaten its flank, while 2 RTR dealt with the head of the column. At 0850 hours Strong reported that he was engaged by ten enemy tanks and supporting artillery. At 0910 the rest of 2 RTR came forward to his aid. Later Strong reported that eight enemy M-13s had been knocked out. Plough recalled:

> We were hull-down below the low ridge. Two groups of M-13 tanks from the 1st Ariete Armoured Division, recently arrived at Benghazi, attacked our position. The first group in two waves was destroyed without loss to us.
> The second group about 40 minutes later advanced down our right flank and three of our A-13s moved across to the Arab grave cairns and tombs. About the same time a few M-13s advanced down the east side of the road and knocked out Lieutenant Henry Dumas's tank. I joined him for a few minutes while he took over one of his other troop tanks. [Dumas's radio operator was killed and two of the crew wounded but they were picked up by a light tank of the 3rd Hussars.] This second group of M-13s was also destroyed or withdrew from the action. The Italian tank crews were 'green' with little battlefield experience. Their tactics were poor. We were lucky. We had protection from the mound and road defile, they had none and had to advance across open ground.

Nevertheless the Italian guns put a heavy barrage on to the 'Pimple'. However, the eastward flank enemy attack was sufficiently strong to force 'A' Squadron to withdraw to the Mosque ridge about a mile east of the road to avoid being cut off. Here a further seven M-13s were knocked out. Major James Richardson arrived in the nick of time and by clever battlefield manoeuvring and hard fighting raked the enemy's flank.

The two squadrons claimed a further eight M-13s. Thus emboldened, Richardson asked Lieutenant-Colonel Harcourt for permission to attack and retake the 'Pimple'. He led 'C' Squadron on a circuit to attack from the north and after a bitter struggle recaptured the mound and claimed a 'kill' of ten more Italian tanks. While this counter-attack was going in, Harcourt ordered Major Strong's 'A' Squadron to turn south and catch the enemy column that had succeeded in breaking through. For 5 miles 'A' Squadron's cruisers chased up and down the line, shooting up ten more M-13s and even more MET. Lieutenant Norman Plough's tank and his troop had been in the thick of the fighting. 'Topper' Brown, his 2-pdr gunner, described the action:

It rained very heavily for most of that night – my duty was the second half of the guard and I was soaked, even wearing my greatcoat. We were hull-down behind a low rise and just as it began to get light Lieutenant Plough suddenly said: 'They're here, reverse!' Whilst the driver [Corporal 'Barney' Barnes] was reversing I managed to get into my gunner's seat and the next thing I saw as I looked through my sights was an M-13 about 30yds away, coming straight towards us. Without thinking I pulled the trigger of the 2-pdr but I didn't even see any tracer. I thought: 'Oh my God, I've missed.' I gave it another one, but just then one of the crew climbed out of the top so I shot him. Daylight shone through the hole made by my first shot – was I relieved! We were so close that the tracer hadn't time to light up. Another M-13 came up almost alongside it so I hit that one as well; knocking both out took less than a minute.

Practically all morning we never stopped firing at wagon loads of infantry or tanks. I haven't a clue how many enemy I killed, but it must have run into hundreds. We definitely had a score of 20 M-13s at the end of the day . . . At times we were getting overwhelmed and

2 RTR group after the battle, February 1941. (*Norman Plough*)

had to keep withdrawing to the Pimple. One time we came around the right of the Pimple and stopped. My orders were to traverse left and I then saw at about 600 yds an M-13 coming towards me on absolutely flat ground. Just as I was about to fire Taff said, 'There are only two rounds left.' I cursed but fortunately hit the tank with both . . . We had started out with 112 rounds of 2-pdr .97 in the racks and 15 extra . . . We then went back for more ammo – I was also nearly out of .30, so you can understand the amount of firing that I had done.

Next thing we were back in the thick of it again. I can honestly say that I didn't at any time feel scared; this I attribute to being so busy, also to the calm commands of my commander. We literally didn't have a quiet moment all day. If we weren't firing at guns or tanks we would pull up behind a wagon-full of infantry and just pour dozens of BESA into the packed wagon. They simply didn't have any idea, or maybe they were petrified. I can recollect each tank I knocked out quite vividly, also several of the infantry wagons. When we pulled back after dark it was sheer relief. My eye ached with the strain of looking through the telescope for about thirteen hours without a break.

At about 1115 hours 'A' Squadron's five tanks returned to the main battle area only to find that another large column was now approaching and both squadrons were running short of ammunition. Brigadier Caunter ordered the 3rd and 7th Hussars to keep up the pressure from flank and rear respectively. 'A' and 'C' Squadrons were merged under Major Richardson and took over all the ammunition from RHQ's four tanks. Three out of twelve M-13s were knocked out but heavy Italian field-gun fire hit four of the remaining 2 RTR cruisers, including Richardson's. Lieutenant-Colonel Harcourt ordered the composite squadron out of the mêlée and back to the Mosque again where Major Woollcombe's LAD lorries were waiting with POL. But three cruisers had to be abandoned on the way back. By 1415 hours replenishment was completed and the composite squadron went back into the battle to a point a mile south of the Pimple. On the flank the 3rd Hussars were greatly helped by 'B' Squadron 2 RTR who were on 'exchange'. Their six cruisers claimed three M-13s for the loss of one tank. Lieutenant Roy Farran of 'B' Squadron 3rd Hussars (part of 2 RTR) wrote:

> Jim Richardson put his eight cruiser tanks around the pimple-shaped mound on which stood the mosque of Beda Fomm, he broke up wave after wave of Italian tanks. The M-13s were coming in along the line of the road in batches of thirty tanks, but each time their attack met disaster when they encountered the cruisers around the mosque. Their crews were brave enough but their tactics were almost too crude to be sane.

By 1530 hours Richardson's composite squadron had been forced to fall back again from near the Pimple to a rallying point 3 miles to the south. 'F' Battery RHA came into action from the Mosque ridge with great effect, so the four remaining 2 RTR tanks returned to the Pimple and held their place in the line until 1800 hours; then, heavily outnumbered and short of ammunition, the survivors fell back eastwards under cover of a smokescreen to replenish from Woollcombe's LAD near the Mosque. The Brigade second-in-command, Colonel Horace Birks, wrote: 'For two miles north of "The Pimple" the road and its borders presented an extraordinary sight – knocked out tanks, abandoned tanks, ditched tanks, burnt-out vehicles, dead and dying Italians with many trying to surrender.'

Some of the huge Italian column evaded their tormentors during the night, and some moved west to try to escape by a track along the coast. But Combe Force, acting as long-stop further south, caught the Italian 'refugees'. Just after daylight on the 8th twenty M-13s led a column that burst through the 2nd Rifle Brigade defences until D and F Batteries RHA halted them in their tracks. Soon white flags were fluttering and tens of thousands of Italians surrendered.

Graziani's army was smashed. The Italian legions were no more. General Tallera was killed. The famous General 'Electric Whiskers' Bergonzoli was captured. Major Strong described the littered battlefield as 'just like Hampstead Heath after a bank holiday'. 2 RTR collected 15,000 prisoners and much loot, including rather smart cars and a few equally smart ladies! Almost unbelievably, their casualties were just three killed in action and four wounded. A total of 101 M-13 tanks were found on the battlefield, mostly in front of 2 RTR. While 48 had been hit by 2-pdr shells and 8 by other guns, 6 were uncertain and 39 had apparently been abandoned intact. It was a famous victory.

Major M.J. Woollcombe and the LAD were magnificent. The 2 RTR fitters and drivers of the supply trucks loaded with ammunition, oil and petrol came right up into the battle zone to effect repairs and refuel tanks. Major Strong's tank was serviced by a lance-corporal and two ORs who carried spare track pins and plates and essential tools in an open truck. Captain P.R.C. Hobart, the adjutant, wrote: 'Our 'B' Echelon commanded first by Max Solly then by John Bonham-Carter was wonderful. They never failed to contact and replenish us each night and drove continuously by night and day hundreds of miles often over frightful going!'

After the action Majors Woollcombe and Richardson were both awarded the Distinguished Service Order and Major Strong won the Military Cross. SSM Priest, Corporals Gibbs, Nunn and Brand, and Troopers Cox and Hughes were each awarded the Military Medal.

CHAPTER TWENTY-FIVE

Operations Brevity
and Battleaxe

After Beda Fomm 2 RTR was withdrawn to the Delta and later re-equipped with the usual mixture of A-9s, A-10s and A-13s, most of them in a poor state. The original 'B' Squadron loaned to the 3rd Hussars was returned and the Hussars got back their own light squadron. At the same time the regiment moved from the 4th Armoured Brigade (Black Jerboa) to the 7th Armoured Brigade, which was destined to become a 'Green Jerboa' formation for the rest of the war. Compliments came from GOC 7th Armoured Division, Major General O'Moore Creagh, about their fine performance at Beda Fomm. The 26 officers and 434 ORs arrived at Mersa Matruh via Tobruk and Alexandria, and then moved on to Sidi Bishr camp, 10 miles east of Alexandria. Major R.F.E. Chute and the quartermaster met them with fifteen lorries, and some leave parties went to Cairo or Alexandria. After a variety of rather mundane tasks – garrison guards, working parties at the docks, escort parties for Italian prisoners – and various courses, the regiment received a draft of 8 officers and 68 ORs and began to prepare itself for the next action, Operation Brevity.

Operation Compass had been an overwhelming success. But victory changed to humiliating defeat in just a few months. Churchill decided to send an expeditionary force to help Greece fight off Mussolini's assault via Albania. This automatically reduced General Wavell's strength in the Western Desert. Two of his best generals (O'Connor and Neame) had been captured. The British tanks were worn out with excessive track mileage. The biggest single factor was the Führer's decision to back up his ally's failures in Africa by sending a professional panzer commander, General Erwin Rommel, with equally professional troops (and the assistance of the Luftwaffe) to drive the Axis forces forward to the Delta. 2 RTR were, of course, little more than pawns in this grand design. Operation Sonnenblume ('Sunflower') was the Afrika Korps' main operation which had brought the panzers (and their Italian allies) sweeping up to the outskirts of Tobruk by early April 1941. The Greek government surrendered on 25 April and General Wavell decided to launch Operation Brevity on 15 May towards Sollum and Bardia, in the hopes of relieving the now heavily besieged Tobruk. Corporal Peter Watson of 'A' Squadron 2 RTR wrote:

'C' Squadron 2 RTR tank crew in the desert, 1941. (*Richard Clifton*)

After Beda Fomm we handed over what remained of our tanks to another regiment and went back to Egypt 600 miles across desert in a lorry. Very rough going that was. We re-equipped in Egypt with old tanks done up in the Ordnance Depot's workshops. We were still getting our old surviving tanks, still inefficient, under-gunned, under-armoured and completely worn-out. Back to the desert again for [another] Libyan frontier campaign.

Lieutenant-Colonel R.F.E. Chute now commanded a regiment equipped with twenty-nine reconditioned tanks, mainly A-9 and A-10 cruisers. 2 RTR and 6 RTR were the main formations of 7th Armoured Brigade. 2 RTR went back into the fray on 12 May and soon fifty enemy MET including tanks and armoured cars were reported east of Bir Habata and a further seventy MET around Bir Dignaish. The role of the regiment, on the left wing of the British attack, was to advance to Sidi Azeiz, 12 miles north-west of Capuzzo and, cut the enemy's line of retreat. At 1000 hours on the 15th 'A' Squadron went into action against 12 enemy AFVs, which later became 30 AFVs and 20 MET. 'A' Squadron went through a gap in the frontier wire, met a German tank patrol and exchanged fire. One German Mk IV was knocked out in exchange for a cruiser hit. 'C' Squadron went to watch Capuzzo, which was reported captured but was then recaptured by the enemy. Aggressive movement by Captain Mark Rudkin's A-13 troop forced the enemy to withdraw. 'A' Squadron then patrolled across the Capuzzo area near Sidi Azeiz. Enemy bombing was heavy during the day but caused no casualties. Due to the lack of spares some of the elderly tanks had to be towed back to their leaguer. Sergeant Kenneth Chadwick wrote 'our tank

Gun cleaning in the desert, 2 RTR, 1941. (*Richard Clifton*)

state was 24 fit after a fashion'. Thick mists made for poor visibility and Lieutenant-Colonel Chute ordered 'C' Squadron to attack the head of an enemy column and then withdraw. 'C' then engaged 8 Mk III and 4 Mk IV tanks. Shortly before last light the enemy withdrew as they were bombed by the RAF. The next day 2 RTR withdrew 10 miles, leapfrogging squadrons, to Sidi Suleiman, with twenty-two cruisers in 'a shaky condition'. The German commander Oberst von Herff put up such a spirited performance that Operation Brevity ended as a minor disaster with twenty Matilda tanks destroyed and over a thousand British casualties. Halfaya Pass was recaptured by the Germans and fortified with a line of the newly dug-in 88mm anti-tank guns.

On 28 May 2 RTR reorganised itself once again as a composite squadron. The brand new Crusader tanks which arrived from England were allocated to 6 RTR.

★ ★ ★

Operation Battleaxe followed a month after Brevity. Its object was the capture of the Halfaya-Sollum-Capuzzo area by 4th Indian Division, supported by 4th Armoured Brigade. Meanwhile 7th Armoured Division, including 7th Armoured Brigade (2 RTR and 6 RTR), had to protect the Indians' southern flank and, as their first objective, capture Hafid Ridge, which lay just on the west side of the frontier wire, 5 miles west of Capuzzo.

Early in June the regiment was in Mersa Matruh, with 'B' Squadron again detached to the 7th Hussars. They returned on the 4th, arriving at Bir Thalata with thirteen A-13 cruiser tanks and their 9 officers and 133 ORs. 'B' Echelon brought up seven A-9 cruisers which had been lent to the 7th Hussars for training. They were in poor condition and lacked wireless sets and tank telephones.

Operation Battleaxe started on 14 June with the Cherry Pickers in front and to the left of 2 RTR, which had moved off at 1430 hours and arrived at Kireigat at 2000 hours. RSM Duvall brought up an echelon convoy including POL. The tank state was 'A' Squadron 15, 'B' Squadron 15, 'C' Squadron 4 and HQ Squadron 4, giving a total of 38 rather mature cruisers. The advance continued on the 15th at 0315 hours and by mid-morning the leading elements had reached Hafid Ridge and reported it clear of enemy. However, the Cherry Pickers claimed their leading squadron had been heavily fired on from Hafid Ridge. Visibility was very poor. 'B' Squadron met heavy fire after reaching the first of three crests and was forced to withdraw. The enemy had twelve field and anti-tank guns well placed in defence. At 1145 hours 'A' Squadron and an RHA battery renewed the attack as 'B' Squadron drove in from the flank and swept at full speed through the enemy guns, shooting them up and only losing one cruiser in the process.

Lieutenant-Colonel Chute spotted further guns behind the next crest and ordered the squadrons to wheel south and get out. But 'B' Squadron was already in trouble, as Major Scoones related: 'The squadron wheeled right to overrun the enemy and all the anti-tank guns, which included some 88mms (less one) were either overrun or destroyed. A simultaneous attack

2 RTR concert party, Mersa Matruh, July 1941. (*Norman Plough*)

by another armoured unit on our left flank [6 RTR] never materialised and the attack by 'A' Squadron was not pressed home.' Captain V.D.C. York behaved courageously in trying to rescue Captain Duncan's crew from their burning tank. Duncan was severely wounded and his crewmen died. Sergeant Cross's tank was hit and Troopers Meadows, Miller and Goddard under heavy machine-gun fire were taken prisoner. 'B' Squadron was actually in among the enemy positions. Five tanks failed to hear the order to retire and were never seen again. They were probably the tanks lacking wireless sets. That night 2 RTR's strength was down to 19 tanks, having lost half its number in the battle. Their neighbours 6 RTR were down to 18. But the war diaries say that by the morning 2 RTR was up to 28 and 6 RTR to 20. Corporal Peter Watson of 'A' Squadron wrote:

> These campaigns used to last about six months. The Germans had a lot more tanks than us [not exactly true!]. Mk IIIs and IVs which were vastly superior to ours [not exactly true!], so we used to go up to the wire, the frontier, this huge fortification of barbed wire between Libya and Egypt. There we used to establish contact with the enemy every day and have a little bit of battle. We used to run along a ridge below the level of the sand and pop up, let the enemy see our turret, then we popped down, go along a bit and look up again, trying to deceive them into thinking we had lots and lots of tanks. One day at sun-down in our laager, the camp, the enemy came up on our left flank. He heavily slaughtered us. Phew! We only managed to extricate ourselves by withdrawing through our own [RHA] 25-pdrs firing alongside us at the enemy.

During the night the regiment was reorganised into a composite squadron under Captain D.M. Wilkie MC with 7 A-10s, 3 A-9s and 5 A-13s. They stayed on the wire north-east of Sidi Omar, having been forced back by a strong German thrust into the 6-mile gap which separated them from 6 RTR. Panzer Mk IVs with strong artillery made a fierce attack on 6 RTR, which by nightfall had only nine remaining Crusaders. By the end of Operation Battleaxe the brigade had only 25 tanks left in action. In the second day of the battle losses in the brigade were 7 tanks knocked out and another 16 disabled by fire. 2 RTR withdrew to Bir Kireigat, 15 miles east of the frontier wire.

Lieutenant-Colonel 'Pip' Roberts, GSO2 at 7th Armoured Division HQ, wrote: 'At last we knew that 6 RTR had to withdraw after heavy casualties. The German withdrawal was a trap. Many anti-tank guns had been left in concealed positions around knocked-out vehicles and held their fire until the tanks were within "killing" distance and quickly knocked out eleven with others disabled.' The 6 RTR War Diary noted: 'Although 2nd Tanks fought a magnificent rearguard action until nightfall, they were unable to hold up the rapid German advance.' Sergeant W. Davidson, Sergeant L.A. Vincent and Trooper E.R. Woodward each won the Military Medal for their bravery in the battle on 21 November.

Operation Battleaxe became a byword for blundering. By retaining command of the battlefields, Rommel's real tank losses were only 13 destroyed! The British armoured brigades claimed 100, but themselves lost a total of 91, of which 64 were Mk I Matildas.

CHAPTER TWENTY-SIX

Operation Crusader

Four days after the end of Operation Battleaxe General Auchinleck, GOC in India, changed places with General Wavell. Despite Churchill's anxiety for action in North Africa, the cautious 'Auk' waited five months before he felt his forces were strong enough to give battle again. British forces were built up to a strength of 115,000 troops, including a further ten armoured regiments. Meanwhile Rommel also received reinforcements, including many medium panzer Mk III cruisers, and built up his tank-busting 88mms to thirty-five.

Still commanded by Lieutenant-Colonel Chute, 2 RTR spent this time training, on courses, guarding (variously mine spotting, boom defence and Ministry of Defence duties), uncasing, assembling and driving vehicles that arrived by sea, and enduring inspections, notably by General A.C. Cunningham, GOC 8th Army, Major-General W.H.E. 'Strafer' Gott, GOC 7th Armoured Division and Brigadier G.M.O. Davey, OC 7th Armoured Brigade. On 3 November the C-in-C General Sir C.J. Auchinleck and Lieutenant-General A.R. Godwen-Austen, Commander XIII Corps, visited and inspected 2 RTR. There was also much sport and local leave, of course.

The 7th Armoured Brigade (2 RTR, 6 RTR and 7th Hussars) was one of three such brigades in the 7th Armoured Division. This made for an impossibly unwieldy formation. 2 RTR was equipped with forty-five cruisers and moved from Mersa Matruh to the Piccadilly point. The grand strategy for Operation Crusader, with overwhelming tank strength of 774 (including 210 Mk 1 Matildas), was to destroy the Axis army. Rommel had three Italian divisions as well as 15 and 21 Panzer and 90th Light Divisions with a tank strength of 388. The odds of two-to-one looked reasonable! The problem was that Rommel actually had by now 558 tanks, of which two-thirds were panzers Mks III and IV (plus the thirty-five 88mm anti-tank guns).

The 7th Armoured Division's main task was to capture the airfields of Sidi Rezegh and El Adem, 25 and 20 miles respectively south-west and south of Tobruk, both sited on escarpments. The Tobruk garrison would then leave their lair to link up with XXX Corps and force the Axis troops to retreat westwards.

On 18 November 1941 the centre column, 7th Armoured Brigade, leaguered about 10 miles north of the Trigh el Abed and 20 miles south of Sidi Rezegh. A motor track down the 100ft-high escarpment led via a

Norman Plough's knocked out A-13 tank at Sidi Rezegh. (*Norman Plough*)

second escarpment towards Tobruk, 12 miles away. After refuelling in the morning 2 RTR, having discarded the canvas screens that camouflaged the tanks as lorries, led the advance on Sidi Rezegh. The very soft sand bogged down both the tanks and the wheeled vehicles, so a detour to the west was made. At 1500 hours 6 RTR took the lead; its tanks soon reached and overran the Sidi Rezegh airfield, capturing nineteen enemy aircraft. Corporal Peter Watson of 'A' Squadron wrote: 'Re-equipped again with the same collection of worn-out tanks we went back to the desert for the second Libyan campaign. There was quite a lot of army [this time]. Our tanks were disguised as lorries with a framework with sacking over it. We crossed the wire at Fort Maddalena, an Italian fortress in the desert.' Watson saw the German airfield where 'planes were taking off and landing. We roared in and shot them up. We ran over the tails of the planes that tried to get away.' Lieutenant N.M. Raven led a night patrol to defend the leaguer, 'after 'C' Squadron crews enjoyed themselves smashing everything on the airfield with sledgehammers and pickaxes,' recalled Major M.F.S. Rudkin. His narrative continues: 'About 11.30pm, when the leaguer had settled down for the night, the tanks refuelled and the crews fed, the sound of diesel lorries could be heard a few hundred yards away to the north. Shortly afterwards the sounds of digging could be heard from the west.' The War Diary noted: 'During the night the leaguer was approached by a German patrol which was driven off and six prisoners taken by a scout-car troop under Sergeant Hopwood. Enemy movements all night; they appeared to be working, quite openly, with no regard to noise made, and seemed to be bringing up guns of some sort from the valley to the north of the regiment's position. Three times during the night small-arms fire was directed into the leaguer and was returned by sentries. All this activity kept everybody awake and inside their tanks.'

On breaking the leaguer in the morning considerable fire came in from enemy anti-tank guns; two cruisers were hit and burnt out and a third was missing. 'A' and 'C' Squadrons were engaged for most of the morning. Second Lieutenant R. Titlestad's troop of 'A' Squadron destroyed two of the enemy guns, for which he received the first of his two Military Crosses. As the light improved the enemy's fire became so severe that both 2 RTR and 6 RTR were forced to withdraw a short distance after suffering a number of casualties. Major Rudkin noted ruefully: 'This was not a very good start to Cambrai Day.' It was touch and go until the 7th Armoured Division's Support Group arrived at 1000 hours to reinforce 6 RTR on the southern edge of the airfield and 2 RTR on the ridge behind. The Tobruk garrison was ordered to break out on the 21st, and 7th Armoured Brigade was ordered to strike north to meet the 70th British Division. But at 0800 hours, half an hour before the attack was due to start, two large German armoured columns were seen approaching from the south-east. Brigadier Davy sent the 7th Hussars and 2 RTR hurriedly off to confront this new threat. Lieutenant-Colonel Chute ordered 'B' Squadron under Major

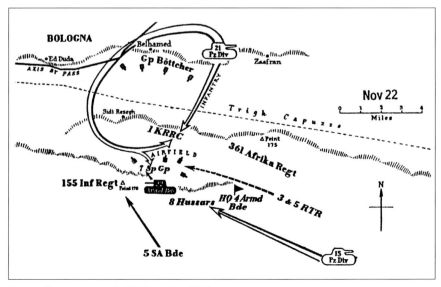

Rommel's counter attack, 22 November 1941.

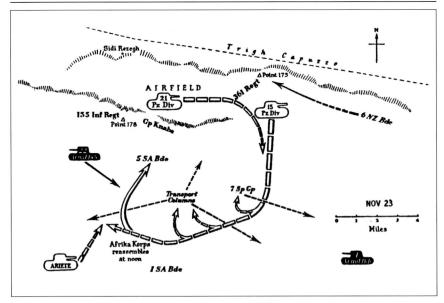

The First Battle of Sidi Rezegh, 23 November 1941.

Woollcombe and 'C' Squadron under Major Rudkin to make a converging attack on the advancing 15 Panzer Division. Rudkin wrote:

> Before fire could be opened, the enemy sighted us and at once turned about and retired at high speed. Many of the enemy tanks were Mk IIs, though there were large numbers of Mk IIIs and IVs in the rear. 'B' and 'C' Squadrons at once gave chase and slowly closed the gap between the two forces. At this stage 'A' Squadron also joined the chase between 'C' Squadron on the left and 'B' Squadron on the right. Some excellent shooting was had by all and a total of fifteen enemy tanks were knocked out, many of the crews being overrun and captured. Enemy fire was poor, and it was obvious that they were not adept at firing on the move, because what return of fire there was, was extremely inaccurate. Had our tanks been fitted with stabilisers, there is little doubt that many more enemy tanks would have been knocked out. However, the chase covered about two miles but was called off when the enemy were seen to retire behind a screen of 88mm guns and other tanks in hull-down positions. This action, which was most successful, raised morale to a very high level, as only one of our tanks had been hit and the crew of this escaped unhurt.

The panzers had turned away to the north to replenish fuel and ammunition. In the afternoon they came back to the attack, having probably lost fifteen tanks in the morning. This time they reached the high ground near Garaet el Nbeidat and from a distance of 2,000 yards poured in fire from anti-tank guns and tanks on 2 RTR. Deployed in line the remaining twenty-six cruisers, including some Crusaders, returned fire but the enemy tanks were mostly just out of range of the A-13 and A-10's 2-pdr guns. In this fire duel 2 RTR lost a dozen tanks and many crews. Six enemy tanks were put out of action and many more hit. Eventually 22nd Armoured Brigade arrived with their ninety tanks and the fifty enemy tanks (including many lights) withdrew north-eastwards in heavy rain and, later, darkness. By nightfall Davy's battered 7th Armoured Brigade had just ten 7th Hussar 'runners', six from 2 RTR, one from 6 RTR and three from Brigade HQ. At first light a composite squadron of twelve tanks was formed under Major Rudkin while Major G.F. Yule formed a protective troop of 'non-runner' tanks whose guns could still fire. The CO and adjutant RHQ on the 22nd were trying desperately to reorganise and to find crews to man any tank replacements received. Lieutenant-Colonel Chute noted:

> On the afternoon of the 21st the enemy succeeded in pinning us in on *two* sides with anti-tank guns while he attacked us *frontally* with his tanks. Once again cruiser tanks had to be used as I [infantry] tanks against an enemy with plenty of anti-tank guns. These tactics must have led to very heavy casualties. The enemy Mk III tanks were awkward customers to take on with A-13s unless they could be caught by surprise in the flanks *without* their anti-tank guns in action as was done in the early morning of the 21st.

During the 21st and 22nd the Deutsche Afrika Korps had reinforced the Sidi Rezegh area and the tide of war was veering Rommel's way. Major Rudkin's composite force was increased by three Crusaders of 6 RTR and joined Brigadier Jock Campbell's Support Group. At 0730 hours on the 22nd the 15 tanks were grouped near Campbell's HQ on the south-east corner of the Sidi Rezegh air strip, facing east, north and west. 22nd Armoured Brigade with 79 tanks was in support on a ridge 2 miles to the south while 4th Armoured Brigade with 108 tanks lay 6 miles to the south-east near Bir el Reghem. When an enemy column of thirty Mk IIIs and Mk IIs got within about 3,000 yards – well out of gun range – Brigadier Campbell, a brilliant and very brave, if not reckless, leader ordered 2 RTR to attack. Previously he had talked to a group of RTR soldiers including Sergeant 'Chinky' Charlie Gibbs, and now he said to Gibbs: 'Go get those three Mk IIIs and I'll give you something to be proud of.' Gibbs did just that – and later received the Military Medal.

Brigadier Jock Campbell RHA won the Victoria Cross at Sidi Rezegh, urging 2 RTR into the highly confused battle in his efforts to prevent the 7th Armoured Division's Support Group being overwhelmed. Major Rudkin, OC 'C' Squadron, recalled:

> Brigadier Campbell seized Major Rudkin's arm and said – 'See that. Attack – and I like speed.' Within three minutes the squadron in line moved off and advanced towards the enemy tanks, Brigadier Campbell travelling with the leading tanks in his staff car. He stood up, waving flags and encouraging the tanks on. The enemy, on seeing this squadron, at once wheeled left to about 1,200 yards, during which time enemy shells and tank fire were directed against our tanks. Deeming the distance now close enough for an effective shoot, the squadron slowed down and halted. Brigadier Campbell was very angry, apparently expecting the tanks to carry out a cavalry charge against the enemy, who outnumbered us by more than two to one . . . One of our tanks had its gun damaged and reversed about 200 yards to put it right. Brigadier Campbell drove over to it, got out of his car, and, livid with rage, threw stones at it, shouting at it to get back into action. After about five minutes the squadron withdrew about 200 yards by reversing, as the enemy fire was heavy. As 1,400 yards was beyond effective 2-pdr range, the tanks ceased fire, the enemy following suit. Brigadier Campbell drove back to his HQ.

The squadron had no communications with Support Group or anyone else. The wireless was only netted to all tanks in the squadron. So the squadron was in no position to receive orders from Support Group HQ, being placed about halfway between the Support Group and the enemy forces. The squadron second-in-command, Captain Plough, was therefore sent back to receive orders. When he reported at the HQ, Brigadier Campbell was still extremely angry that the squadron had not charged right into the enemy. Captain Plough explained that we would have achieved nothing and that it would have been suicide. Whereupon Brigadier Campbell replied, 'That's what you are soldiers for – to die.' He then gave orders that the squadron would hold their present position at all costs. If any tank withdrew a yard, he said, he had given orders for his guns to open fire on it. For the next two hours the squadron remained in position, praying that the enemy would not advance and feeling more frightened of 'Jock' Campbell and his guns than they did of the enemy. Ammunition was running low and the whole position was most uncomfortable. Eventually a portion of A1 Echelon managed to get through and dump ammunition on the ground, from which each tank in turn refilled.

Just as the last troop of tanks was refilling with ammunition, a lot of firing started up behind in the area of the aerodrome. On looking round, Major Rudkin could see a force of about 80 enemy tanks attacking Support Group from the west, and it had already advanced to within a few hundred yards of the aerodrome. The guns of the Support Group were firing at them over open sights at about 600 yards' range. Without waiting for orders, the squadron immediately about-turned and joined in the battle on the high ground at the north edge of the aerodrome. The whole scene was like an artist's impression of a battlefield. All 16 enemy aircraft on the landing ground, which we had destroyed three days previously, had caught fire and had destroyed several of our guns which had been in position under or behind the aircraft. Several enemy tanks were ablaze. Round the blazing aircraft were 25-pdrs and anti-tank guns firing over open sights.

By now the tank commanded by Corporal Peter Watson of 'A' Squadron, with Sergeant Sid Buswell as his tank commander, was unserviceable (only one track, couldn't steer, no reverse gear and the 2-pdr gun wouldn't fire!). The technical adjutant agreed it was not fit. But a few tanks arrived from Brigadier Davy's HQ and Watson was soon back in action:

So we had the Germans in front firing on us. We were outgunned by the German tanks by about a mile as we only had worn out 2-pdrs on ours. That meant that for the first mile of an attack they could hit us but we could not hit them. We had to do a cavalry charge kinking left or right to avoid the shots. With artillery support we started another attack. We raced across the desert towards the Germans. If you're in a tank and an armour-piercing anti-tank shot just misses you, it sounds like this: 'Meeoow!!' If it hits, you hear just a thud, you don't feel much, but if it penetrates you feel just a little shake and depending where it lands, you either survive or you don't. We got hit in the engine. We put out the fire with an extinguisher. That was good. We moved off again and then we got too many hits right in the engine. We carried a hundred gallons of high-octane petrol. The flames shot up 30–40ft high and if you're not out in a few seconds you are dead.

Wounded and burned, Corporal Watson was rescued by an RHA portee and taken back to a field dressing station that was being shelled at the time. Then he travelled back by South African ambulance to Cairo where a Harley Street burns and skin specialist worked his magic on the corporal's injuries.

Back on Sidi Rezegh airfield there was total chaos. The smashed aircraft were burning fiercely, as were knocked out tanks and gun portees. The Support Group had placed its 25-pdrs among the wrecks. Mortars fired outwards and enemy mortar fire came inwards. Major Rudkin's A-15 and A-13 non-runner tanks were firing. Two of them were knocked out by a 'friendly' A-15 Crusader; one went up in flames, the other was towed away. Captain Norman Plough's troop managed to get on to high ground and supported the South African infantry in an attack. The composite squadron was reduced to seven tanks by dusk. On the 23rd Major Yule's force had joined with the remains of Major Rudkin's survivors. Lieutenant Roberts arrived from out of the blue to join them, and then there were sixteen 'runners'. Second Lieutenant Davison's echelon party brought ammunition and POL and the first rations the tank crews had had for three days. Advancing with HQ 7th Armoured Brigade to Bir el Chelb to support the South African forces, 2 RTR encountered yet another large force of enemy MET and tanks. The action continued until dusk and then there were twelve tanks left! During the 24th Major Yule picked up five A-15s from 22nd Armoured Brigade, which were quickly in action against a large enemy column of tanks and MET. The German Mk IV tanks forced Yule's group aside as their 75mm shelling was very accurate. Also Davison's A1 Echelon of soft vehicles needed protection. The nomadic group then linked up with twenty-three Stuart Honeys of 5 RTR; joining up with the 22nd Armoured Brigade they leaguered at Bir es Sausenna. Rommel – that bold 'Chancer' – launched an armoured drive with 21 Panzer Division to reach the Trigh el Abd, and covered 60 miles in just five hours. The 15 Panzer Division, starting late on its drive eastwards, brushed aside Major Yule's little force which continued to harry the panzer advance. Brigadier Alec Gatehouse's brigade with 3 RTR, 5 RTR and the 8th Hussars also joined in, like hunting dogs after a tiger. Intermittent skirmishes took place on the 25th and 26th and the Second Battle of Sidi Rezegh took place over three days starting on the 27th, but not with the same large-scale brutal intensity of the first battle. At mid-day on the 27th the 2 RTR composite squadron around Bir Sciafsciuf encountered a huge column of tanks and MET advancing along the Trigh Capuzzo road. The column was shelled by RHA batteries but forty enemy Mk III and Mk IV tanks attacked the composite squadron. Lieutenants Roberts and Greenhill had their troops in good positions; holding their fire to 800 yards' range, they destroyed four tanks and damaged many others, but in turn lost two cruisers. Captain Ramseyer brought back urgent stores from base HQ. Meanwhile Rommel, furious that his dash for the wire had missed all its objectives, was heading north towards Sidi Rezegh again!

On the 28th battle was resumed against a vastly strengthened Desert Rats division. The 22nd Armoured Brigade, of which the 2 RTR composite squadron was now a part, was up to fifty tanks, plus Major Yule's fourteen, half of them Crusaders and half A-13s. A flank attack on 21 Panzer Division did some damage but Lieutenant Robert's tank was hit and he was wounded. Sergeant Carrie and the fitters worked all night with splendid results. On the 29th and 30th spasmodic small actions took place, inflicting and receiving hits and damage. Nineteen enemy tanks were claimed as destroyed by the brigade. 2 RTR now moved to Maddalena and Major J.R.D. Carlton left with an advance party for Cairo, leaving Lieutenant

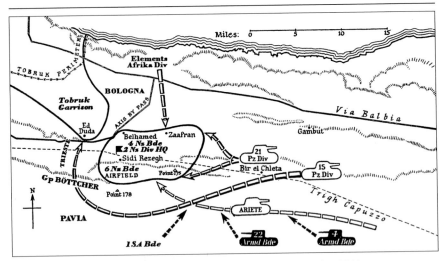

Operation Crusader. The Second Battle of Sidi Rezegh, 27–9 November 1941.

E.J.R. Brotherton and thirty ORs to escort the prisoners to Matruh. Second
Lieutenant J.R.C. Elmslie and thirty-seven ORs left for the desert on a
special salvage mission. And on 16 December Major Yule and the composite squadron returned to link up with the rest at Abbassia camp.

Operation Crusader and the two battles of Sidi Rezegh had been relatively
successful. Tobruk was relieved, but Rommel took his undefeated panzer
divisions westwards to fight another day. 2 RTR had suffered 8 officer
casualties and 66 ORs, 17 of them killed in action. A brigade memorial
service was held in All Saints' Cathedral, Cairo, on 28 December.

Towards the end of Operation Crusader, Alan Moorehead and Alexander
Clifford, with Randolph Churchill, visited the Sidi Rezegh battlefield. Every
few hundred yards there were graves – with the dead man's belt or perhaps his
helmet flung down on top of the fresh earth, and over it a rough cross made of
bits of packing case. Sometimes there were mingled German and British
graves, as though the men had fallen together, still locked in combat.
Sometimes the dead were laid alongside the blackened hulks of their burnt-out
tanks. The tanks themselves still smouldered and smelt evilly. Their interior
fittings had been dragged out like the entrails of some wounded animal.

A month was spent near Cairo. Leave was granted, regimental and cadre
courses were started and guard duties were frequent. An officer and eighty-
four ORs were detailed to guard the British Embassy, the CMP Barracks
and the 63rd General Hospital. Curiously though, three M-3 Stuart, or
Honey tanks arrived for driving and maintenance instruction. This was a
new beast for 2 RTR. Major J.R.D. Carlton MC returned on 29 December
from a conference. He was informed that the 7th Armoured Brigade was to
embark for an unspecified destination.

CHAPTER TWENTY-SEVEN

Burma, 1942

A 2 RTR troop commander wrote the following account of the regiment's final days in the Delta.

The 7th Armoured Brigade spent Christmas 1941 in Cairo. It was a pretty hectic time – meeting up with old friends and doing the high spots: The Carlton, Shepherds, Bardia, Dolls Cabaret, Groppies for tea dances, the Auberge de Pyramid, Mena House, Tommy's Bar for iced tinned beer, and Gazeira. Taxis and garrys conveyed us from one place to another, usually a taxi by day and a garry at night for the garry was cool, comfortable and allowed one to enjoy for a few moments the romance of a starry Eastern night. But at night we were always happy and full of song. On Sunday we rested and many of us attended service at Cairo Cathedral which, although Eastern in design, reminded us of our own churches at home.

Early in January of the New Year the brigade moved out to Tahag, on the banks of the Sweet Water Canal. We found a veritable city of canvas stretched out across the broad wastes of sand; encaged prisoner-of-war camps, RASC dumps, Training Centres, Ordnance Depots and at intervals alongside the tarmac road a string of Shaflos' cinemas. Within days we were reinforced and re-equipped. Officers and men came from the UK and tanks (the light Stuarts, or Honeys) from America. Bush telegraph worked night and day keeping us informed of our new destination. Everything indicated the Far East, for the tanks were painted a dark green. No time was to be lost in preparing for a move.

Through the heat of the day we worked in the tank park. All vehicles had to be painted this dark green colour, drivers familiarised themselves with the workings of a radial engine, gunners stripped down, dry cleaned and greased up the 37mms and Brownings, and operators and tank commanders got down to learning the American W/T procedure. There were tool kit checks, kit inspections and the colonel invited troop commanders to submit designs for the stowage of tank kits and etceteras, paying particular attention to the placing of camouflage nets, bed rolls, steel helmets and haversacks.

In the evenings we leisurely retired to the Mess, or sometimes to the open air cinema. The Mess was homely for we had a brick fireplace built into the tent side-wall and the PMC hung up 'Esquire' pictures – until the colonel finally disapproved of his taste. We sat in camp chairs round the wood fire reading *Penguins* and listening to the wireless. 'Lord Haw-Haw' was then at his best and 'Lili Marlene' was sung on every foreign station. (In the Mess at the time of writing were Colonel Chute, Norman Bourne, Sam Tyrell, Norman Plough, Henry Dumas, Paul Hunter, Willy Davidson, 'Jock' Mutch and Claud Duvall.) The success of the cinema largely depended upon the weather. The slightest wind blew up the sand, the sand got into the sound track and the projector. The result was pandemonium and then the native vendors got cracking with the 'Nutchs, lemonade, velly good.'

Presently, this leisure was put aside when orders came through for the brigade to move. On 28 January the Honeys were loaded on to the tank flats at Tel-el-Kebir – destined for the docks at Suez. By the 27th the brigade was embarked, troops aboard HMT *Ascanius* and equipment on four MT ships. We only knew that our destination was the Far East, probably Singapore. But morale was very high.

Standing on the boat deck that first night, looking out across Suez, the waterways, the entrance to the Canal and the desert beyond, one realised very deeply the vital position that Suez commanded and the part that it played in the Allied efforts in the Mediterranean theatre. Its oil refineries were half lost in a pall of black smoke, ships' masts stood up behind the grey wharf sheds like a forest of leafless trees, winches rumbled under the strain of heavy

Members of tank crews aboard ship, Egypt to Burma, 1942. In the background is HMS *Gloucester* that later sank in the Bay of Bengal. (*Richard Clifton*)

loads, and native dhows laden with crates and bales lay hidden in the still oily quagmires of the back waters. Down on the quayside were numberless crates labelled 'Ford Spare Parts', 'Chevrolet Engines', 'Liberty Aero Engines, handle with care'. And in the wharf sheds were truck tyres, tractors, sacks of wheat, sugar, rice and flour, boxes of tinned foodstuffs and pyramids of grease and oil drums. Out in the waterways tugs and lighters darted about their various courses and deep sirens gave warning of the approach and departure of ocean vessels. Almost blocking the entrance to the Canal lay the *Georgic* three-quarters submerged; the result of enemy air attack. In the hold was captured German equipment.

Our convoy of five ships, escorted by the destroyer HMS *Ajax*, put to sea on 30 January with all caution and secrecy that the moment demanded. To be at sea again was to experience relief and freedom.

The 'A' Squadron vehicles were in the *Mariso*, *Birchbank*, *African Prince* and *Trojan*. The CO was Lieutenant-Colonel R.F. Chute, with Major George Yule (known to Indians and Gurkhas as 'Chota Burra Sahib') as his second-in-command. Major N. Bourne was OC 'A' Squadron, Major J. Bonham-Carter OC 'B' Squadron and Major M.F.S. Rudkin OC 'C' Squadron.

A friendly visit to Colombo was remembered for 'the sweet tang of sandalwood from off the coastline of white beaches and tall emerald trees'. After the fall of Singapore the 7th Armoured Brigade (which included the 7th Hussars, also equipped with light Stuart tanks), via Java, entered the mouth of the River Irrawaddy on 21 February 1942. 'In line we sailed the 15 miles up-river to Rangoon. Somewhere in that direction, we knew not how far, were the Japs. The sun rose very quickly and the great golden Schwedaguang Pagoda, standing behind Rangoon, became a beacon of flame.' The voyage of 4,600 miles was over. The Japanese were rampant; they had taken both Kawkareik and Moulmein, 100 miles due east of

Rangoon across the Gulf of Martaban. On the quayside to greet the convoy were just two people, Brigadier J. Anstice DSO and his ADC 'Watt' Tyler.

Captain Norman Plough, second-in-command to Major Mark Rudkin of 'C' Squadron, wrote:

> Pilots boarded the ships to take us up-river. The countryside was abandoned with no sign of life anywhere. Ships' crews and brigade troops landed and using the ships' derricks unloaded all the brigade vehicles [including 115 Stuart tanks and countless 25-pdr guns and Bren-gun carriers]. We then discovered that Rangoon city had also been abandoned, except for prisoners released from local jails. Japanese air-raids and rumours that the Burma Corps were retreating had caused the evacuation. 'B' Echelons of all brigade units then ransacked the warehouses in the docks, city stores for food – and several large petrol tankers.

'The 2 RTR Echelon in Burma consisted of a hundred vehicles for which three or four miles of road by day and nearly two miles by night were required,' wrote Sergeant Kenneth Chadwick. He went on:

> Rangoon became our own OFP, NAAFI and Woolworth's during the first week. Our 'shopping' expeditions provided us with cigarettes, drink of incredible variety and books for ourselves, vehicles, tins, trailers, etc. Our RASC Company carried our entire supply of ammunition, our requirements of petrol (high octane for the four fighting squadrons and MT spirit in HQ Squadron vehicles and in two trailer tankers each of 400 gallons 'acquired'). From the Rangoon branch of the Burma Oil Company some 3,900 2-gallon petrol cans were 'obtained'. Water was not fit to drink locally except from selected wells. We started with one 230-gallon water cart for the whole regiment, later increased by a 400-gallon BOC tanker. Water had to be provided for the four squadrons, 'A' Company of West Yorks infantry and a troop of gunners (Essex Yeomanry) a total strength of some 800 men. The cart was often required to obtain and issue more than 1,000 gallons a day. Most men were not used to the rather humid conditions and heat in Burma.

Chadwick also noted that there were few maps, and in some areas no maps at all: 'The follow-my-leader principle had to be relied on. Dispatch riders were invaluable as there were few signposts and most were incomprehensible. The new 19 wireless set did not stand up well to the climate. At times the regiment carried almost all the wireless traffic for the 17th Indian Division.'

Major M.F.S. Rudkin 'commandeered' some money on arrival in order to have a pay parade!

Brigadier Anstice told his senior officers that the Japanese had few tanks and their Type 94 and 95 light tanks were of poor quality. Nor did they have an adequate anti-tank gun, which was reassuring. It was definitely not good tank country. The country has two substantial rivers running north and south, the great Irrawaddy and, 50 miles to the east, the Sittang. The few roads and tracks led through rice paddy fields, under water in the rainy season and baked hard in summer (but with many banks and obstructions). And beyond the paddy fields was the jungle, almost impenetrable for tanks.

On 23 February 'B' Squadron hurried to Waw, a small village 20 miles north-west of Pegu and two days later 'C' Squadron took over. Major Rudkin burned the deserted village in order to defend a wooden bridge.

Burnt-out vehicles near Waw. (*Norman Plough*)

Meanwhile the Japanese 213 and 214 Infantry Regiments had forced the huge vital bridge across the River Sittang to be blown, leaving on the wrong side many British, Indian and Gurkha troops who were killed or forced to surrender. Churchill described this as 'a major disaster'. Captain Norman Plough encountered many infantry stragglers from the Sittang débâcle. 'Most had abandoned their personal weapons except the Gurkhas who all carried their rifles and machine-guns after swimming several rivers.'

The next day 'A' Squadron (OC Major N.H. Bourne), patrolling with the Cameronians north of Payagyi, killed fourteen Burmese 'dacoits' armed with Japanese weapons. On 1 March 'B' Squadron moved towards Tazon, and 'C' Squadron towards Waw. Battalion HQ moved to Payagyi, newly equipped with no. 19 wireless sets. The next day Second Lieutenant Yates's troops patrolled an irrigation canal and came under heavy fire from 75mm guns that knocked out two Stuart tanks, killing two troopers and wounding another in a third tank. Troopers Brown and James distinguished themselves. On the 2nd 2 RTR was in action with the West Yorkshires to try to recapture Waw village, but the attack was not successful. Norman Plough recalled: 'Our squadron had an attachment of 4th RHA with two 25-pdr guns and with our 37mm guns and machine-guns set fire to and destroyed most of the Japanese positions. This action continued for two days. We lost two tanks and several were damaged by heavy Japanese mortar fire.'

The Japanese resumed their offensive on the night of 3/4 March, and Major Rudkin's squadron was vigorously attacked at first light in heavy mist.

Their tanks were surrounded and overrun by yelling Japanese who advanced right up to the tanks, some carrying explosives attached to long poles which they attempted to drop into the turrets. However, the Stuarts' machine-guns and the tank commanders' Tommy guns produced deadly fire. Fortunately, the 7th Hussars, who were due to relieve 2 RTR, were now quite close. Major Rudkin wrote:

> I therefore gave orders for each tank to find its own way back to RHQ across country. The going was extremely bad and obstacles were tackled for which the tanks could never have been designed. It was a nightmare journey as one could not pick one's route owing to the mist, and the odd sniper who infiltrated across the road behind us kept the heads of the tank commanders down. By a miracle every tank arrived back safely although the crews were bruised and shaken.

'A' Squadron remained at the level crossing at Khyaiklha and the other squadrons south of Payagyi.

On 5 March Arthur Fearnley, a young troop leader in 'A' Squadron, was sent to rescue the brigade commander of 63 Infantry Brigade, who was with his HQ staff and three battalion COs in Pegu, then surrounded by Japanese forces. Brigadier Wickham and his staff were reluctant to leave but eventually decided to use two Indian scout-cars. 'About mid-day the small column set off southwards down the road, Sergeant Barnes's tank leading, then mine, then the two scout-cars with my corporal's tank bringing up the rear. About half a mile south of Pegu the road passed under a rather narrow bridge. All was surrounded by thick jungle. Beyond the bridge a British truck was slewed across the road.' It was obviously an ambush site. 'Heavy machine-gun firing broke out. The leading tanks passed the obstruction and continued down the road.' Fearnley's tank was hit, and lurched off the road down an embankment. Corporal MacDonald fired a few bursts from his Browning but he was badly wounded. The driver Trooper Ross recalled: 'I saw with horror that the back of his skull had disappeared.' Fearnley saw two Japanese soldiers crawling in the undergrowth and shot at them with his revolver. The radio operator Trooper Bossom, also badly wounded, guided Fearnley as he managed to restart the Stuart and drive it up on to the road and through several road-blocks. 'The tank was festooned with the cores of armour-piercing machine-gun bullets. We had a dead driver, a gunner with a severe chest wound, and a wireless operator with a shattered right leg. Such is the resilience and organisation of a tank unit that within an hour, I had a new tank, a new crew and we were back in business.' Sadly the brigadier and the three Battalion COs were all killed in the ambush. Fearnley was awarded an immediate Military Cross.

On 5 March 2 RTR withdrew to Hlegu for a few days' rest, but the Japanese 33rd Division moving rapidly in its drive to capture Rangoon had erected a formidable road-block across the main road north of Hlegu. Since most of the 17th Indian Division, all of the 7th Armoured Brigade *and* General Harold Alexander (visiting and now commanding all forces in

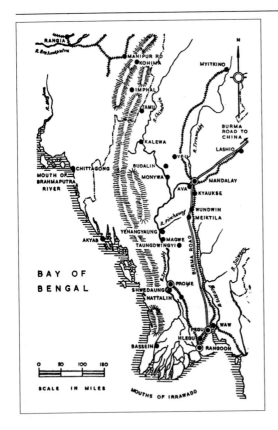

Burma, 1942.

Burma) were waiting to get clear of Rangoon, urgent action was needed. Successive attacks all failed, including the last by Major Bonham-Carter's 'B' Squadron supported by Essex Yeomanry guns. At first light on 8 March Bonham-Carter discovered the enemy had gone – a major blunder by the Japanese General Iida. The retreat north continued towards Prome. Corporal Peter Watson of 'A' Squadron, last heard of seriously wounded in a Cairo hospital, had rejoined his unit.

> We were fired upon, machine-gun fire and mortar fire, but we got out [through the road-block]. We then participated in the longest retreat in the history of the British Empire, but there was one instant that terrified us. An infantry patrol had just gone out one night and they didn't turn up the next day. They were found with their throats cut, their arms cut off . . . . that sort of thing is very demoralising. Anyway we started our retreat. There was no chance at all that we could beat the Japanese: all we could do was to delay them. Hundreds of miles away lay Assam with its mountains. At a certain time the monsoons would come. India would be safe if we got there at the same time as the monsoon broke. That was the plan.

2 RTR provided the main rearguard through Gyobingauk, Paundge and Wettigan, north-east of Prome. On 13 March Lieutenant-General Bill Slim, appointed by Wavell as the new Corps Commander, arrived at Prome and visited all the troops under his command. Slim then wrote:

Brigadier Anstice's 7th Armoured Brigade was also under Cowan's command and I was delighted to see it and note its condition. Its two regiments of light tanks, American Stuarts or Honeys mounting as they did only a 2-pdr gun and having very thin armour which any anti-tank weapon would pierce, were by no means ideal for the sort of close fighting the terrain required. Any weakness in the tanks, however, was made up by the crews. The 7th Hussars and 2nd Royal Tank Regiment were as good British troops as I had seen anywhere. They had had plenty of fighting in the Western Desert before coming to Burma and they looked what they were – confident, experienced, tough soldiers. Their supporting units, 414 Battery RHA, A Battery 95 Anti-tank Regiment and 1st Battalion West Yorkshire Regiment were up to their standard.

Chinese troops of General Chiang Kai Shek's Nationalist Army had entered Burma to assist in the defence of their major supply route, the Burma road, and were under great pressure at Toungoo in the River Sittang valley. On 18 March the 17th Division and 7th Armoured Brigade halted in the Nattalin area to cover the concentration of the 1st Burmese Division at Prome. Two days later the Chinese Army launched its attack but pressure from the Japanese 55th Division persuaded Alexander to ask General Slim to take the offensive to relieve the pressure on the Chinese. A disaster followed as half of the armoured brigade was trapped between road-blocks at Shewedaung. The 7th Hussars lost 10 Stuarts, the Essex Yeomanry 2 guns and the unlucky Duke of Wellington's Infantry took 112 casualties. Eventually helped by 'A' and 'B' Squadron 2 RTR the road-block was broken. Over 300 vehicles had been destroyed or captured. 'C' Squadron held a line astride the road near Prome for the 63rd Brigade to come through. Major Rudkin wrote:

At about 0700 I moved about half a mile east of Brigade HQ, and suddenly saw a column of about 500 of the enemy marching due north about 1,500 yards away. This enemy force had some horses and towed guns but were mostly infantry marching in close column. I at once reported the column to RHQ by wireless and ordered two troops with Squadron HQ to give chase. We were unable to get closer than 2,000 yards owing to a dry river bed which we were unable to cross, and I moved the squadron back to 48 Brigade's position. Had we managed to get within range of this column there is little doubt we could have inflicted heavy casualties on the enemy as he was marching in close column and seemed unaware of our existence.

When we were about 300 yards short of 48 Brigade HQ very heavy and accurate mortar fire started to fall around the tanks and this fire soon spread to Brigade HQ. It was evident that a strong attack was coming in. The heavy mortar fire caused some disorganisation, as the HQ was trying to pack up and move, with the result that there was very little control. As the fire increased, the withdrawal became a rout with the infantry straggling back disorganised up the road. The squadron tried to do all it could to cover this withdrawal, but there was no enemy to be seen, only this devastating barrage of fire.

Meanwhile, as 48 Brigade was withdrawing, 'A' Squadron 2 RTR was in position about 2 miles to the north at Ngabain, and the squadron leader, Major N.H. Bourne, had also sent out patrols to the east. Both patrols made contact with the column that had been spotted by Rudkin earlier that morning, one beating off an infantry attack that was inexplicably made in extended order and the other shooting up a column of mules!

Lieutenant-Colonel Chute went sick and Major George Yule took over command. Almost immediately he suggested that two of his squadrons should ferry the tired and exhausted infantry of 17th Division the 12 miles

2 RTR group in jungle. (*Norman Plough*)

to relative safety at Dayindabo. So 'B' and 'C' Squadron ran a shuttle service with 'A' Squadron providing a rearguard. For eight hours the Stuarts drove back and forth, moving some 2,500 men over distances from 5 to 12 miles. The record was set by a Stuart tank carrying thirty-five Gurkhas!

'A' Squadron had to cover difficult terrain and often the tanks had to tow one another out of dried-up river beds. The withdrawal continued through Allanmyo to Taungwingyi. Corporal Peter Watson of 'A' Squadron recalled:

> All the way up that road for hundreds [*sic*] of miles the Japs used to encircle us and set up road-blocks. Names like these occur to me – Pegu, Tongoo, Tharawady. We went on to Magwe airfield. We had had no air support whatsoever. We found a number of planes loaded up with bombs, right across the airfield. In the barracks, half-eaten meals, half-drunk glasses of beer, beds not made. It was the *Marie Celeste* all over again . . . We had a battle in that airfield during which time the army had to destroy all the bombs that were left. The Chinese Army came over and flew away a number of planes. They were not very good mechanics!

Near the village of Myaungbintha 'B' Squadron was covering the embussing point of 16th Brigade at about 2100 hours on 7 April when the crews heard noises that sounded like tanks moving through the village. At midnight, with the embussing completed, Major Bonham-Carter sent back two troops to act as escort and the remainder as rearguard. The strange tank noises started up again in the village and three vehicles which sounded like Stuarts appeared round a bend several hundred yards down the road with their lights full on. The rear troop of 'B' Squadron promptly engaged them, claiming one definite and two possible hits. They were almost certainly Hussars tanks captured by the Japanese at the Shwedaung road-block. The Japanese now had the capacity to listen in on the brigade's radio frequencies so a basic code was introduced that was known only to 'B' Squadron, and included such words as the sergeant-major's nickname! From 11–14 April the regiment was in action much of the time, with 'A' Squadron beating off a night attack on 48th Brigade. Despite the persistence of snipers at first light the Stuarts launched a small counter-attack on the village of Thadodan. One tank was hit and set on fire but the crew escaped. Then 'C' Squadron and RHQ in close country came under fire from two 75mm guns deployed nearby. The Essex Yeomanry FOO's first ranging round landed almost on his own OP! Lieutenant Banner took his troop to the south to try to spot the guns. Held up by a dry river bed Banner dismounted to reconnoitre on foot and was never seen again. Near Alebo 'B' Squadron with infantry carried out a sweep and destroyed a Japanese patrol in the open. The next day a 'C' Squadron patrol caught a Japanese mule convoy carrying 75mm ammunition and shot it up. Checked by 48th Brigade, the Japanese bypassed it to the west and pushed up the Irrawaddy valley, seizing Migyaungye and threatening the vital oil installations at Yenaungyaung and Chauk. On 13 April the 7th Hussars relieved 2 RTR, whose tanks went north along the road to Magwe to go into reserve. The battle for the oil-fields had started on the 11th and lasted for a week, and inevitably the regiment became involved. There was to be no rest for them, only more fighting. In the afternoon of the 13th they had to fight their way over the Yin Chaung bridge east of Kokkogwa, which was covered by a Japanese 75mm field gun. By stages 2 RTR picked up the KOYLI and ferried them to Milestone 310 to help cover the west flank of the main withdrawal. Major Rudkin's journal continues:

> On 14 April 'B' Squadron, who were still detached, inflicted casualties on the enemy while they were trying to recover transport of the KOYLI's which had been ambushed the night before while trying to reach their infantry. The transport had been abandoned in the village of Tokson and 'B' Squadron sent one troop, 8 Troop, with the KOYLI drivers.
>
> On approaching the village the tanks came under considerable machine-gun fire and it was evident that the village was strongly held. As there were no infantry with the tanks it was not possible to put in an attack. The KOYLI drivers were therefore sent back and the village was engaged by the tanks and the gunners. At least fifty of the enemy were killed. This was confirmed by some of the KOYLI who were at the far side of the village unknown to the tanks. They had tried to contact the tanks to plan an attack on the village, but the tanks had retired before contact was made as the liaison officer from the infantry had gone missing on his way.

On 16 April both 'B' and 'C' Squadrons covered the withdrawal of the two infantry brigades, the 1st and 13th, which were under increasing pressure from the enemy, who ambushed another column of lorries and made 'B' Squadron's tanks a specific target for their mortar teams, causing them to change position constantly.

> Several other enemy columns were reported moving northwards and 'C' Squadron was ordered to assist 'B' Squadron. 'C' Squadron moved off and advanced south from the lateral

Ferrying infantry through the Burmese jungle. (*Norman Plough*)

road running east from Magwe to try to cut the road running north-east into Magwe. The squadron advanced on a front of about a thousand yards so as to try to make contact with the enemy columns moving north and to try to link up with 'B' Squadron on their left. The country in this area had some very thick areas which were interspersed with some large open stretches. Visibility was therefore sometimes only a few yards, and sometimes up to five hundred yards.

'C' Squadron advanced about two miles but found great difficulty in linking up with 'B' Squadron who were withdrawing on their left. 'B' Squadron was continually reporting enemy moving north and north-east up the road to Magwe. One troop of 'B' Squadron was fired on from a village near the main road, one tank being hit by a 75mm. The tank was not knocked out and managed to shoot up the crew of the gun and damage it. At the same time the centre troop of 'C' Squadron was fired on from a village a short distance to the west. Second Lieutenant Timmis's tank was hit six times at very close range by a 75mm, and Timmis, with the remainder of his crew, was killed. The driver, Trooper Russell, was seen to get out after the first shot.

On 16 April Captain James Lunt of the Burma Rifles reported:

The 2 RTR did sterling work ferrying back the exhausted infantry, picking up the wounded and constantly counter-attacking to delay the advancing enemy. Moreover theirs was the only reliable communication available to General Bruce Scott and his harassed brigade commanders. Two tanks were lost but it is virtually certain that without the brilliant work of 2nd Royal Tanks 1st Burma Division would never have got clear of Magwe. That evening Slim ordered most of his precious 7th Armoured Brigade to withdraw through Yenaungyaung to beyond the Pin Chaung.

General Slim gave the fateful orders for the destruction of the oil-fields and refinery on 15 April. A million gallons of crude oil burning with flames rising 500ft. Over all hung a vast sinister canopy of dense black smoke. It was a fantastic and horrible sight.

North of Yenaungyaung lies the Pin Chaung, a dry river bed which was the scene of a Japanese ambush. Sergeant Gibbs of 'C' Squadron had to repair a petrol stoppage and had bumped into a Japanese road-block. Quite soon it became apparent there were three road-blocks slicing up the long column. In the front were 7th Armoured Brigade HQ, half of 'B' Squadron and 'A' Company of West Yorks. Then a road-block. Then 'C' Squadron and half of 'B' Squadron and the whole Burma Frontier Force. Then a road-block. Then the 1st Burma Division and 'A' Squadron 2 RTR. And finally another Japanese road-block!

The columns were three and four deep for a mile in length. At first light half of 'B' Squadron and the West Yorks broke through and freed most of the 'log jam'. The Essex Yeomanry 25-pdrs plastered the Japanese positions. And astonishingly the Chinese 38th Division at long, long last arrived. A plan was agreed that 'C' Squadron with the Chinese would attack across the Chaung to try to relieve the still-trapped 1st Burma Division.

Accordingly, at 0615 hours on 18 April, Major Rudkin reported to 38th Division HQ:

There was little activity except for the cooking of breakfast and it seemed most unlikely that the attack could start on time. I asked the British liaison officer with the Chinese what was

Chinese military friends. (*Norman Plough*)

happening and he informed me that as the Chinese realised that they would not be ready to attack at 0630 hours, they had put their watches back one hour, so that officially they were still attacking at 0630 though the time would in reality be 0730. They had, therefore, not lost 'face' by being late.

The plan was that a troop of tanks would follow the leading troops of the leading Chinese battalion and give what support it could. Another troop was to follow the leading infantry battalion and assist the leading troop if required. The tanks would be almost entirely road-bound owing to the going off the road.

At 0730 the assaulting Chinese moved forward off the ridge on a front of about four hundred yards, the leading troop keeping very close behind on the road. On foot near the tanks was a Chinese interpreter who carried out liaison between the tanks and infantry.

After advancing about half a mile the leading tank was hit by a Japanese 75mm gun situated on the road just north of the Pin Chaung which was firing straight up 300 yards of road. The tank was disabled but there were no casualties.

The Chinese advance continued and by afternoon had almost reached the line of the ford on the Pin Chaung which was still held by the enemy. The Chinese had had heavy casualties, especially among officers, as it was the custom for Chinese officers to lead, whatever their rank. It was finally decided to hold positions about half a mile north of the crossing and continue the attack next day.

The 1st Burma Division's advance north to Yenaungyaung was still stalled by a road-block to Myaunghla, although Major Bourne's 'A' Squadron did sterling work supporting their 1st and 13th Brigades. It was the turn of 'B' Squadron on the 19th to support the Chinese 38th Division. Major Bonham-Carter was told they would be ready at noon, which meant 1300 hours – which actually meant 1500 hours! The attack went well and Thwingon was attacked and taken with the help of 'B' Squadron, numerous Japanese being killed and 200 British and Indian prisoners released. The 1st Burma Division was fortunate. A friendly Burmese told 'A' Squadron of an obscure track round the Japanese eastern flank. The tanks and wheeled vehicles drove along it but the 1st Burma's transport got bogged and had to be burned. The field artillery could not get through, only animal transport. After three days' fighting 'A' Squadron rejoined the regiment after having been cut off. For his part in the fighting escape Major N. Bourne was awarded the Distinguished Service Order.

From 19 April the 38th Chinese Division was involved in further fighting south of the Pin Chaung and then withdrew to the Kyaukpadaung area covered by 'A' and 'B' Squadrons which then moved to Meiktila to turn their Stuart tank tracks. 'C' Squadron stayed with the Chinese for a week. Captain Norman Plough recalled:

We were part of a small mixed brigade supporting the Chinese infantry division in the area of the Magwe oil-fields. They had marched several hundred miles from Mongolia down the Burma road. Major Mark Rudkin commanded our Stuart tanks, a troop of RHA 25-pdrs, a troop of anti-tank guns, LAD section with a recovery vehicle, one water and one petrol tanker, a 'B' Echelon section [and] a medical unit with one ambulance. We reported to General Sun Li Jen, their divisional commander. We discussed tactics and agreed that our tanks would carry into action 10–15 soldiers on each tank, penetrate as far as possible, drop them off and cover their attack with all tank weapons and RHA 25-pdr guns. This type of action went on for several days. Major Rudkin often bravely walked into the jungle with the Chinese infantry to locate the positions of the Japanese mortars which caused most damage to us. Every evening after returning to the Chinese HQ, we discussed the day's operations

Retreat from Rangoon to Imphal.

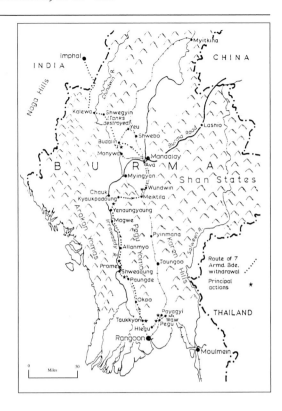

and Chinese casualties. Our medical unit concentrated on helping wounded soldiers. The general was most grateful for this help. He personally interviewed each soldier who returned and rewarded anyone who killed a Japanese. The Japanese PoWs were collected together and tied to posts, their ankles, hands and necks noosed. In the morning most of them had fallen forward and strangled themselves.

Major Rudkin, Captain Plough, Lieutenant Kebble, Second Lieutenant King, SSM Philpotts and Sergeant Hine were each awarded Chinese Medals of Honour. On their last day under the command of the Harvard-educated General Sun, he asked Major Rudkin how many men were in 'C' Squadron. A little later the Chinese handed him 85 rupees, one for each man as a reward for their hard week's actions! Near Pyawbe Major Bonham-Carter of 'B' Squadron set off with two scout-cars to liaise with a Chinese unit which was under pressure. Rounding a corner of the road, they found themselves staring into the muzzles of three Japanese tanks at a distance of 75 yards.

Fortunately for the men in the scout-cars they were genuine Japanese tanks, not captured Stuarts, and they all missed when they fired. The scout-cars turned and escaped but Bonham-Carter 'dealt' with the enemy tanks. The 7th Armoured Brigade withdrew into leaguer north of Wundwin. The Japanese had cut the Burma road at Lashio, 130 miles north-east of Mandalay, and were threatening to cut off all the Allied troops. So on

'C' Squadron 2 RTR, Chindwin River, May 1942. (*Richard Clifton*)

28 April 7th Armoured Brigade retired across the Irrawaddy River by the Ava bridge, but not before a day-long battle around Ngathet and Wundwin, in which 'A' and 'B' Squadrons (the latter with Captain Dumas in command as Bonham-Carter was recovering from a severe snake bite) were both in action. The enemy had, unusually, a fair number of anti-tank guns and four or more tanks. Two Stuarts were knocked out while a third overturned in a nullah and had to be abandoned. Throughout the night 2 RTR continued their ferry service carrying the infantry of 63rd Brigade northwards. Corporal Peter Watson of 'A' Squadron wrote:

> Jenangyaung, the oldest oil-fields in the world, were the next port of call. Hundreds and hundreds of oil derricks right across the landscape all burning, Dante's inferno. We fought a battle there aided by the Chinese Army. From there we crossed the river near Mandalay and got to a place called Monywa where we had another battle with the Japs. [I remember] the smell of putrefying flesh. It was hot and humid and there were dead bodies everywhere. The sun got to them and that cloying smell of flesh putrefying is dreadful.

The Ava bridge lies just south of Mandalay, which had been devastated by Japanese bombers. It was full of deserted stores, fuel dumps and camps, all now burning furiously. Two days later there was another crisis. Burma Corps HQ at Monywa due west of Mandalay had been almost surrounded by the Japanese. Tank support was urgently required to repel the 33rd Japanese Infantry Division, now eagerly marching north after capturing Yenaungyaung. The brigade was sent rapidly to the rescue on a 140-mile march, mainly at night, via Ettaw. 2 RTR arrived near Budalin on 2 May. 'A' Squadron was sent to Alon to cover the river and 'C' Squadron arrived to protect their left flank. The Stuarts' 37mm guns fired AP shot at Japanese barges on the river. The plan was for the troops trapped in Monywa to make their way northwards while the tanks acted as a rearguard on their retreat north.

Captain Norman Plough, second-in-command of 'C' Squadron, noted:

> Our last contact with the Japanese was in the area of Monywa. We were ordered to support a British infantry regiment holding a line across flooded paddy fields. We soon came under heavy mortar attack. The steep muddy earth banking about 2ft-high around each section of the paddy fields restricted our movement to less than 5mph. We had two tank casualties, one with a broken track, the other severely damaged by mortar fire. If a mortar shell landed on top of a Stuart's turret most of the crew would be killed by concussion. Within half an hour the defence line was broken and our infantry retreated in disorder. All we could do was to provide heavy machine-gun fire to hold the Japanese penetration.

The 215th Japanese Infantry Regiment was very aggressive and their tank company (equipped with both Japanese tanks and captured Stuarts) was very active. Major M.F.S. Rudkin described the 2 RTR rearguard action: 'The regiment withdrew at very slow speed up the road [from Monywa] for the next four hours. The speed was governed by the marching infantry in front who had animal transport with them.' One Stuart tank shed a track in the heavy going and Rudkin left another to guard it while the crew effected repairs. At 0400 hours tanks were heard moving towards the RTR leaguer. The NCO commanding the guard tanks in the leaguer assumed they were the stragglers returning – until he heard excited Japanese voices inside one tank (a captured Stuart) that shot and set on fire a genuine RTR tank, burning and killing the crew. According to Major Rudkin:

> The road to Kalewa was only about 12ft wide, through thick and hilly country. In many places there were ravines on one side and the surface being soft many vehicles were lost over the side. Broken-down vehicles were also pushed over the side to keep the road clear. There were many sharp corners and many soft river beds. The many inexperienced drivers in the column added to the hold-ups and breakdowns. Eventually after 24 hours in which we'd covered 54 miles, the regiment formed a leaguer about 11 miles from the ferry on the Chindwin. Three tanks had engine seizures beyond hope of repair and were abandoned after being destroyed [on 6 May]. Little time had been spent on maintenance for eleven weeks, during which many tanks had covered 2,400 miles.

Major J. Bonham-Carter, now second-in-command of the regiment, returned from a recce of the Chindwin River ferry. The recent rise in the river level left little hope of ferrying any tanks across. At the ferry point the river was only 400 yards across but the landing on the opposite bank was 4 miles upstream. The 7th Hussars managed to raft across one tank called 'The Curse of Scotland', but the ferry crew threatened to strike if ordered to tow another raft over. Then RSM Denton managed to get four 8-cwt trucks across laden with walking wounded. But, 3 miles short of the ferry, orders were received to destroy (but not to burn in case of air attack) the remaining seventy Honeys of the brigade – except initially for those of 'A' Squadron. Major N.H. Bourne in the final action supported the gallant little Gurkhas who were fending off the Japanese fighting patrols on the heights overlooking the ferry point. Corporal Peter Watson of 'A' Squadron wrote: 'When we awoke at first light – bang, bang, bang! The Japs were there on the opposite side of the river and on top of a peak. The Gurkhas, dear friends, whom we had fought with, took over. They went across the river, found a bamboo pole and put a flag on top. As the Gurkhas went up the hill attacking the Japs with their kukris and rifles the flag was raised higher and we were ordered to fire above the flag, which we did. Everyone in the area fired.' The 'A' Squadron tanks then met the same fate as the others. The engine sump and radiator drain plugs were removed and when the oil and water had run out the engines were run at high revs until they seized completely. Inside the tanks' (and other vehicles') wiring was stripped out, junction boxes smashed, radios broken up, the guns stripped down and the firing mechanisms broken or buried. Sledgehammer blows distorted the gun barrels. Ammunition was taken away and hidden in the jungle.

2 RTR was turned into an infantry force and divided into platoons of 28 men, NCOs and ORs, carrying twelve days' rations and weapons. The British 25-pdrs were brought down to the water's edge and kept firing to the last moment before they were ferried upstream. After a huge last barrage the remaining guns and tanks were destroyed. General Slim wrote: 'We had saved one-third of the guns (28), some of the best (8) mechanical transport and 4-wheeled lorries but the loss of [70] tanks was a terrible blow. True they were worn out, obsolete, hard to replace in India but they held such a sentimental place in our esteem for what we owed them and their crews that it was like abandoning old and trusted friends to leave them behind.' They had smashed through twenty road-blocks, losing forty tanks in the process. It was a bitter moment for both tank battalions. They had lost forty-five tanks in the eleven-week campaign, about half to enemy action and half to accidents (such as toppling into deep chaungs) or mechanical failure. Major Rudkin of 2 RTR noted that 'the Japanese weapon which did most damage was their 50mm mortar. They used this with extreme accuracy and they penetrated the top of the tanks where the armour was thinnest. One tank of 'B' Squadron stopped for a few moments in an open bit of ground and within one minute received six direct hits. The Japanese 75mm gun used over open sights was fairly effective and stopped a tank but this did not penetrate the front, it often penetrated the side or rear and would only damage the front. About a quarter of the tanks hit by 75mm guns were knocked out.'

Captain Norman Plough recalled:

We started the march to Imphal in an organised column with a few of our own vehicles, reorganised as infantry. All ranks carried their revolvers and rifles, some with tommy-guns. The going was rough through the foothills of the mountain range with many small rivers to cross. This kept us clean after the hot and humid days of the march. We mostly moved at night, it was chilly and often very wet. The monsoon season had arrived.

Of the evacuation Field Marshal Wavell wrote:

2 RTR 'B' Echelon. (*Norman Plough*)

The vast majority of the refugees were ill-clad and ill-equipped. The movement took place at the height of the monsoon in one of the wettest parts of the world; the country through which it was made could hardly have been more difficult. It was almost unknown, almost trackless; the thick jungle was infested with all the tropical plagues of mosquitoes, leeches, flies and similar pests; there were long, steep ascents and descents; deep, swift, swollen rivers lay across the path; there were no local supplies of food available.

Corporal Peter Watson remembered:

We started walking about 2 o'clock that afternoon. We were led by a local Burmese who knew the way. We went along the river bank, sometimes through thick bamboo jungle, sometimes wading up river beds, sometimes up sheer mountains. During the night it was inky black and we were still walking. In single file or double file we would walk, day after day, mile after mile. When we destroyed the lorries they gave us some food, a tin of bully beef, a tin of herrings in tomato sauce, one sock filled with rice, another sock filled with sugar. We handed them in as we went forward to the cooks and got grub from them. We were wearing nothing more than shirts and shorts and walking through torrential rain [the monsoon had started] most of the day. Sometimes the sun came out and we stood there in nothing to dry off.

Many suffered from dysentery and everyone lost weight. Watson had foot rot in his left leg and jungle ulcers all up his right leg: 'I could hardly walk, but I was so frightened of the Japs so I kept going. After about ten days the column reached Milestone 108, a barren hillside not far from Imphal, and stayed there for a week. Then a convoy of RASC vehicles carried the regiment to the railhead at Dimapur, and from there they travelled by rail to Dhond near Poona. Watson wrote: 'At Dimapur there was nothing for us – no food, no tents, nothing. The army in India had written us off. They thought we would not survive and they did not bother.'

Sergeant Kenneth Chadwick wrote about 'B' Echelon's experience in the Burma campaign:

LAD at Waw working on a Stuart engine. (*Norman Plough*)

With 'B' Echelon now becoming a petrol canning factory, a ranch, a fire brigade, an infantry battalion and a crystal gazer, there seemed little else to do but enjoy Burma. Responsibilities grew as it received the sick into convalescence, attached troops into its ration – and cigarettes – strength, and Chinese into its hair. There were suckling pigs to be caught, killed and roasted, even the sergeant-major's duck served well in the end. The crickets and the Tokto lizards nearly drove us mad, as did the mosquitoes and flies.

On the jungle march forty-eight cases of dysentery and fever were reported.

General Wavell visited on 24 May but had no real news to impart. The retreat from Burma was followed by 2 RTR's odyssey in India, through Dimapur, Lumding, Shillons, Gauhati, Assansol, Dakakavi, Tori, Lohardagi camp, Kuru and Dhond. The regimental strength was 21 officers and 336 ORs but in July numbers were increased by drafts from the UK of another 200 ORs. Local leave was granted to Poona and hospital convalescents returned to their units. Courses started and General Lee tanks arrived and were exchanged for General Grants. In September 1942 it became known that the next move would be to Iraq. Captain H. Dumas collected a draft of eighty-five men from the 25th Dragoons. On the 13th the regiment started to move in five parties towards Bombay docks under Lieutenant D.M. Spencer-Smith.

For eight months 2 RTR (and the 7th Hussars) had struggled in Burma (and Assam and India) against heavy odds. They had been highly praised by Churchill, Wavell, Alexander and Slim. Each regiment lost about sixty or seventy casualties to Japanese action. 2 RTR lost seventeen men killed in action; they lie buried in St George's Church, Mingaladon.

CHAPTER TWENTY-EIGHT

Odyssey to Iraq and Syria

2 RTR sailed from Bombay's Alexandria docks on 21 September bound for Paiforce, in the Middle East. As Corporal Watson wrote: 'We then embarked from Bombay up the Persian Gulf to Iraq and stayed in the desert for some time in case the enemy broke through the Caucasus to seize the oil-fields in Iraq and Iran.' 2 RTR embarked on HMT *Neuralia*, with the tanks in *Risaldar*, and Captain H.R.G. Corkery and twelve ORs left to supervise the loading of 'A' Squadron's tanks on the MT *Belray*. Lieutenant-Colonel George Yule took over as the officer in charge of troops and ships. After a week at sea the convoy reached the mouth of the Shat al Arab on the 30th, then went on to Margil and entrained for Az Zubya. Pilferage from vehicles in transit had been considerable. 2 RTR arrived at its new winter camp at Habbaniyah (30 miles west of Baghdad). All the key towns and villages which 2 RTR detachments visited – Shu'Aiba, Bar Jisiya, Al Mahmudiya, Al Musayyab – were railway points between the Arabian Gulf port of Abadan and Baghdad. November 1942 was spent training. Major P.W. Stratton, OC 'B' Squadron, organised courses for NCOs to take PT classes, while other NCOs went to Baghdad for driver/mechanic and WT instructors courses. A regimental wireless net was held and codenames introduced which still survive! The CO was Nero, his RHQ was Nero 2-6, Ajax was OC 'A' Squadron, Badger OC 'B' Squadron and Cyclops OC 'C' Squadron. Huntsman was the scout-car troop and Duck was 'B' Echelon.

Stuart tanks and armoured cars arrived. Calibration of guns and field firing took place amid sandstorms and heavy rain. Major M.F.S. Rudkin took seven tanks – a composite squadron – off to Middle East OCTU at Insawiya near Mosul for three months. Cambrai Day on 20 November was celebrated adequately. Indian, Polish and Iraqi officers arrived on attachment. In February 1943 the regimental strength was twenty-nine assorted tanks. For six long unhappy months the Green Jerboa Rats exercised, fired on ranges and organised wireless schemes amid occasional sandstorms south of Baghdad. In that hot, dusty, colourless station in Iraq, hockey and soccer provided some relaxation, and in April 1943, despite the severe heat, cricket was played. Tank crews familiarised themselves with ageing General Grant tanks and the lighter Stuarts. General Sir H. ('Jumbo') Maitland-Wilson, GOC Paiforce, visited the brigade on 11 December, and the GOC 5th Indian Division welcomed the brigade on

'C' Squadron main guard, Latfia camp, Iraq, January 1943. Back row, left to right: Sergeant Wilson, Troopers Thompson, Leach, Clifton and Craig. Front row: Troopers Flynn, Bath and Roland. (*Richard Clifton*)

2 RTR officers visiting Roman ruins in Baalbek, Lebanon, August 1943. (*Peter Dey*)

Christmas Day and presented medal ribbons for actions in Burma. Sand-fly fever or malaria claimed a hundred or so victims from the brigade. Exercise Scotter took place on 20–23 April in the Karbala area.

On 6 May the brigade sent their tracked vehicles by rail to Basra for embarkation and the two tank regiments began a six-day march by road and desert from Latayflya, Wadhi Mobdil and Rutba staging camp to Mafraq, averaging 120 miles per day, reaching Acre on the 11th. Rather surprisingly the whole regiment went on a week's leave to a camp in Beirut!

On 26 May nineteen Crusader tanks were collected from 9th Armoured Brigade. Having come hundreds of miles west from Baghdad, the regiment embarked on yet another odyssey, this time heading north to Silver Fox camp at Aleppo via Damascus and Homs – over 250 miles. The divisional commander now ordered that 2 RTR should be equipped for the first time with fifty-two Shermans and the light squadron with Stuarts. After a month in Aleppo, in July they returned south via Hamah to Baalbek, 50 miles north of Damascus. The men endured endless training, night schemes, courses and mountain exercises at Slennfe as Shermans and Stuarts arrived in penny packets. Road-blocks were set up at Homs, Baalbek and Chounlar for internal security.

Lieutenant-Colonel George Yule now had a new second-in-command, Major J.P. Zacharius, who took command of HQ Squadron. One small excitement occurred when, in the summer of 1943, 7th Armoured Brigade was ordered to disarm the Greek Brigade. There was some fighting. The Moscow-led ELAS group was at loggerheads with the Republican anti-Communist group. They squabbled so violently that no Allied commander would have them under his command!

Lieutenant Peter Dey joined 2 RTR at the end of August 1943 and commanded 1 Troop, 'C' Squadron. 'Shermans and Stuart tanks started to arrive. TEWTS and field firing took place at Slennfe on the Turkish border. The Baalbek valley was covered with sharp rocks and carpeted with a layer of fine red dust which periodically blew up into a whirlwind and swept through the tented camp, felling tents and distributing paperwork from regimental and squadron offices all over the valley.' Dey took his troop on 'a delightful excursion up the Orontes River, living off the abundant fruit trees growing wild along the river bank and bartering some of our issue rations for milk, eggs and other products'. The brigade was visited by ubiquitous ENSA parties, and excursions were made to see the Roman remains, as well as to Beirut and the Bain Militaire for a swim in the lagoon.

On 28 September 1943 7th Armoured Brigade left Syria for Egypt. Their march through Palestine needed very careful security measures as Jewish insurgents were active. They raided the British forces' armouries – if they could – to steal arms and ammunition. On arrival in the Delta on 2 October both regiments were brought up to strength at Fayid in men and equipment – including new Shermans, Stuarts and Daimler scout-cars. In November the 7th Hussars became, for a time, the reconnaissance regiment of 10th

Armoured Division. 6 RTR, under command of Lieutenant-Colonel A.C. Jackson, rejoined the brigade, as did 1 RHA and 2 RB. Each troop now consisted of two Shermans and two Stuart tanks. Out of the fray now for eighteen months, and having absorbed many new recruits and unfamiliar equipment, the brigade had a strenuous Egyptian winter.

New tactics – direct fire as forward artillery in support of infantry – had to be learned. The desert arena was not of much help since the brigade's eventual destination would be somewhere in Europe. Desert colouring on tanks and vehicles was painted over with the sombre hues needed for the close, green battlefields to come. A 'dry-shod' combined operation using armour and infantry took place at Fayid, followed by a 'wet-shod' fortnight's course at Kabrit.

By 31 October the brigade, commanded by Brigadier O.L. 'Minnow' Prior-Palmer, was up to strength, with fifty-two Sherman M4A4 tanks and new Daimler scout-cars for the recce troops for each armoured regiment. The brigadier was a stickler for turn-out and discipline and imported a Guards drill instructor. The drill courses and daily parades were not popular, but 'Jumbo' Maitland-Wilson approved the divisional parade turn-out on 22 December.

One exercise was carried out with the 84th Anti-Tank Regiment RA to prove the effectiveness of self-propelled guns to reinforce static anti-tank defences

Exercise Tussle 'C' Squadron 2 RTR, January 1944. Corporal Petitt, Trooper Rider (wireless operator), Trooper Smith (driver). (*Peter Dey*)

Exercise Tussle, Bir Beida. Captain Davidson (adjutant), Lieutenant Kirkbride, Lieutenant Bruce 'C' Squadron 2 RTR. (*Peter Dey*)

against tanks. Another tactic practised was the avoidance of ground attack by enemy aircraft in desert conditions without cover by turning tanks in tight circles at maximum speed to create an impenetrable dust cloud. Sergeants Brooks and Basham taught 2 RTR mine- and booby-trap clearance on courses at Fayid.

After Christmas 1943 several exercises – Fig Picker, Octopus, Kipper and Tussle – took place at Bir Beida near Jebel Ataqa. Exercise Tussle saw 10th Armoured Division matched against the 6th South African Division. In February wet-shod combined operations training started at Kabrit, involving wading, loading and unloading landing craft. Major Morrell of the Lancashire Fusiliers lectured about operating in Italy – which was clearly their next destination. On 18 March Exercise Formidable took place: it was a full-scale assault based on a D+1 landing on a beach and live ammunition was used. 1 RHA fired their 105mm field guns. Some shells dropped on to 2 RTR and 6 RTR Shermans but luckily without causing casualties.

In the spring of 1944 the brigade had for the second time to disarm a Greek detachment – a naval one – at Kabrit on the Suez Canal, and in April, training now over, the brigade moved to Muhaggara on the coast of the Gulf of Suez to await embarkation.

The Italian Campaign, 1944

2 RTR handed over its tanks and transport to the 7th Hussars and tentage supervised by RQMS Young. Then they moved to Port Said and on 30 April 1944 set out in the landing craft *Drake* and *Wolfe*. The Green Desert Rats – 7th Armoured Brigade – with its tanks, artillery, sappers and support services sailed in the *Reina Del Pacifico* and *Champollion*. They headed first north through the Suez Canal then west to Taranto on the heel of Italy.

So on 4 May 2 RTR 'invaded' Italy and marched to Dowler camp. The senior officers went on to San Vito to plan the relief of 50th Battalion RTR in the area of Treglio. Sherman tanks were collected together with some 'cut-off' Stuarts for recce troop. A week was spent calibrating guns on the Archi ranges. On 18 May 2 RTR came under command of the 4th Indian Division. Moving 250 miles north with the brigade by rail and road, via Bari, Foggia and Termoli, 2 RTR was soon in action at Guardiagrele and Lanciano south of Pescara. Targets were enemy MET, SP guns, Spandau machine-gun nests and enemy-occupied houses. 'A' Squadron supported 1/4 Essex on the 26th into Lepiane, over heavily mined and boggy ground. It was not easy retraining for warfare in close country with so many rivers and streams, intensely farmed and providing excellent cover for the defenders. The RAF, obviously unaware how far the Allies had advanced, helpfully dropped propaganda leaflets on 'C' Squadron's area!

The squadrons took up their positions along the static front on the Adriatic, their tanks harboured among olive groves and oak woodlands. The Central Mediterranean Training Centre at Benevento (between Naples and Foggia) was valuable for commanding officers and squadron commanders to bring newcomers up to date on 'required' tactics for the Italian front. Target spotting, working with and without infantry, and range practices were all on the agenda.

On 11 May the Fifth and Eighth Armies were to open the battle for Rome and the beleaguered Allied beach-head forces in the Anzio pocket would attempt to break out. Kesselring had now fortified the Caesar, Hitler, Gothic and Gustav lines of defences. The Allied strength, after the withdrawal of three divisions for Operation Overlord and seven for Operation Anvil, was twenty-eight divisions of many nationalities, compared to the Germans' twenty-three. General Alexander wanted a local superiority at the point of attack in the order of 3:1 to ensure success, since the four lines were well structured and heavily defended.

In June the regiment concentrated at Castel Frentano before an action to cut the main Rome–Pescara road, 20 miles to the north-west. 'C' Squadron moved to Villanova in mid-June. Captain F.B. Richardson MC patrolled to the north-west to within 3 miles of Popoli, and investigated Torre, a small town 'governed' by four ex-prisoners of war. Richardson was fêted and made a speech from the town hall balcony!

On 22 June Lieutenant-Colonel George Yule was posted to the Senior Staff College at Camberley. Sergeant Chadwick wrote: 'RHQ operators were Lieutenant Fry, Sergeant Patch, Troopers Holland, Dixon and Kelly. A typical message would be: "N17 to QLC Pighead. 20 Jerries heading south; Singapore, left 3 squares and up. 40 Fascists heading south. 4 with MGs. Sunray [the CO] is away and no one knows where. It doesn't seem worth worrying about and the driver can use his common sense".' Lieutenant Peter Dey of 'C' Squadron wrote:

We were now under command of 4th Indian Division at the eastern end of the Hitler Line, stuck in mountainous ground covered in undergrowth while the battle raged for Cassino at the western end. Limited success was achieved by all three squadrons supporting infantry attacks at Lepione and Guardiagrele but no real progress was made until Cassino fell and the Germans fell back to their next line of defence north of Rome. The Germans on the east coast now fell back to conform and 'C' Squadron followed up without resistance as far as Chieti in what became nicknamed the 'Vino Hunt' because of the tremendous reception they received in every village along the way. In the meantime 'A' Squadron advanced to try to cut the Rome–Pescara road. The road had been demolished in a number of places but diversions were being created by Italian engineers and 'A' Squadron was able to advance to the Pescara River. They were now placed under command of the Utile Division with the task of protecting the Italian engineers. In the meantime the rest of the regiment had concentrated at Castel Frenato and on 27 June it moved to join 6 RTR and 8 RTR at Venafro north of Naples. At the same time Lieutenant-Colonel George Yule handed over command of 2 RTR to Lieutenant Colonel Lascelles.

On 1 July the brigade, now concentrated at Venafro, was visited by GOC 5 Corps, Lieutenant-General Allfrey, and during the next two weeks there was a demonstration of bridge-laying followed by practice at crossing obstacles and a number of TEWTS. On 18 July the regiment moved to Fiuggi via Cassino and Ferentipo. Sadly Tom Kirkbride, the adjutant, was trapped under his tank when it overturned on the journey and his arm had to be amputated. On arrival there was a brigade exercise followed by a demonstration of Duplex Drive Valentine tanks swimming on Lake Bracciano. At the time Churchill was thinking of an assault on southern France, no doubt using DD tanks which operated splendidly on the smooth water of the lake but none of us fancied using them in rough water.

The decision to switch the main thrust by Eighth Army to the east coast and to do so without alerting the Germans meant that the move across the Apennines had to take place in darkness and all vehicles had to be leaguered up and camouflaged by first light. Wireless silence was strictly enforced and no movement was allowed in the open. For the tanks this involved three night moves starting on 14 August. The roads over the mountains were narrow, dusty and tortuous and drivers were restricted to shaded front and rear lights.

In mid-August the regiment spent four days near Lake Bracciano, before moving north 250 miles to San Severino, then to Sassoferrato and to an area south-east of Urbino. The period 19–28 August was spent training with 167th Brigade at San Severino. By this time 7th Armoured Brigade (2 RTR,

6 RTR, 8 RTR and often 7th Hussars) was under command of the 56th (London) Division. Plans were made for the breaking of the Gothic Line, well fortified inland from Pesaro on the Adriatic. The Italian forced labour had had plenty of time to create defences 35 miles long in front of the River Marecchia running inland south-west from Rimini. There were many other river barriers running in parallel that had to be forced – the Metauro, Arzilla, Foglia, Conca, Marano and others.

On 3 September the regimental leaguer east of the River Foglia (2 RTR was part of Minforce), was heavily shelled, despite good camouflage, causing twenty-three casualties, including six killed.

The regiment supported the 1st Welch Regiment, part of 167th Brigade, in its attempt to force a bridgehead over the River Conca, to include the capture of the villages of Croce and San Savino. Moving from Morciano down the slopes of Montefiore on 5 September, Lieutenant J.C.C. Stanton of 1 Troop, 'A' Squadron, approached Croce only to be greeted by heavy enemy machine-gun fire. The 9th Royal Fusiliers asked for help so Major E.J.R. Brotherton, now OC 'C' Squadron, with 2 Troop under Lieutenant I.F. Peet and supported by 'A' Squadron, attacked the village. The 'C' Squadron tanks were all damaged or disabled by heavy shell and mortar fire, but 'A' Squadron advanced into Croce. The only road ran along the top of a bare ridge commanded by enemy observations posts which deluged the ridge with accurate fire. Enemy snipers and bazooka teams fought with fanatical fervour. The Royal Fusiliers were grouped around the church and during the evening the enemy infiltrated back into the village. 8 RTR tried to approach Croce from the Conca valley, and 2 RTR withdrew at 2000 hours. Major Dumas of 'A' Squadron went into Croce with Lieutenant D.T. Grantham's 4 Troop to try to extricate Sergeant Herbert's tank. Their mission failed. The regiment had eight casualties, including five missing. The next day Major J.P. Zacharias led 'B' Squadron in support of the London Scottish from Trebbio in their attack on the Il Palazzo ridge north of Croce. Lieutenant A.C. Walker's 3 Troop tank became ditched. His third tank was mechanically unfit in leaguer. Under cover of smoke Captain R.H.L. Tyler, Major Zacharias, the SSM, Lieutenant Walker and 2 Troop all reached their objective. The remainder of 'B' Squadron under Captain R.W. Stephens waited in Trebbio. During the afternoon SSM Buswell's tank was hit on the cupola by a mortar bomb, killing the SSM and the operator and wounding the gunner. A little later another mortar bomb exploded close to Major Zacharias's tank. He was severely hurt and died of his wounds later. The next day Captain Stephens with two troops of 'B' Squadron supported the 8th Royal Fusiliers from Trebbio in an effort to recapture Croce. The Fusiliers had already received heavy casualties through shelling and infantry/armour communications were poor. At 1730 hours Stephens' troops were in Croce without infantry support, so the tanks at last light withdrew to leaguer in Trebbio. The battle for Croce raged throughout the 8th. Three enemy tanks or SP guns and

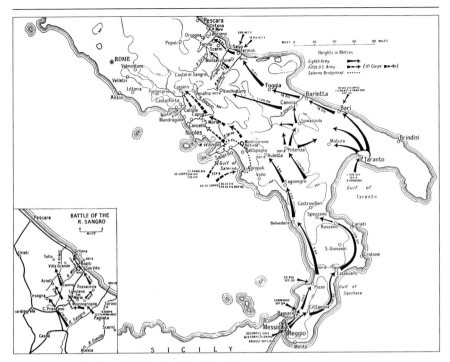

The invasion of Italy and the Battle of the River Sangro.

some anti-tank guns around the village engaged the remaining tanks of 'B' Squadron. All were out of action by mid-day, three damaged by shell fire and three ditched. The infantry could provide no protection and all the tanks had to be abandoned and 'B' Squadron suffered five casualties. Captain A.J. Fearnley of 'B' Squadron was the liaison officer with the artillery, 8th Royal Fusiliers and the London Scottish. Captain J.R.C. Elmslie of 'A' Squadron, with Lieutenant D.T. Grantham's 4 Troop, remained in Croce all day under constant mortar and shell fire, this time supporting the London Scottish. Corporal Jenkins' tank was damaged, as was Elmslie's. Croce was eventually captured, but it had been a long, bitter fight. Kesselring still had many first-rate panzers and Panzer Grenadiers. 2 RTR had spent three days fighting them.

The infantry and tanks in the Croce and San Savino area had sustained very heavy casualties from OPs and enemy guns on the high ground around Gemmano, Montescudo and Monte Columbo. If these heights could be captured, then the pressure on the villages between the Rivers Conca and Marano would be reduced. This led to the action at the Fabri Ridge, which took place on 13 September. At first light 2 RTR (Major H. Dumas's 'A' Squadron and Major E.J.R. Brotherton's 'C' Squadron) would support 2/7th Queens Battalion in the assault on the Fabri Ridge from La Serra to Serra Fabri. Captain P.S. Hunter was liaison officer in a Stuart tank with the commanding officer of the 2/7th Queens. The following is Captain Elmslie's account of the battle:

After the opening of the battle of the Gothic Line, the Germans had fallen back to a defensive position, at the southern end of which was the village of Croce. From Croce a second ridge, the Fabri Ridge, ran north for about a mile.

On 13 September the infantry, 2/7th Queens, were attacking due west, their start line being along the Coriano Ridge. The slopes were too steep and the country too thick for tanks. 'A' Squadron therefore started from a separate position to the south and advanced round the head of the valley to join them on the objective while 'C' Squadron gave fire support.

The start was slightly delayed by the fact that there were still enemy on the infantry start line to the right, but we moved off just after first light. There was a very heavy concentration of artillery fire in the valley, together with a smokescreen to shield us from observation from San Savino. This, together with the half-light, made it very difficult to see more than a few yards, and we were worried by the fact that we had no infantry with us and would have to manoeuvre among enemy positions without being able to see them until we were well within bazooka range. But we had no casualties from this cause, and found out later that we had very good reason to be thankful for the poor light. Three tanks stuck in the ploughed land within a few yards of the start-line, but these were the only casualties we had in getting up on to the objective. The right leading troop was hung up by bad country in the valley, and the two remaining tanks of the other leading troop got up on to the ridge completely by themselves. They had come right through the main infantry positions and then had to turn and fire backwards among the tanks of the rest of the squadron in order to help them to get forward, which they soon did. We found afterwards that the route by which we had travelled was occupied by more than 300 enemy infantry, who were taken completely by surprise.

In about ten minutes from the start of the attack, the nine remaining tanks of the squadron were all concentrated at the northern end of the Fabri Ridge. As the light grew and the smoke cleared, we saw that we were splendidly placed: looking back at the whole of the enemy's reserve positions, along the Coriano Ridge, and overlooking any movement that he made. The main positions had been attacked during the night, and most of them, including San Savino, should have been cleared by dawn; but all the ground we could see behind us was still in enemy hands. No one else had had the success that we had. We were actually on Fabri Ridge for about two hours before any infantry joined us; they had run into enemy infantry as soon as they had moved off from the start line: 'C' Squadron being unable because of the steep ground to support them closely, and we equally unable because we should have been firing back towards them and did not know their positions well enough to do so safely.

We had a number of excellent shoots at enemy moving about in and behind San Savino, and during the morning an enemy Mk IV tank appeared moving down the hill. We must have fired about 80 or 100 rounds from all the tanks in the squadron at it, and hit it repeatedly. The crew abandoned it. We also brewed up a half-track near some haystacks which caught fire, revealing two enemy 88mm anti-tank guns concealed in them.

Suddenly an enemy anti-tank gun (probably an SP) concealed in one of the farmhouses to the north opened up and with his first round hit Corporal Jenkins' tank and set it on fire. The rest of us moved back to dead ground where the infantry were digging in.

By now the area had been cleared of enemy fairly well and our troops were established on the reverse slope. At the top of the ridge was a house which we shot up and a number of enemy in it surrendered. About every half an hour thereafter throughout the afternoon the same thing happened so that by the end of the day we had got about fifty prisoners from this one place.

Enemy along the hedgerow at the top of the ridge and from mortar positions over the far side kept causing trouble. We bounced delayed-action shells on the crest and put 2-inch mortar bombs over it, but none of our infantry actually got to the crest so we were unable to get observation of these enemy mortars. We remained to help the infantry consolidate and were relieved about 3am, by which time, nearly 24 hours since we started, every man in the squadron had fallen asleep.

2 RTR M4A1 Sherman II crossing the Rubicon, Italy. (*Tank Museum 2556/A6*)

But 'A' Squadron had problems. Lieutenant J.W. Brown's 2 Troop tank developed a steering failure, while Sergeant Bermingham's of 3 Troop was ditched. The remaining tank of 2 Troop transferred to 3 Troop under Lieutenant A.R. Tollington. Corporal Morris and his gunner of 1 Troop were killed when a shell hit the cupola of their tank. Sergeant Barber of 3 Troop was wounded by the blast when a farmhouse was destroyed by the RAF. Lieutenant Sansom's and Corporal Watkins' tanks, both of 1 Troop, were disabled by enemy mines. 'A' Squadron, now reduced to four tanks (including that of the OC Major Dumas), helped capture Cerasolo and found a crossing over the River Roncone. The 25-strong enemy garrison holed up in Cerasolo Church were persuaded by Dumas (via a Pole) to surrender. 'A' Squadron had five casualties during the day but took their objective. From 18–20 September the advance to the Coriano Ridge took place, with 8 RTR and the 7th Hussars leading. Both these regiments were in action and took casualties while 2 RTR and 2/5th Queens retained their bridgehead over the River Marecchia. Heavy rain made the ground impassable to tanks except on roads. Captain J.R.C. Elmslie and Lieutenant A.R. Tollington of 'A' Squadron found good firing positions and Lieutenant Peter Dey led a recce party of 2/5th Queens along the proposed centre line. For three days the regiment was shelled much of the time and it rained heavily. They saw no action, but suffered five casualties wounded. On the 22nd 8 RTR handed over to 2 RTR all their fit tanks – 12 Shermans and 5 Stuarts. The GOC 8th Army sent a message to the CO, Lieutenant-Colonel

Lascelles, congratulating the regiment on their actions at Palazzo, San Savino, Croce, La Menghino and Fabri Ridge. But there was a bitter blow for the regiment, when two experienced squadron commanders were killed in action on consecutive days.

During the night of 14/15 September the regiment's recce officer Captain R.M. Tyrell and Lieutenant M.H. Rodway carried out valuable reconnaissance of the River Valinno under enemy shell and mortar fire. The sappers attempted to make three crossing points over the river but failed. A smokescreen put up on the 15th allowed the thirteen tanks of 'B' Squadron to cross the stream and establish a bridgehead, although four tanks got bogged down. Tank strength then was 25 'fit' and 7 'unfit'. 'B' Squadron then did a good job supporting 167th Brigade in the capture of Mulazzano and the crossing of the River Marano on 16 September. Captain R.L.D. Tyler, the 'B' Squadron liaison officer, travelled in his Stuart tank with the CO 9th Royal Fusiliers. Captain A.J. Fearnley, the second-in-command, supported the 7th Battalion Oxford and Bucks advancing towards Trarivi. 2 RTR then leaguered at Il Casone. The next day it was 'C' Squadron's turn to help capture Monte Olivo. Lieutenant D.A.R. Bruce's Sherman was hit by a 75mm anti-tank gun and two of the crew were captured. Captain C.A. Windsor and three other tank commanders had ditched tanks. Lieutenant Peter Dey in 1 Troop supported the 1st Welch Regiment in the final successful attack on Monte Olivo on the 17th. On the same day Major Dumas's 'A' Squadron supported the London Scottish in their attack on Cerasolo. Captain P.S. Hunter was liaison officer with the infantry.

'C' Squadron and RHQ were on the high ground south of San Savino giving effective support to 'A' Squadron. As 2/7th Queens were taking heavy casualties from numerous machine-guns and snipers, Major Brotherton's 'C' Squadron, although handicapped by the steep slopes, moved forward on the left flank, but then suffered tragic casualties. Their second-in-command, Captain F.B. Richardson, was killed in his tank by a sniper, while Major Brotherton was severely wounded in his tank and died of wounds at the advanced dressing station. The CO then ordered Captain R.W. Stephens to take command of 'C' Squadron with Captain C.A. Windsor as his second-in-command. Lieutenant D.A. Bruce assisted the reserve company of the Queens to get over their start line. Sergeant Fitzpatrick of 1 Troop set on fire an enemy SP assault gun, while Lieutenant Bruce's troop demolished a house from which soldiers emerged in numbers to surrender.

During the battle on the 13th 'A' Squadron eliminated a Mk IV tank, an SP 75mm gun, two 88mm anti-tank guns, three half-tracks and a small car. On the debit side Corporal Jenkins and Trooper Adams died of wounds, despite great assistance from Lieutenant Brown and Trooper Dobbinson. It was nevertheless a most successful operation, despite these grievous losses.

After two days out of the line Lieutenant D.T. Grantham, the regiment's intelligence officer, attempted to find feasible cross-country routes ahead.

'C' Squadron 2 RTR Sherman II with 76mm gun and Sherman 17pdr Firefly in Italy. (*Tank Museum 5617/F5*)

Major C.A. Windsor took over HQ Squadron from Major Norman Plough, who became OC 'C' Squadron with Captain J. Greenhill as his second-in-command. The main crossing of the River Marecchia was carefully planned, with 'A' Squadron supporting the 2/7th Queens and 'B' Squadron the 2/5th Queens in advances to the Rivers Rubicon and Fiumicino and the capture of Castelvecchio. Lieutenant Grantham and Captain Tyrell were responsible for marking the tank track routes for 'A' and 'B' Squadrons respectively. Progress was slow but Lieutenants Sansom and Tollington of 'A' Squadron both engaged many targets until their ammunition ran low. Although Castelvecchio was occupied by the 2/5th and 2/7th Queens, enemy tanks penetrated their positions and forced their withdrawal. Despite the use of AVRE Arks for bridging the River Salto 'A' Squadron could not get forward to help the infantry and a number of enemy Panthers inflicted damage on the 'A' Squadron tanks. Sergeant Fitzpatrick was killed and Sergeant Bermingham (of 1940 Western Desert fame) was wounded, as were four ORs. Three tanks were damaged or ditched. Lieutenant Dey and Lieutenant Peet of 'C' Squadron around La Pieta engaged many targets, although three tanks became ditched and heavy rain fell continuously. During the 29th and 30th the enemy withdrew from Castelvecchio and Savignano. During the next week the enemy brought up tanks and SPs at night to cause nuisance value. A huge luxurious villa with thick walls on the top of the Castelvecchio Ridge was used as an OP by every FOO in 56th Division. Its cellars sheltered the Italian owners, including a countess. The hall was used as a cookhouse with at least a dozen stoves in constant use. The lower floors were used by the medium machine-guns of the Cheshire Regiment and they inflicted great misery on the German infantry in their rain-filled slit trenches. The ground floor included a billiard table which doubled up as a bed for Major H. Dumas, OC 'A' Squadron. Bridge could also be played in another tastefully furnished room! All this luxury within 200 yards of the enemy! 'A' Squadron used the OP facilities on 2, 3 and 4 October and 'C' Squadron on the 5th, and considerable damage was inflicted.

On a recce into Savignano Lieutenant Sansom's 1 Troop of 'A' Squadron encountered a Panther tank and despite hitting it on several occasions failed to disable it. Despite very thorough planning between 4 and 7 October for a joint attack on Gatteo with 43 Gurkha Brigade, the operation was cancelled on the 7th. With the rest of the 7th Armoured Brigade, in mid-October 2 RTR went back to Porto Recanati to refit. Later Sergeant Bermingham was awarded the Military Medal for his bravery in the action against the Panthers near Savignano on 1 October. By now the Squadron HQs had received Shermans equipped with 105mm guns. Each troop now had two tanks fitted with 76mm guns and one 17-pdr Sherman Firefly capable of dealing with Panthers.

The last three months of 1944 were relatively peaceful, much of the time being spent on the coast south of Ancona, on maintenance, cleaning of vehicles, courses (wireless, gunnery, driving and maintenance) or on leave to the regimental leave centre, and the exciting Python leave scheme to the UK was announced. Lieutenant J.W. Brown, Corporals Hindle and Gebhard, and Troopers Lee and Stapleton were first to go, followed by Major H. Dumas and eighty-three others. They moved first to Rome, then Naples and back to England. Many of the Western Desert veterans had spent four years 'battling with panzers' abroad. Major-General Whitfield, GOC 56th (London) Division, inspected the regiment on 26 October. Cambrai Day was celebrated in style as the local vino around Porto Recanati was plentiful! Then came a move to the brigade area at Forlimpopoli, south-east of Forli, 75 miles to the north-west. Here field firing took place. For three dull, drizzly days the regiment supported 25th Indian Brigade, 'A' Squadron with the 4/11th Sikhs, 'B' Squadron with the 1st Kings Own and 'C' Squadron with the 3/18th Garwhalis. On 2 December three low-flying Focke-Wolfe 190s rudely strafed the area. A recce to Faenza was made on the 12th and Major Chapman went to liaise with the 9th Lancers. New 'Funny' AFVs arrived: an Ark (basically a bridge-laying Churchill tank); a fascine carrier; a Weasel armoured carrier for use in water or swamps; and several Platypus grousers which were allotted to 'A' Squadron. A senior chaplain from Eighth Army held a Christmas service and then it was the New Year and back into action.

CHAPTER THIRTY

The Italian Campaign, 1945

The Germans still held two pockets of land on the east side of the River Senio in front of the Genghiz Khan Line. These positions, some 5 miles wide by 3 miles deep, were to be cleared by 7th Armoured Brigade. V Corps intended to hold the river line for its winter boundary. Armour supporting a New Zealand infantry brigade would achieve this objective in Operation Cygnet. The waterlogged ground had frozen solid so the tanks had need of their Grousers. These metal blades, which gave additional gripping power when fitted to the Sherman tracks, were time-consuming to fit, and it took a full crew two days of hard work to fully equip each tank, as each Grouser had to be fitted separately. Major J.R.C. Elmslie wrote of the experiments made in the winter of 1944 on the Platypus track (an extension fitted to Shermans), which doubled the width of the tank track tread to reduce ground pressure. New fascines (2ft 6in in diameter) were made of wooden branches that were compressed to fill in ditches, streams and other tank obstacles. The Tabby consisted of special binoculars using infrared rays to help tank commanders see at night.

Operation Cygnet was the responsibility of 2 RTR, the 10th Hussars and the 2/6th Queens Infantry mounted in Kangaroos (turretless Sherman tanks). 'C' Squadron was to clear the start line, then 'A' and 'B' Squadrons would advance (with 'A' on the right, 'B' on the left), with 'C' mopping up behind them. Because of the shortage of artillery ammunition large-scale support would come from the Tactical Air Force. On 4 January 'C' Squadron cleared the start line through the New Zealand Brigade. A smokescreen was fired to show the RAF the bomb line – a very wise precaution. Major Arthur Fearnley, OC 'A' Squadron, advanced for about a mile through thick smoke. Lieutenant Tony Pinnell of 3 Troop overturned his tank in a bomb crater. His two troop tanks did not know the operation codewords and were of little help. Lieutenant 'Jacko' Jackson of 2 Troop broke down and had to transfer, so 1 Troop then took the lead. Captain Elmslie, second-in-command of 'A' Squadron wrote:

The attack went very smoothly. We moved cross-country beside one of the roads, avoiding casualties from mines. 'C' Squadron lost a tank crossing a mined road. We used air photographs rather than maps and called down air-support on practically every house as we reached it. A cab-rank was kept overhead throughout the day and we used every sortie that the RAF were able to lay on. We got first-class support, usually only a hundred or two hundred yards ahead of one's tanks.

A sawn-off Honey recce tank followed up for use as an ambulance. Commanding it was Corporal MacGregor, who was confronted by three Germans manning an Italian Semovente SP gun. They immediately surrendered it to him – although he and his crew were unarmed! Sergeant Henderson's tank in 4 Troop was hit by a bazooka and the crew baled out. Sergeant Eighteen, the 2 Troop sergeant, got his turret flap caught in the wire of overhanging vines – a frequent hazard in wine-growing areas of Italy – and suffered concussion. Elmslie's wireless operator, Corporal Levy, refused to use the crimping machine to link 105mm shells and cartridges together. Being very conscientious he kept the Sherman tank crew up until 0500 hours crimping all the rounds by *hand*. Captain Elmslie continued:

> After the RAF had shot up or bombed each house, we fired a few rounds into it and then moved on to the next, leaving the infantry to mop up . . . The enemy opposition was practically nothing because of the extraordinary effect on their morale of the air and tank bombardment. There were four enemy battalions in front of us and at least 500 PoWs passed through the New Zealand line.

By about 1400 hours the advance had reached the line of houses about a mile from the river bank. The final attack was delayed but successful, although the German defenders dug in along the far banks of the river and stayed there for the rest of the winter.

Lieutenant Peter Dey, of 1 Troop, 'C' Squadron, recalled: 'The plan was simple. 2 RTR was to lead the advance to clear the Cassanigo pocket, from south to north, with 2/6th Queens following in Kangaroos to deal with pockets of resistance, while 169th Brigade moved in behind the armoured group to pick up prisoners and secure the river line. There was thick fog and visibility was down to five yards.'

Dey's troop sergeant strayed into a farmyard and his tank was bazooka'd, luckily without casualties. Lieutenant Dey carried a grenade in each hand, ready to deal with any Panzerfaust team, but 'luckily the fog cleared [and] the Germans were completely taken by surprise. They had never encountered infantry operating from Kangaroos. Over 200 PoWs were taken. A number of tanks and SPs were captured for the loss of only two tanks and a few minor casualties to the infantry.' 'A' Squadron was based in the village of Malmissole; the villagers were very friendly and so Twelfth Night – 6 January – was celebrated in considerable festive style!

A snowstorm after Operation Cygnet left 8 inches of snow on the ground. On 12 January 2 RTR transferred to 43rd Gurkha (lorried) Brigade, which was then in Corps Reserve. Major-General Horace Birks, in charge of Royal Armoured Corps squadron training, visited four days later. Recce parties went to look at the area between the Montone and Lamone Rivers in front of the German Genghiz Khan defence lines. 'B' Squadron moved to Pideura where sappers bulldozed fire positions. On the 30th 'A' Squadron helped a Polish unit in an attack as the enemy withdrew from his positions beyond the River Senio. In February the melting snow soaked the ground, making tank movement very difficult, but the regiment moved on 17th/18th from Forli to Faenza, a town on the main Bologna–Rimini road.

From 20 February for three weeks the regiment was involved in small actions in which various troops supported brigades of 56th (London) Division. They were engaged in clearing enemy out of dug-outs, cuttings, farmhouses and the built-up outskirts of San Severino. Often targets were fired on indirectly with 105mm HE fire, particularly machine-gun posts on the embankment of the River Senio. Castel Capucci, Bulzacca and Cotigaola were targeted areas. On 1 March Lieutenant-Colonel H.A. Lascelles DSO, the CO, left to become GSO1 Royal Armoured Corps. Lieutenant-Colonel P.H. Hordern MBE took command for the rest of the war (and beyond). Early in April the regiment was in Brisighelia, just west of Forli. The appalling winter eventually came to an end and the campaigning season was imminent. General McCreery's Eighth Army was ordered to push V Corps through the Argenta Gap (on its right seaward flank) with the Polish Corps forcing the lines of the Rivers Senio and Santerno. Kesselring still had ten German divisions well established in his heavily mined Genghiz Khan Line. The allied forces now included Indians, New Zealanders, Poles, a Jewish brigade and Italian troops. 7th Armoured Brigade was under command of II Polish Corps but 2 RTR (and 14/20th Hussars with infantry-carrying Kangaroos) was a pursuit force with the 43rd Gurkha Brigade, used as lorried infantry. Elements of 26 Panzer Regiment (equipped with 40 Mk IV Specials), 508 Heavy Tank Battalion (40 Tiger tanks), 1 Battalion 4 Panzer Regiment (about 35 Panthers) and 242 Assault Gun Brigade (SP guns including Semovents) formed the main opposition ahead.

The main offensive started on 9 April. The brigade was to support 8th Indian Division during their crossing of the Senio on either side of Lugo, due west of Ravenna. The terrain here was a large flat plain, with hamlets, farmhouses and vineyards dotted about. The irrigation system may have been perfect for the farmers, but it consisted of various ditches, streams and canals that usually presented very tricky obstacles to tanks. They usually ran south-west to north-east across the line of advance. The larger canals and rivers (and the Po was very wide and fast-flowing here) needed major bridging and/or rafting operations. General Vietinghoff was now in command of the German forces, as Kesselring had been promoted to Commander-in-Chief West. He had no fewer than twenty-three German and, rather surprisingly, four Italian divisions, thus outnumbering the Allies. Despite this numerical advantage, Vietinghoff had major problems to contend with: the RAF and USAAF dominated the skies, and the German armour was restricted by a shortage of fuel.

2 RTR was to engage in an armed pursuit from a bridgehead to be established west of the River Santerno towards Medicina, east of Bologna, and possibly beyond. They were now involved in action for a long week, from 13 to 19 April, in what became known as the battle of the Argenta

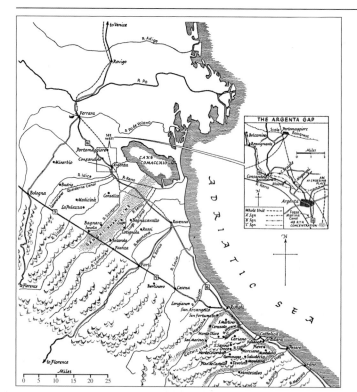

Battle for the valley of the River Po.

2 RTR M4A1 Sherman II, Medicina, Italy. (*Tank Museum 4327/E1*)

Gap. Supporting 2/8th Gurkha Regiment, 2 RTR set off from Santa Lucia on the 13th. Major J.R.C. Elmslie was OC 'A' Squadron, with Major A.J. Fearnley and Major C.A. Windsor commanding 'B' and 'C' Squadrons respectively. The Canale del Molino was crossed using fascines, but Major Elmslie was wounded in the thigh. The next day 'A' Squadron swung west to cross the Fosso Gambellara. Captain P.S. Hunter took command of the squadron, moving towards the River Sillaro. Captain G.C. Sansom spotted an AFV on the other side, but neither he nor the RAF could destroy it. Lieutenant G.P. Barnett was wounded by mortar fire, while dismounted to look for a crossing point.

'B' Squadron cleared around Castruzza, and RHQ at Loghetto received a stonk of heavy and accurate large calibre shells. 'C' Squadron was in reserve at La Vigna, but moved up to cross the Scolo Ladello Canal. A hostile battery at Crocetta smashed a 'C' Squadron Sherman and in turn was destroyed by medium guns and cab-rank Typhoons. Later on the 15th an SP knocked out both Lieutenant V.D. Samuel's Sherman, from 'C' Squadron's 2 Troop, and the troop corporal's tank. On the 16th 'A' Squadron met up with the 14/20th Hussars and carried the 2/6th Gurkhas across an Ark bridge laid in the River Sillaro before moving into the outskirts of Medicina. In the process 1 Troop became ditched and was surrounded by bazooka men. Captain Fane-Hervey was severely wounded. They advanced again on the 17th, moving up the Budrio–Medicina road until 'A' Squadron reached the Torretto–Gaiana Canal. Here heavy opposition was met and the regiment suffered eight casualties.

With 6 RTR on the right and 8 RTR on the left, 2 RTR crossed over the Lugo Canal to help in the capture of Solarolo. They reached the Santerno on 11 April, giving much help to the hard-pressed infantry. 2 RTR followed up with the 43rd Gurkha (lorried) Brigade. A week later they were across the Sillaro, had occupied Medicina and had reached the Qualderna Canal south of Budrio, just east of Bologna.

Captain J.R.C. Elmslie of 2 RTR described 'A' Squadron's last action in Italy:

The enemy was definitely in retreat, but rearguards of their 1st and 4th Parachute Divisions were putting up strong resistance in well-chosen positions. The ground in this area is cut up by a series of rivers, canals and ditches and heavily planted with tall vines. At intervals there are unexpected patches of completely open ground, across which an enemy anti-tank gun could kill as the tank emerged suddenly from the vines.

At first light on 16 April A Squadron 2 RTR (P.S. Hunter) acted as advanced guard to 14/20th Hussars (half tanks, half Kangaroos), carrying 2/6th Gurkha Rifles in a 10-mile advance to Medicina. At 6am A Squadron led across the Sillaro, which though practically dry had very steep banks. Two Arks had been put in one on top of the other, but the ramps were still at an extremely sharp angle. The leading tank slipped and the driver stalled his engine leaving the tank at a sideways angle half-way up the exit ramp. At this moment an accurate enemy salvo arrived slap on the crossing, but the driver managed to straighten up and drive forward off the ramp.

The squadron commander decided to go straight across country and avoid all roads, which were expected to be heavily mined. As a result there were no tank casualties from mines or anti-tank guns the whole day. The 14/20th Hussars on the other hand followed the main road, and suffered considerably, as every small bridge was blown and mined and often covered by anti-tank fire.

The squadron advanced on the left of the axis with two troops up. At La Palazza the leading tank bogged in a deep ditch. A German armed with a bazooka who crawled up the ditch to snipe at the tank was killed before he could fire. An SP gun flashed out of the houses, fired twice at one tank, missed it, and disappeared northwards. No. 1 Troop commander (G.C. Sansom MC), by following its tracks was able to cross the ditch, and throughout the whole day the track marks of this troop of hostile SPs, which paid us much attention, also saved us much reconnaissance time in finding crossing places.

'A' Squadron received orders from OC 14/20th Hussars to hold back in Medicina. No. 1 Troop, however, was too fully occupied shooting up enemy-held houses at point-blank range, and cooperating with a platoon of Gurkhas against barricaded and sandbagged houses. Wireless messages did, however, eventually penetrate through the fog of battle, and No. 1 Troop also unwillingly withdrew.

'C' Squadron crossed the Scolo Acquarolo early on the 19th and had two tanks knocked out by AP fire. Lieutenant Eagle's tank was bazooka'd, and he, Sergeant Westmoreland and Trooper Crowther were all killed. Lieutenants Dey, Mitchell and Rodway observed indirect shoots from various OPs in houses, from 15th Field Regiment RA and 78th Medium Regiment. Sergeant 'Yomto' Thomas was awarded the Military Medal. At nightfall the regiment was withdrawn from the line and leaguered south-east of Medicina. Moves forward took place to Maccaretolo, then across the River Po to Canda, arriving there on 30 April.

In the battle for the Argenta Gap 2 RTR had six officers wounded and one killed, ten ORs wounded and four killed. Ten tanks were knocked out, six of them from 'C' Squadron, the other four from 'A' Squadron. Among many awards three Military Crosses were gained. Most of the Allied armour including 2 RTR could not continue the hot pursuit to Venice and Trieste because of the lack of tank bridges across the Rivers Po and Adige. The end of the hostilities saw the regiment move on to Monselice, Pernumia and Latisana. On 12 May a wheeled vehicle column of 2 RTR moved as fast as it could to Villach in Austria via Treviso and Udine. Kenneth Chadwick described their sojourn in Austria in *Seconds Out*.

2 RTR had come a long, long way from the outbreak of war – serving with the BEF in France, at Beda Fomm and in the Western Desert, in the Burma campaign, wandering in the deserts of Iraq and Syria and then travelling up the whole length of Italy, crossing rivers and canals, mountains and swamps, smashing through all the enemy's defence lines and battling with Hitler's panzers all the way to Austria. It was a magnificent record!

★ ★ ★

A FINAL DEDICATION

We are the D-Day Dodgers way out in Italy,
Always drinking vino, always on the spree!
Eighth Army skyvers and the Yanks,
Six Armoured Div with the tanks,
For we are the D-Day Dodgers,
the Lads that D-Day dodged.

We landed at Salerno – a holiday with pay,
Jerry brought the band to cheer us on our way,
We all sang songs, and beer was free,
We kissed all the girls in Napoli,
For we are the D-Day Dodgers,
the Lads that D-Day dodged.

The Volturno and Cassino were taken in our stride,
We didn't go to fight there, we just went for the ride!
Anzio and Salerno were all forlorn,
We didn't do a thing from dusk till dawn,
For we are the D-Day Dodgers,
the Lads that D-Day dodged.

On our way to Florence we had a lovely time!
We ran a bus to Rimini through the Gothic Line,
Winter sports and snow!
Then we went bathing in the Po,
For we are the D-Day Dodgers,
the Lads that D-Day dodged.

If you look around the mountains, through the mud and rain,
You'll find the battered crosses, some of which bear No Name,
Heartbreak, toil and suffering gone!
The boys beneath they slumber on,
For we are the D-Day Dodgers,
the Lads that D-Day dodged.

(in date order)

T/Major N.C.B. Fellows MC
1/Lt R.W. Edwards
Capt W.R.E. Hughes DSO
Capt W.D. Yeo
Lt R.C. Richards
Lt A.T. Hughes
T/Major W.G.S. Benzie MC
W/Lt J.H. Ellison
T/Major J.A. Hotham
T/Capt E.P.H. Gane MC
Lt R. Adams
2/Lt D. Lawrence
Capt D.M. St. C. Thom
5857251 Tpr Williams D.W.
3597533 Tpr Dobson R.
7907978 Tpr Dennisen F.
7888125 W/Sergeant Hulme W.T.
7887268 Tpr Parker S.R.
7889605 Tpr Clark C.E.
7915816 Tpr Crighton R.
788196 Tpr Ratcliff C.C.
7909369 Tpr Bennett F.
7886462 Tpr Osborne A.
7910054 Tpr Stanton P.T.
7887830 L/C Lovatt E.W.
7887438 L/C Humphreys G.V.
7939519 Tpr Nash J.H.
4530146 Sergeant Hambro
892059 Tpr Hudson J.C.
7903230 Tpr Crocombe W.
788601 Sergeant Hughes J.
7910100 Corporal Curtise R.F.
7915088 Tpr Buckley A.
4270607 Tpr Clough F.
7887544 L/C Jenkins J.E.
7912339 Tpr Warburton R.E.
7943054 Tpr Movat W.
7942139 Tpr Barton W.
841906 Tpr Makin A.S.
4614678 Tpr Boothroyd R.
7889936 Tpr Gould G.
330161 Tpr Rafferty G.A.
7931346 Tpr Greenwood D.K.
7888735 Tpr Fletcher H.
7941468 Tpr Hill G.N.
7886915 Tpr Armstrong J.
7946227 Tpr Vaughan A.W.
7909532 Tpr Jury G.A.
7940240 Tpr Carter W.W.J.
7944211 Tpr Hargreaves G.
7943950 Tpr Brasaley J.W.
7888234 W/Corporal Wheeler J.
3535722 Tpr Cheetham G.
7887952 Sergeant Wison H.

7892739 Tpr Fletcher-Hearne J.
6142140 Tpr Matcham R.C.D.
7956320 Tpr Shimwell A.R.
7935478 Tpr Smith R.
7946220 Tpr Slater W.
7944224 Tpr Bell H.
7939056 Tpr Fitzgerald M.
420658 Tpr Clarke E.
7908469 Tpr Young P.D.
7888104 Tpr Emms G.
7896160 Tpr Knapton W.
826408 W/Corporal Leehan E.A.
59106 L/Sergeant Corbett C.G.
7914791 Tpr Nicol J.R.
7899305 Tpr Spencer W.
7896424 Tpr Rushton T.J.
3527904 Tpr Boult C.M.S.
7887916 Tpr Cameron J.
557326 Tpr Howe A.P.S.T.
3717775 Tpr Bispham G.
7912380 Tpr Jones R.A.
7942410 Tpr Amatt W.
7902679 Corporal Collins C.G.
7888139 Tpr Weller A.H.
7885425 Sergeant Shinnie J.M.
3970614 Tpr Brown W.E.
7942978 Tpr Carrol T.J.P.
5443213 Tpr Trees L.C.
7907924 Tpr Bulmer L.
7941094 Tpr Wemyss C.J.
7887090 Tpr Mackay A.
7884686 Tpr Pittam H.F.
7883988 W/Sergeant Whitlam G.
553308 Tpr Thompson J.H.
7942376 Tpr Sheldon J.
7885381 W/Sergeant Clarke G.A.
7886127 L/Sergeant Noon T.
7892721 Tpr Hill R.W.
7936884 Tpr Patterson C.
547664 W/Corporal Weeds B.J.
353586 Tpr Nicholson J.
3969744 Tpr Denny F.J.
7883328 W/Sergeant Horsfield G.C.
7902491 Tpr Bramsdon R.
7989601 Tpr Robbins J.
7911089 Tpr Beck J.
3391661 Tpr Swift W.
7941489 Tpr Moores J.
7908815 W/Corporal Jones H.
7943418 Tpr Williamson D.J.
7887043 SSM Horne G.
7905942 LULC Jeffries R.
7903151 Tpr Jones J.L.
7937855 Tpr Harris R.F.

APPENDIX B: 1 RTR ROLL OF HONOUR, OFFICERS AND MEN, OCTOBER 1943 TO MAY 1945

(as mentioned in despatches, in date order)

W/Capt G.F. Cordy-Simpson
T/Capt B.S. Young
W/Lt D. Elgar
W/Lt A.M. Walker MC
T/Capt R. Frost
Capt F.M. Wainman (RAMC)
W/Lt R. MacGregor DCM, MM
2/Lt E.S. Kershaw
T/Capt H.M. Stephens MC
Capt H.A. Wells (RAMC)
W/Lt J.M.P. Ley
2/Lt A.F. Piesse
Tpr Albala J.
Tpr Armin F.
Tpr Atkinson D.
Tpr Barwick R.
Tpr Blades L.
Tpr Booth L.
Tpr Burnell F.A.
Tpr Carloss F.
Tpr Calvert W.
Tpr Cross W.
Tpr Crossan J.
Tpr Costigan J.
Tpr Charlesworth J.
Tpr Chinar E.
Tpr Carruthers F.
Tpr Davies J.
Tpr Driver E.
Tpr Ellis P.
Tpr England R.
Tpr Edwards V.
Tpr Eccles P.
Tpr Foster E.
Tpr Foxcroft A.
Tpr France F.
Tpr Gardner R.H.
Tpr Gibson J.A.
Tpr Gibson R.
Tpr Hartley H.
Tpr Hespen K.
Tpr Justice J.W.R.
Tpr Jones D.
Tpr Jones M.
Tpr Kendrick J.
Tpr Malyon J.
Tpr Morris N.
Tpr Martin D.
Tpr Miles S.
Tpr Naylor E.
Tpr Nunn S.
Tpr Osterfield F.
Tpr Pimm M.
Tpr Price F.E.W.
Tpr Povey R.

Tpr Rawlins R.W.
Tpr Robbins N.
Tpr Roberts K.G.
Tpr Richmond J.
Tpr Smith R.
Tpr Swift W.
Tpr Sullivan J.
Tpr Savery H.
Tpr Stone M.
Tpr Smalley J.
Tpr Sandford W.
Tpr Thompkins R.F.
Tpr Thompson A.
Tpr Thompson C.
Tpr Watton A.J.
Tpr Wilson R.
Tpr Wrighton L.
SSM Brown D.
Sgt Botterill G.V.
Sgt Davies A. MM
Sgt Ferguson G. MM
Sgt Goodban G.
Sgt Loosemore J.
Sgt McConnachie J. MM
Sgt Montgomery R.
Sgt Shelcott H.
Sgt Tibbles W.
Sgt Webster A. MM
PLS Forrest J.
PLS Spencer D.
Cpl Ashton W.E.
Cpl Braendli J.
Cpl Cowley D.
Cpl Eisbruch S.
Cpl Ferguson J.
Cpl Fraser A.
Cpl Glenton A.
Cpl Hague J.
Cpl Huitt R.S.
Cpl Maybury J.
Cpl Mitchell E.
Cpl Pryke G.P.
Cpl Thomas P.
Cpl Warraner J.
Cpl Wilkins H.E.
PLC Arno J.
PLC Betts H.
PLC Bullet L.
PLC Charleson G.
PLC Dennis V.
PLC Field E.
PLC Oxley W.
PLC Spaull B.
PLC Vaughan K.
L/C Smith R.

(as mentioned in despatches, in date order)

Bar to DSO
Lt Col R.M.P. Carver

DSO
Lt Col R.M.P. Carver
Lt Col F. Brown
Lt Col P.R.C. Hobart
Maj J.J. Dingwall

Bar to MC
Maj A.R. Leakey
Maj C.A. Holliman (KIA)
Maj C.L. Sproull
Capt J.M. Storey

MC
Maj C.A. Holliman (KIA)
Maj N. Fellows (KIA)
Maj L.G. Heynes
Maj G.J.W. Pedraza
Capt A.R. Leakey
Maj F.D. Pile
Maj W.L. Mather
Capt C.L. Sproull
Capt G.M. Storey
Capt E.P.H. Gane (KIA)
Capt J. Mears
Capt G.T. Withers
Capt N.F. Canham
Capt E.W.C. Smart
Capt D.W.A. Ambridge
Capt H.M. Stephens (DOW)
Lt R.W. Stedman
Lt D.W.F. Hallam
Lt A.M. Walker

DCM
Lt T. Harland
Lt R. McGregor (KIA)
SSM J. Moat

BEM
Sgt L. Allen
Sgt T.F. Stacey
L/Sgt P.J. Brennan

Order to Leopold II with Palm
Lt T. Harland

Croix de Guerre
Maj J.M. Storey (French)
Sgt H.J. Smith (French)
Lt T. Harland (Belgian)
Sgt L. Allen (Belgian)

Bar to MM
SSM S. Caulfield

MM
Lt D.W. Beedon
Lt R. McGregor (KIA)
Lt Green
SSM C. Alexander
SSM S. Caulfield
SSM L. Dauncey
SSM J. Dunnett
SSM G. Horne (KIA)
SSM J. McConnachie (KIA)
SSM G. McKee
Sgt H. Bennett
Sgt N. Jenkins
Sgt H. Lincoln
Sgt A.W. Davies (KIA)
Sgt A. Webster (KIA)
Sgt F. Williams
Sgt R. Craig
Sgt A. North
Sgt H. Cornish
Sgt D. Johnstone
Sgt J. Donelly
Sgt E. Stennett
L/Sgt A. Bamford
L/Sgt H. Jones
Cpl G. Anderson
Cpl H. Scott
Cpl H. Bressloff
Cpl W. Walpole
Cpl W.L. Clarke
L/Cpl K. Peterson
Tpr L. Bowden
Tpr R. Spedding
Tpr H. Jones

MID
Lt Col R.M.P. Carver
Lt Col P.R.G. Hobart (twice)
Maj G.J.W. Pedraza
Maj B.C. Forster
Capt H.R.R.R. Bailey
Capt R. Frost (KIA)
Capt B. Young (KIA)
Capt H.M. Samuel
Capt A. Edwards
Capt W.D. Yeo (KIA)
Capt F. Gutteridge
Lt A. Geneve
Lt I.E. Green
Lt R.W. Stedman
Lt E.W.C. Smart
Revd M.W. Willson
WOI J. Ransom
WOII L. Shadbolt
WOII C. Agase
RSM C.V. Coke

SSM J. Haven
SSM E.E. Brown (KIA)
QMS J. Bund
QMS W. McArthur
MQMS A. Tew
Sgt T. Sharp (twice)
Sgt J. McConnachie (KIA)
Sgt H. Lincoln
Sgt I. Loosemore (KIA)
Sgt G. Horry
Sgt F. Abbott
Cpl D. Mottram
Cpl L. Glaser
L/Cpl J. Richards
Tpr J. Lockett (KIA)
Tpr J. Jenkins
Tpr R. Gibson
Tpr I. Kelly
Tpr H. McQuinn
Tpr E.L. Watkins
QMS A. Wheatley (REME)
Sgt P. Creek (REME)
Cpl J.W. Tibbetts (RCS)

Maj T.S. Craig
Maj J.K. Greenwood
Tpr J. Firth
Tpr F.A. Mason
Sgt J. Holmes
Sgt G. Barnes
Sgt L. Allen
Capt D.W. Brunning

C-in-C's Certificate
Sgt E.S. Liversedge
L/Cpl E.G. Broughton
Sgt H.D. Still
Tpr G.L. Fox
Sgt G.L. Johnson
L/Cpl J.W. German
PLS C.F. Ramsey
PLS A.G. Kelly
Cpl W.H. Guest
L/Cpl C.G. Murgatroyd
Sgt A.J. Berman
Cpl R. Beattie
RQMS T. Betts

DSO and Bar
Lt Col R.F. Chute

Bar to DSO
Lt Col Harcourt DSO

DSO
Maj J.A.C. Richardson
Maj M.J. Woollcombe
Maj N. Bourne
Maj J.A. Bonham-Carter
Lt Col H.A. Lascelles
Lt Col P.H. Hordern

MC and Bar
Maj J.R.D. Carlton
Capt R. Titlestad
Lt H. Fane Harvey
2/Lt E. Duncan

MC
Maj J.L. Marsh
Maj E.J.R. Brotherton
Maj H. Dumas
Maj C.A. Windsor
Capt D.M. Wilkie
Capt G.T.A. Strong
Capt M.F.S. Rudkin
Capt R.M. Tyrrell
Capt Rogers
Capt J.S. Walters (RAMC)
Lt G.D. Addison
Lt A. Fearnley
Lt Pete
Lt Samson
Lt Rodway

OBE
Lt Col G.F. Yule

MBE
Capt W.H. Davidson
Capt F.C. Churchman
RQMS L.G.W. Reynolds

BEM
Sgt E.S. Hickin

DCM
Cpl E. Hughes
Tpr W.T. Cox

MM
Sgt Thomas
Sgt A.C. Burton
Cpl W. Hunt
Cpl G.P.K. Brand
Sgt Cae
Sgt Gibbs
Sgt Wall
Sgt Bermingham
Cpl Nunn
Cpl Embleton
Cpl Mason
Cpl Jenkins
Cpl Pemberton
Tpr Thompson

Chinese Decorations (Medal of Honour)
Maj M.F.S. Rudkin MC
Capt N.T. Plough
Lt Kebble
2/Lt King
SSM Philpotts
Sgt Hine

Mk VI light tank: crew 3, weight 5.24 tons, maximum speed 35mph, range 130 miles. Developed from Carden-Lloyd series of light tanks and carriers. Armament 1 x .5in Vickers MG, 1 x .303 Vickers MG. Engine: Meadows 89bhp. Period 1936–41.

Cruiser Mk I (A-9): crew 6, weight 12.8 tons, maximum speed 25mph, range 150 miles. Armament 1 x 2-pdr (close-support type had 3.7in mortar) and 1 x .303in Vickers MG. Engine: 6-cylinder AEC, 150bhp. Period 1937–42.

Cruiser Mk II (A-10): crew 5, weight 14 tons, maximum speed 16mph, range 100 miles. Armament 1 x 2-pdr (close-support type had 3.7in mortar) and 1 x .303in Vickers MG. Engine: 6-cylinder AEC, 150bhp. Period 1938–42.

Cruiser Mk III (A-13): crew 4, weight 14 tons, maximum speed 30mph, range 90 miles. Armament 1 x 2-pdr and 1 x .303in Vickers MG. Engine: Nuffield Liberty 1, 340bhp. Limited numbers produced. Period 1939–42.

Cruiser Mk IV (A-15 Crusader): crew 4 (later 3), weight 19 tons, maximum speed 27mph, range 100 miles. Armament 1 x 2-pdr (1 x 6-pdr on Crusader Mk III), 2 x 7.92in Besa MG. Engine: Nuffield Liberty, 340bhp. Period 1941–44.

Stuart I (light tank, US M-3) 'Honey': crew 4, weight 12.5 tons, maximum speed 36mph, range 70 miles. Armament 1 x 37mm, 2 x .30in Browning MG. Engine: Continental 7-cylinder radial, 250bhp. Period 1941–44.

Grant I (medium tank, US M-3): crew 6, weight 28.5 tons, maximum speed 26mph, range 144 miles. Armament 1 x 75mm (in hull), 1 x 37mm (in turret), 1 x .30in Browning MG. Engine: Continental 9-cylinder radial, 340bhp. Period 1942–44.

Sherman I and II (medium tank, US M-4): crew 5, weight 30 tons, maximum speed 24mph, range 85 miles. Armament 1 x 75mm, 2 x .30in Browning MG. Engine: Continental 9-cylinder radial, 400bhp. Period 1942–45. (Crews preferred the diesel version, as the petrol type was more likely to catch fire.)

ARMOURED CARS

Rolls-Royce: crew 4, weight 3.8 tons, maximum speed 50mph, range 150 miles. Armament 1 x MG. Period 1940–41.

Morris CS9/LAC: crew 4, weight 34.2 tons, maximum speed 45mph, range 240 miles. Armament 1 x Boys, 1 x Bren LMG. Period 1936–42.

Bibliography

Chadwick, Kenneth, *Seconds Out* (Privately Published)

Delaforce, Patrick, *Churchill's Desert Rats: From Normandy to Berlin with the 7th Armoured Division* (Sutton, 1994)

Delaforce, Patrick, *Churchill's Desert Rats 2: 7th Armoured Division in North Africa, Burma, Sicily and Italy* (Sutton, 2002)

Delaforce, Patrick, *Monty's Marauders* (Tom Donovan, 1997)

Farran, Roy, *Winged Dagger* (Cassell, 1998)

Fletcher, David, *Tanks And Trenches* (Sutton,1994)

Forty, George, *Leakey's Luck* (Sutton, 1999)

Forty, George, *The First Victory* (Nutshell Publishing, 1990)

Liddell Hart, B.H., *The Tanks* (Cassell, 1959)

Masters, David, *With Pennants Flying* (Eyre & Spottiswoode, 1943)

Moorehead, Alan, *African Trilogy* (Hamish Hamilton, 1946)

Roach, Peter, *The 8.15 To War* (Leo Cooper, 1953)

Roberts, G.P.B., *From The Desert To The Baltic* (William Kimber, 1987)

Index